STOP.
STATE
POLICE.

STOP. STATE POLICE.

A Road Dog's Perspective

RETIRED MOTOR TROOPER CHRIS "BOMBER" BOMMARITO

MILL CITY PRESS

Mill City Press, Inc.
555 Winderley Pl, Suite 225
Maitland, FL 32751
407.339.4217
www.millcitypress.net

Library of Congress Control Number: 2023-919343

Paperback ISBN-13: 978-1-66288-673-7
Hard Cover ISBN-13: 978--166288-674-4
eBook ISBN-13:978-1-66288-675-1

TABLE OF CONTENTS:

PROLOGUE

A QUOTE from one of my favorite TV shows, *Game of Thrones*. In the last episode Tyrion Lannister says, "Stories—there's nothing in the world more powerful than a good story; nothing can stop it, no enemy can defeat it!" I would like to tell some stories that highlight my career as a Michigan State Motorcycle Trooper / Road Dog.

What led me to become a Michigan State Trooper working for what used to be one of the premier law enforcement agencies in the country? Many would question if that's still the case today. The Michigan State Police is a full-service agency that was formed in 1917 during World War I like most other State Police / highway patrol agencies. There are State Police posts within seven (used to be eight) districts that cover/ patrol every part of the State of Michigan. They eliminated the fourth district, which was in the center of the state near Lansing, before my time joining the State Police. The buildings/work sites that Troopers work out of are called posts because Troopers were posted there after attending the State Police Academy in Lansing. Some other state agencies around the country refer to the worksites as barracks or stations. Growing up as a young kid, I was most familiar the Detroit, Pontiac, New Baltimore, Richmond, and Romeo posts. Well, I did become a Michigan State Trooper having a great career with a great agency that was gradually losing its luster. I had an English teacher in high school that told us to keep journals of our lives no matter what career path we took. She coached the girls varsity basketball team and was one of my favorite teachers. I took her advice; I kept scrap books with different news clippings from the start of my career till the end, when I retired after 23 years as a road trooper (Road Dog), the best with 15 years as a Motor Man on the motorcycle unit. I was fortunate to be able to buy two years of my military service in the US Army and leave at 23 years instead of 25. I didn't keep scrap books from my time in the Army; I guess I knew deep down the military would not be my lifelong career.

Never in my younger years did I think I would become a Michigan State Trooper. Growing up as a young kid, I would see Troopers at the state fair in Detroit, the Cherry Festival in Romeo, or at Detroit Lions games in Pontiac. I also mainly saw Troopers stopping cars on the freeway in Metro Detroit. They always commanded respect with their sharp, crisp uniforms and their cross-draw holsters. The Troopers were the badasses! As a kid seeing those distinctive blue patrol cars with the red bubble police light on top caught your eye more than other police cars. They were also the only police cars that had the hood light with big red letters saying "STOP" and "**State Police**" in white lettering to either side of the "STOP." I included this in the title of the book because it has great significance on what that "Hood Light" meant to me as a young Trooper and what it meant at the end of my career. If you got stopped by a Trooper, you were in a world of shit! At least that's what we thought.

Looking back at my life, there were various experiences that affected my future career as a trooper, such as family, divorce, death, school, and military. All these things form the person you are and will become. "Sliding doors": if you pick one door, one thing might happen, but if you pick the other door, something else happens; such is life.

I was born at Bon Secoure Hospital in Grosse Pointe, Michigan, and raised in South Detroit in 1968, just like the Journey song "Don't Stop Believing." My parents divorced when I was five years old. I was the youngest, having three older siblings. Yup, I was the baby of the family with two older brothers: James, three years older; Dominic (Donny), five years older; and Kathleen, seven years older. Donny was diagnosed with muscular dystrophy when he was around five years old. He was confined to a wheelchair the rest of his life, dying at the age of 15. My brother's death when I was only nine years old had a jarring effect on me. I was confused and so sad not understanding why he had to die so young. I guess it kind of desensitized me to death to a point at a young age. My future wife, Michelle, and I named are son Dominic, after his uncle Donny, in honor of his short-lived life. My mother had nine half-brothers and -sisters. Her younger brother, Robert, had also died at 15, from drowning when he went to Boy Scouts camp at Crystal Lake up north in Michigan. He jumped in the lake of the dock with his other Scout buddies, got hung up in sea weed, and never came up, drowning at the scene. His death was a horrible loss to our family with my grandmother Ruth never being the same after his death; how could anyone be?

We lived on Marlboro St. in Detroit, which at the time was racially mixed with both white and Black families. We attended Catholic schools until my parents divorced. My brothers and I both had white and Black friends we hung with. We would go out in front of their house and yell their names for them to come outside to play. "Dewaynee," "Laru," come on out and play. We actually had face-to-face contact and played outdoors on the block and in the alleys of Detroit, not like the social media interactions kids have today. We generally stayed around our block not wandering to other blocks in the area. The neighborhood started to go South when my parents decided to divorce in 1973. Crime and violence in the area definitely spiked fast, so we got out of the city when getting out was good. There was a shooting down the street, and robberies of local businesses were on the rise. This period after the Detroit riots in the 60s was known as White Flight.

My parents had a tumultuous divorce, violent at times. I know my father had always accused my mother of cheating on him, which I think led to the split-up. All of us kids were in a car with my mother when my dad, who was in another car, ran into the back of our car. We didn't have seatbelts back then, so we were bouncing around the car like pin-balls. My mother was pissed, as she should be. A DPD (Detroit Police Department) scout car with two male officers inside actually saw my dad run into the back of our car. They made a traffic stop on both vehi-cles to see what was going on. After my mother told the officers what was going on, they removed my father from his car and told him to get lost. They then gave him an ass chewing, telling him to quit the bullshit and advising him he was lucky he wasn't going to jail. He was told to drive one way in his car, and Mother was advised to take us kids and go the other way. No crash report, no arrest for domestic assault, just an ass chewing. "See you later, Pops."

After the divorce was finalized, my father stayed in the city of Detroit buying a small bungalow near Moross and Harper Woods on the east side. He let his uncle Frank move in for a spell. Frank was shot in the face during a poker game when he was a young man. He talked with a slur/grumble that scared the hell out of us kids. My father' aunt Grace married a mafia boss by the name of Pete Licavoli, who was thought to have avoided multiple murder raps throughout his life. WTF? He never came up during my oral interview with the state specifically, but my family connections with the mafia did! When asked if my family had any connections with the mafia, I just stated my parents divorced when I was five years old and didn't have much contact with that side of the family. My dad's neighborhood on the east side of Detroit near Harper Woods had a huge population of Detroit cops and firefighters. The City of Detroit had a residency requirement for city employees for years. My dad had two cops living on either side of him. As crime became worse and the city turned into more of shithole, many of the city workers moved their families to the suburbs, getting apartments to stay in for the residency requirement. The Detroit Police Department actually had a "Residency Unit" of cops that followed cops and firefighters around to make sure they lived in the city.

My mother moved my siblings and me in with her brother, my uncle Larry, and his family, near New Haven, Michigan. She tried to make ends meet having to go on welfare (food stamps) to take care of us kids. My father barely gave her any money for us—no such thing as child support at the time. In today's age my father would have been in a world of shit with friend of the court (FOC) warrants that are issued for nonpayment of child support now. My mother took multiple jobs trying to save money for a place to live while we stayed with my uncle's family. We appreciated them letting us stay with them temporally, but it still sucked. We had three cousins and three of us in the same farmhouse. My uncle's family were Jehovah's Witnesses. Thank God we weren't made to go to church with them. My brother Donny went to stay with my dad for about a year. It sucked being separated at such a young age. I must have gone to at least eight different schools growing up as a kid. When my mother was able to get on her feet after about a year, we lived in various apartments, condos, and rented houses for years. We finally ended up living in a ranch-style house in Sterling Heights, a suburb north of Detroit.

My mother worked long hours as a waitress and bartender at two different bars at one time. She was able to save money, buying into a country Western bar named Filthy J. McNasty's Saloon, located on Mound Rd. near 8 Mile Rd. on the south side of Warren, which borders Detroit. The bar catered to auto workers during the day and urban cowboy types at night. She was able to eventually buy the other parties out of the business and own it by herself, which was a pretty huge accomplishment for a single mother of four. She owned the bar for approximately 20 years eventually selling it to some Arabs that turned it into a party store. I grew up in that bar working as a cook, porter, bar keep, and office manager. When I was 18 years old, I obtained a carry concealed weapon (CCW) permit for business, bank, and home, allowing me transport cash to and from the bank for the business. I purchased a Glock 17 from my mother's boyfriend. Gun laws at the time required you be 21 to purchase a handgun unless from a friend or family, which lowered the age to 18. There was a General Motors stamping plant and Dodge truck plant across the street from the bar. Auto workers would come in and cash their checks and have lunch. I would transport sometimes amounts of $25,000 to $40,000 in cash. Damn, as an 18-year-old that was a pretty huge responsibility. Growing up in a honky-tonk bar, I saw many bar fights, broken bottles over heads, and police response for various reasons.

I was on the side of the bar in the parking lot unloading my gun to put in the trunk when a young Warren police officer approached me. I advised him what I was doing, which was not required by law at the time; the next thing I know, he's jamming me up against the back of the car frisking me. I told him I had a CCW permit and explained what I was doing. He told me to shut up, ran me and my Glock serial number with his Dispatch, and kicked me loose. He took all of my three magazines and emptied all the bullets into the floor board of my trunk. What a dick, totally uncalled for when I was totally legal. That shitty police contact/experience stayed with me when I later became a trooper! If I came across somebody with a CCW, now called conceal pistol license (CPL), I never busted their balls or ran the serial number on the radio with Dispatch to sound cool. If people actually disclosed as required by Michigan law, I was fine with that. If they weren't carrying their weapon, I would ask why not, which would get a surprised reaction. I always told people they should carry their guns; law enforcement can't be everywhere all the time, especially nowadays with all the school shootings, terrorist attacks, etc.

My father was an insurance adjuster writing estimates for vehicles that were involved in crashes or stolen and/or stripped for parts. He did that for years, which he actually seemed to enjoy, making good money and even getting a company car every two years. He ended up leaving the insurance business and opened up a body shop (automotive collision) on Harper in Detroit, naming it Bommarito's Collision. Even in the early 70s, this was not the greatest neighborhood for a business. His business and home were both located in the ninth precinct, the worst for crime in the city. There were constant shootings and robberies up and down Harper, where his business was located. One of his employees actually shot and killed a guy in the alley behind the shop that tried to rob him—holy shit, only in D-town (Detroit). As we got older and started driving, my brother James and I would take our cars down to my dad's shop to do auto body work and have them painted. I had a 1977 Nova for my first car, and my brother also had a 1975 Nova that used to belong to my mother. His was a two-door manual V-8 that was cooler-looking and faster than my four-door straight V-6.

As most kids in the 70s and 80s, I grew watching a lot of TV, good or bad—who knows—but I think better than today, with kids having their faces buried in the phones constantly! I liked movies such as *Mad Max, Top Gun,* and *Excalibur.* There were good guys and bad guys, and I wanted to be a good guy! All brothers fight when they are younger, but once, my older brother James hit me so hard in the back I could barely breath. I told him, "One day I'm going to grow up become a State Trooper and arrest you!" I don't know why I said, "Trooper," when it could have been "cop" or "deputy." Who knows? It's just what came out. I must have been psychic? He did some ride-alongs later on in my career me bringing that up and us both laughing about it. Now that I have you in the car I'm going to arrest your ass, Bro! Too funny!

I attended Margaret Black Elementary School, which was actually in our subdivision in Sterling Heights. Wow, a school named after a prominent woman in the 70s. There actually has been equal recognition of prominent women for years. Besides fighting with my brother James, I learned how to fight in my elementary-school years. We would have arguments in class that go out to the ball fields behind to scrap during recess. Bloody nose here, black eye there until a teacher or principal would run out and stop the fights. Another way to get to somebody was during kickball games at recess: a fast kickball mashed to the face tended to wake people up and get their attention.

I attended Melby Junior High School in Warren. My older siblings went to Carleton Junior High in Sterling Heights, and when it was my turn to go there, it was overcrowded, so they bussed us to Melby Junior High, home of the Rebels in Warren. Boy, parents were super pissed off at the Warren consolidated schools for that move. I was kind of pissed too because I wanted to go to Carleton. Sliding Doors, let's see what happens at Melby.

All three years went by fast and furious. Kids started to take the path of geeks, burnouts, or jocks at this level. I decided to open the door to athletics, playing on the basketball team going undefeated in eighth and ninth grade. I also did pretty good academically, mostly As and Bs. I had a couple of fights in junior high. I was in wood shop, and this kid Bill kept poking me with a kite stick. I told him to stop, and he disregarded me, so the next thing that happened was fists a flying and the wood shop teacher tuning us both up. Didn't have to go to the office either. Another fight I had was with my buddy John getting on the bus at the bus stop. He was in front of me and decided to elbow me in the face giving me a bloody nose. I jumped on him grabbing his head smashing it into the retractable school bus windows. The assistant principal was waiting for us to get off the bus at Melby. Oh shit, he grabbed us both by the collars taking us off the bus to the main office. We got an ass chewing and had to pick up trash after school for a week. Both our moms, single parents, were not happy having to pick our happy asses up after school for a week.

Luckily John had an older sister and my older brother James were old enough to drive, so they picked us up after school. I also got in trouble my last week of junior high school with my buddy Ryan. We decided to skip our last hour because we had a substitute teacher. As we were jumping the fence, some idiot pulled the fire alarm. Shit, should we go back and run to the back of the school and get in line for attendance? Nope, we took off running and got busted the next day obviously. At first, we were blamed for pulling the fire alarm; fortunately, a female burnout admitted to it getting us off the hook for that one. Last week of ninth grade picking up trash again! Damn it!

My mother decided she wanted to move from a subdivision in Sterling Heights to a big old farmhouse for us to live in on about five acres in Clinton Township with well water—talk about a huge change. Damn it, moving again for the umpteenth time! I went to Chippewa Valley High School in Clinton Township, another suburb northeast of Detroit. Lots of Italians in Clinton Twp. and at Chippewa. I was considered a half-breed because I wasn't full-blooded Italian. There was actually a gang at the school that wore green, white, and red jackets called the King Louis's. What the fuck, I felt like I was in a 50s movie, *The Lords of Flatbush* or *Grease* with the Thunderbirds. Same shit, different shovel. The house was on a dirt road called Greenfield that ran behind the high school. First time living on a dirt road.

I could see the high school from the front porch, so I walked to school from the house. Chippewa had ninth graders (freshmen). When I left Melby Junior High, I was in ninth grade starting at Chippewa as a sophomore. Chippewa was a good school for the most part. It had three separate buildings, which was cool. The East Building used to be the original high school, the West Building was the newest built, within the last five years, and in the middle of them was the Fine Arts Building, with a huge auditorium for plays, concerts, and so forth. It had state-of-the-art acoustics and accommodations. The high school was actually like a college campus. We had to walk outdoors in between classes. They had smoking patios, which were big concrete slabs offset from the sidewalks, where students could smoke. Pretty progressive for the time. The legal age to smoke in Michigan at the time was 18, but there were freshmen out there smoking with the seniors; the school basically gave them a free pass. You mostly saw burnouts on the patios and every once in a while would see a jock with their varsity jacket on. We would walk by and give them the dumbass look! I tried smoking cigarettes a couple of times—didn't like it, tasted like shit and too expensive; I was a cheap ass that would rather spend my money on other things such as chewing gum instead of smokes. I was walking by one of the smoking patios wearing my varsity jacket with some buds when at the last second out of the corner of my eye I saw a glass Mountain Dew bottle spinning through the air coming at my head. Damn quick duck; that was close. We never saw the prick that threw the bottle; weird got along with most people pretty well. First and only time that happened.

I ended up running track my sophomore year receiving my varsity letter in the 110 high and 440 low hurdles. I was actually pretty fast, beating seniors from other schools. I had a good experience at Chippewa trying to keep low key at the time of *The Breakfast Club* and *Sixteen Candles*. Never had any fights in high school but I had to verbally tune up a sophomore King Louie during an assembly in the auditorium we were called down for. I was a senior and was sitting in a chair with some of my buds when he walked up and told me to move so he could sit there. I had my Chippewa Valley varsity jacket on, feeling a little empowered. I told him to go fuck himself and find another seat. I gave him the mean eye, which worked because he backed off and listened. Another life lesson used many times as a Trooper later on dealing with shitheads that might try and dictate what I'm supposed to do!

We planned on staying at Chippewa and in Clinton Twp. for the duration until an incident occurred, which had another effect on my future life. We had gotten a golden retriever female puppy naming her Casey. She was six months old when I was outside playing with her in the yard. She ran a couple of houses down, and I tried to keep up with her. There was a dog chained to a doghouse in front of a neighbor's two doors down. She went to play with that dog, when the homeowner pointed a rifle out his front door and shot my dog twice. My brother-in-law and I grabbed her and tried to get her to the emergency vet but were unable to make it; she died in my arms.

My mother ran down the street and threw a brick into the front picture window of the house. Sheriff's deputies from the Macomb County Sheriff's Department responded to the scene to investigate the shooting. The cowardly Italian immigrant finally came out their house when the deputies arrived. The guy who killed my dog tried playing stupid saying he didn't understand English. The deputies did the right thing confiscating his rifle and arresting him for illegal discharge of a weapon too close to a residence and cruelty to animals. When we went to court, an assistant Macomb County prosecutor dismissed the charges claiming the brick thrown through the window was equivalent of the dog being shot. What a fucking moron! My first bad experience with a Prosecutor's Office. We decided to move back to Sterling Heights not having good neighborly relations anymore.

We ended up moving back to Sterling Heights in the Utica School District but to a different area from where I grew up at the prior Sterling Heights house. Most of my friends lived over there, so I sold my Mongoose bike and bought a "Jawa" moped to tool around town on. You had to be 15 to get a moped license and just take a written test. That thing was fast for what it was. I had a goofy red helmet with a black visor. Good experience for my becoming a motor officer years down the road. Hey, all the young kids and I were friends of the TV show *Chips*.

I had changed schools so many times, we decided it best if I stay at Chippewa and drive back and forth, so I sold the "Jawa" moped to help buy my first car, which was a 1977 Chevrolet Nova with a straight six-cylinder engine and bench seats. If you took a turn too fast in the

Nova, the front passenger door would fly open. I had a young girl in my Nova right after I got my driver's license at 16. I might have been driving a little fast around the corner when the door opened and she rolled out onto a grassy area by the curb. The car had bench seats and seatbelts, but they had just passed the seatbelt law in Michigan, and she didn't have hers on, although I did. Damn, that was close; if she had hit the concrete curb, who knows what the outcome would have been. I said, "Shit, Renee, are you OK?" She got up, dusted off, and jumped back in the front. Good reason to get that door fixed, I guess! My older brother James actually took the Nova, and I was able to buy a 1977 Chevrolet Camaro, which was pretty sweet for my second car. Two tone with Maroon on top and silver on the bottom

I was a junior and had my driver' license, which made it convenient. There was no school of choice back then; we just left my Clinton Twp. address so I could continue going to school there. I had always wanted to go in the military when I was younger, so I looked into the different branches of the military including every branch except for the Coast Guard. I scored really well on the ASVAB test, which is the test that determines what job or career path you will take in the military. The same test applies to all five branches of service. My Army recruiter said I scored high enough to become an air traffic controller. Cool, I guess being pretty good at video games, why not take that as a Military Occupation Specialty (MOS). The MOS for air traffic control was 93 Juliet for radar operator and 93 Hotel for tower controller. That would come in handy later on in law enforcement when dealing with people claiming to be Vets! Ask them what their MOS was in the military, and they should be able to snap it back instantly. If they don't know it, they are full of shit! What the hell, I joined the US Army Reserve (USAR) on the delayed entry program while still a senior in high school. I was still only 17 years old until after I graduated, so my parents had to sign off on me going in the military. I went to drill weekend at Selfridge Air National Guard Base in Mt. Clemens while in high school until I attended Basic Training and Air Traffic Controller/ATC School after graduating.

Had to put gas in the car and pay for a high school social life in the 80s. My high school buddy, who later in life became a chef, worked at a local bakery before and after school. He asked me if I wanted a job making donuts from 4 a.m. till 7 a.m. weekdays before school. I took that job for about a month but then quit. It was horrible having to get up that early before school and then going to school smelling like donuts. I don't know, maybe girls liked how I smelled. I also applied for a job a McDonalds and was turned down, go figure! Well, I did have my mother's bar, where I worked at and actually used for a school internship when I was a senior in a distributive education class. We had a banquet for the end of year, and I was called up and given a certificate for working at "Filthy J. McNastys Saloon." The look on people's faces and laughter was classic. Hey, I was working for my mother, and it paid the bills.

I graduated from high school in 1986 during the great times. President Reagan was in the White House, the economy was great, and it was actually a blast growing up and going to school during the 80s. Great music, movies, and a sense that everything was pretty damn gnarly. I left for basic training for the Army Reserve at Fort Knox Kentucky, home of Army Armor after the Fourth of July celebrating my 18th birthday doing push-ups on the hot pavement of Fort Knox—that sucked! Basic training was only eight weeks long. I attended the same training with Active Duty, National Guard, and Reserve soldiers, which were all men. I guess they wanted the women kept separate for a multitude of reasons. The active duty drill sergeants busted your balls if you were going in the guard or reserve just a little harder it seemed. Profanity abounded and not even considered out of line for drills to yell at recruits. "Hey, shit for brains, get your head out of your ass," "Don't give up, winners never quit, and quitters never win, you pussies." When we would march, our cadences were strewn with profanity and sexist remarks. "I wish all the ladies were holes in the road, and if I were a dump truck, I'd fill them with my load." Whatever; I didn't mind at the time. It was a shitty yet cool experience at the same time. I actually did really good during basic training graduating as an "honor soldier" maxing out on all my common core tasks with testing and my physical fitness (PT) test, which consisted of a two-mile run for times, push-up, and sit-ups.

Basic Training graduation was an experience! My older sister showed up wearing high heels, tight black spandex pants, and a tight purple top with her cleavage extremely visible. These guys hadn't been around a woman for eight weeks, so they were horny as hell. Supposedly the Army puts "Salt Peter" in our orange juice during Basic, which is supposed to keep us from getting horny! My fellow soldiers started cat-calling her with me yelling at them, "Hey, fuckers, that's my sister you're hitting on." Luckily, she was with her husband, and he was a big, burly good ole boy from Alabama. Too funny, I told her afterward, "Hey Sis, you really look nice but probably not the best place to wear that outfit."

I received a plaque and was supposed to be recognized as an "honor soldier" at the graduation ceremony with my family in attendance. Some drill sergeant from another platoon grabbed me and another private out of formation and made us pass out refreshments instead of marching with my platoon. My drill sergeant, SFC Green, came looking for me with that pissed off look on his face. "Private Bommarito, what in the hell are you doing passing out refreshments? Get your dumb ass over with your platoon ten seconds ago, you moron!" I tried to explain that some other platoon drill had put me on that detail; boy, was he pissed. He didn't care about the other private because he wasn't getting recognized.

After graduating from Basic at Fort Knox, I was able to go to dinner with my family, and then was put on a bus and shipped to Fort Rucker, Alabama, the home of Army Aviation, to attend advanced individual training (AIT) at the Air Traffic Controller school in August of 1986. There were still drill sergeants at AIT, but they were a little more chill than the Basic Training ones. We also had females at AIT—that was an experience. Lots of hooking up going on. AIT was run more like a college curriculum with most weekends off. As long as you didn't step on your dick, you could pretty much count on having most weekends off to party. We were allowed to drink alcohol on base at 18. I graduated from Air Traffic Control School in January of 1987 as a 93 Juliet Radar Operator, again with honors as a distinguished graduate. The school was fun but challenging. Most had been doing something right. Fort Rucker was badass having a shit ton of helicopters everywhere. Black Hawk Lift helicopters, Apache and Cobra attack helicopters, and Kiowa Scouts. The whole atmosphere there was a blast. The fort was located near Enterprise Alabama, which was a small typical military town, not much there. We were about one hour from Panama City, Florida, which was a blast to go to on the weekends. I didn't leave base much during Air Traffic Control School; that would change when I went back to Rucker in 1993 after graduating from college. I returned home to Sterling Heights and for the next six years as an Army Reservist went to Selfridge Air National Guard Base for weekend drill and Grayling Army Base up north for my two-week summer camp.

Now that I was an Army Reservist, it was time to go to college. I also had to get a job, so I got a job at Murray's Auto Parts in Sterling Heights, which was a couple of miles from my house. I also attended Macomb Community College full time, one semester taking 18 credit hours in a semester playing catch-up from being gone for the military. I had received the G.I. Bill to pay for a good chunk of school. I finished my associates degree in general studies, not knowing what advanced career field I wanted to get in, law enforcement or aviation? I had taken some law enforcement classes at Macomb. There were some officers from Detroit Police Department (DPD) in some of the classes I became friendly with. One was only 18 years old, wearing a shoulder holster to class with a .357—man, I thought he was a badass; his name was Chris too. I wasn't desperate enough to go to work for Detroit. I had too much knowledge of the city to work for DPD. My first sergeant in my Reserve Unit was a Detroit police officer, Sherdard Brison. He was a great man who while on patrol attempted to stop an armed robbery suspect in downtown Detroit when the shithead pulled a gun and shot "top," killing him. His female partner was also shot but returned fire, killing the turd as he tried to flee on foot. Everyone in our unit was sad as hell losing our good friend. I had applied to the Sterling Heights Police Department to be a police dispatcher when I was finishing up my degree at Macomb. I went through the application process and was offered the job as a dispatcher just when a Special Forces sergeant came to our Reserve Unit at Selfridge looking for air traffic controllers to go to Honduras, Central America, to support Special Forces Operations. Remember Lt./Col Oliver North, from the Iran/Contra Scandal. There happened to be a war going on between the Nicaraguan Sandinistas and El Salvador contra rebels. This shit was going on during the height of the Cold War proxy between the Soviet Union and the US.

Should I become a police dispatcher or go overseas in a war zone? I was 20 years old, Fuck it—I decided to go to Honduras. My mother and girlfriend at the time were not too happy with me, but what the hell—I thought it would be a great experience. Myself and another air traffic controller from our unit left to go to Central America. We flew down there in January 1989 from Wright-Patterson Air base in Ohio; man, it was cold as hell on a huge Air Force C-5 transport jet. When we got off the plane, it was hot as balls, like something out of a Vietnam movie. "Oh, shit, here we go." Two days after being in the country the same Special Forces sergeant came onto base from his jungle operations. "Hey Guys, got some bad news: they cancelled your mission. You can go back home to Michigan or stay here and work at the Air Force Radar facility." Easy decision, we both decided to stay and work with the Air Force.

The Air Force air traffic controllers busted our balls initially for being Army pukes, but then eventually adopted us like the bastard stepchildren we were. The regular Army guys across base were sleeping in tents eating shit "meals ready to eat" (MREs). We were treated like kings, staying in wood hooches with ice machines and VCRs. We also had beds, not cots, and ate at a full-service chow hall with hot food and a badass salad bar. We worked different shifts at the radar facility and drank a lot of *cervezas* (beer) and tequila when we were off. Every other Thursday there was a moral support activity called "Bimbo Bingo" night. They would bus in two or three buses full of Honduran women to play bingo, drink, and do other things. Many of the Honduran women wanted to marry GIs and return with them to the big "PX" (Post Exchange/America). I couldn't justify bringing a wife home to stay with my mother and meet my girlfriend! Needless to say, we had a great time in Honduras and also left with a badass tan!

When I returned home from Honduras in 1990, I looked at three different universities to attend to obtain my bachelor's degree. Eastern Michigan U, Central Michigan U, or Western Michigan U. I had decent grades at Macomb but not good enough to go to U of M or Michigan State. Plus they were way too expensive at the time. I had no interest in attending schools out of state—way too expensive. I had friends that attended the Big 3, so I took a tour of all three to see which I wanted to attend. I finally decided to go to Western Michigan University in Kalamazoo. Having a background as an air traffic controller, Western seemed to be the best pick. Western had both aviation and criminal justice programs that I could choose from. I had taken mostly general study classes at Macomb, which would transfer to most Michigan universities. I decided to pursue a major in aviation and a minor in business. I figured you could always become a cop with an aviation degree but not an aviator with a criminal justice degree. One of my high school buddies was the "Drum major" for the Western Michigan marching band. I went up one weekend and stayed with a bunch of band geeks in the dorms. They definitely knew how to party blocking rear doors to the dorms open with empty half beer barrels. "Hmm, I think I'll go to Western," I said to myself.

Great times at Western graduating with a bachelor's degree in aviation technology in December 1992. I was a member of the Aviation Fraternity, Alpha Eta Rho, during my stint, which was a blast. We had monthly meetings and took some cool field trips to various airports including Chicago/O'Hare. I had almost switched to a criminal justice major because the aviation classes, which included many math and engineering classes, were kicking my ass. I toughed it out staying with aviation. Attending Western was definitely different than going to community college. Western was a top-notch school with great facilities and instructors. I had just turned 21 when I transferred there making it easy to party maybe a little too much. I lived in the dorms my first year there and then moved to off-campus housing for the remainder. Being a sergeant in the Army Reserve I could have easily enrolled in the Reserve Officer Training Corp (ROTC) at Western but decided not to when I saw cadets picking up trash in the bleachers after football games. Piss on that. My cousin Greg transferred to Western a year after I did. He was involved in ROTC graduating in 1993 receiving his commission as a 2nd Lt. in the active Army. His was branched into Logistics. He tried to talk me into going into ROTC; I decided not to because there was no guarantee of getting the Aviation Branch. They can make you specialize in whatever they want with ROTC.

I did have a shitty life-learning experience at Western, which influenced me becoming a trooper and the type of trooper I would be later on in my life. I had gone to a college party with a group of my close friends and had a little too much to drink. I was 21 at the time, which is no excuse for drinking as much as I did that night. I had started to get tired, so I told my friends I was going out to my car to sleep and when they were ready to leave they could drive us home. I didn't want to crash in a room at an apartment I didn't know ending up with black marker all over my body; been there, done that in the Army. I was approached by a Kalamazoo Township police officer that saw me sleeping in my car in the apartment complex. He contacted me, removed me from the car, performed sobriety tests, and arrested my for drunk driving. I did everything he said not knowing where this was going even blowing into a preliminary breath test (PBT) with a result of .15. Holy shit. I was going to jail for trying to do the right thing and not driving. The Kalamazoo Township police officer exaggerated on his police report a smidgen saying the car was running and I had crashed into a car port. I requested a jury trial, conducted my own investigation taking pictures of my car showing no damage, pictures of the car port showing no damage, and getting sworn statements from local automotive collision shops showing no or recent damage to my car. I told the truth about what had happened and was found not guilty by a jury of my peers. I should never have gone out to the car to sleep, but I never drove that car while intoxicated. I was in the process of applying to attend US Marine Corps Officer Candidate School to become a lieutenant and fly jets (Top Gun envy). The Marine captain in charge of the program scratched me from the process just for getting arrested even though I was found not guilty. Fuck. Now what? Add $5,000 (the cost for the trial) to my college debt getting ready to graduate from Western!

After graduating from Western Michigan University in December 1992, I returned home to Sterling Heights. My mother told me the city was hiring police officers. What the hell, I have a bachelor's degree and Military experience—I should be a shoo-in, right? Wrong! I applied for one of the positions and made it to the Oral Board. This time it was different than three years earlier when I was offered a job as a police dispatcher. There was a female command officer on the Board from DPD (Detroit Police). Hmm, why was she on the interview board for Sterling Heights Police? She was busting my chops about not taking the job as a dispatcher a few years prior. She also asked why a degree in aviation would benefit the city and if I thought all of a sudden Sterling Heights was going to buy a helicopter for me so I could fly it. Oh shit, this interview was going south fast. I could tell by her demeanor I was fucked!

I had some buddies from Western that were flying in the Michigan National Guard near Lansing. They told me there was a MOS in the Army called an AeroScout Observer (AO) where you could fly left seat in OH-58 scout helicopters as an enlisted member co-pilot/navigator, which I already was as a sergeant. That sounded like a job I would like, so I contacted an active duty recruiter advising them of my credentials. They signed me up for AeroScout school with a six-year commitment in the active Army. I figured I could go to AO school and then transition to be an Army warrant officer flying and making a career out of it. A bachelor's degree in aviation, certification as an air traffic controller, I was a shoo-in. Sweet, sign me up. I was on my way back to Fort Rucker in early March 1993 for AO school, which was approximately six months long.

Fort Rucker, the home of Army Aviation, was a blast. Great weather, party in Panama City, Florida, and Southern women abounded. AO school was intense. PT every morning at 6 a.m., and then classes and flight training for the rest of the day. Lots of avionics, math, engineering, escape and evade, aviation training, etc. My degree from Western was definitely a plus in having an advantage over other trainees during the school. Our primary uniforms were olive drab flight suits. Damn, it was like *Top Gun* without the patches. They didn't give us our patches until we graduated and received our duty assignments. There was this aviation supply store in Enterprise called Wings. We had to go to get personalized flight bags for all our gear, maps, whiz wheel (fuel tool), etc. We all put nicknames on the bags. I had "Bomber" put on mine. It was pretty cool to be flying aircraft now and not directing them from a dark radar facility. My flight class had about 20 of us in it—all males; females were excluded from the AO position back then. There were female pilots but not AOs, not sure why. We would march to classes on base then take a bus to flight training at the airfield. Learning to hover in the helicopter was probably the hardest and funniest. The flight instructors would have half the class in helicopters on helipads lined up in row. The other half of the class would be in flight operations watching our classmates out the window. The choppers would lift off the ground nice and steady, and then the instructors would hand the controls over to the trainees. Holy shit, those birds were all over the place. It was funny to watch. We were amazed that no one crashed into each other's side by side. Just like anything else, practice makes perfect, we all became pretty good hovering and flying.

After graduating from AO school at Rucker we received our duty assignments, same that happened toward the end of graduating for the State Police Academy. I had what was perceived but not necessarily true to have shitty luck with both. Some guys go to Hawaii, Germany, Korea, North Carolina, California. I was assigned to the 10th Mountain Division in Fort Drum, New York! Damn it, snow, snow, and more snow! I see enough of the shit in Michigan. Screw it, I'll make the best of it. The 10th Mountain Division did have some hellacious historical battles defeating the Germans during the World War II in Europe. A sizable part of the unit was currently in Somalia when I went there.

I was assigned to the 3/17th Cavalry (Cav) Squadron, which was one of three units under the 10th Aviation Brigade. The other two units were the 10th Attack Battalion and the 10th Lift Battalion. I was happy to be assigned to the Cav getting my first experience being called a trooper! We were a little arrogant wearing Cavalry Stetson hats with our uniforms and flight suits. Remember Robert Duvall in *Apocalypse Now*? That was us.

The Cavalry Squadron was heavier with Scout helicopters and lighter with Cobra Attack helicopters. The Attack Battalion was opposite of us, heavier on Attack helicopters. All the salty guys in my unit had just rotated back from Somalia conducting operation "Gothic Serpent." The 10th Aviation Brigade was constantly brining back helicopters stateside that were shot up with bullet holes and mortar shrapnel. I would see them at the airfield and think to myself, "Shit, I'll be going over there soon." We were due to rotate back to Somalia in January 1994. That never happened due to an Army Ranger mission that went south with many rangers and Special Ops soldiers getting killed by Somali militiamen. President Clinton should have kicked their ass; instead he pulled all our troops out. The movie *Black Hawk Down* pretty much explains what happened. We never went back to Somalia, the shithole that it was. Let the United Nations deal with it.

I received my first Challenge Coin when I was stationed at Fort Drum. They were given by command for an accomplishment or by troops to other troops as a sign of friendship. The Challenge Coin tradition started in the military years ago when troops would lay down a Challenge/Coin at a pub or bar challenging the other military member to show/produce a Challenge Coin. If they didn't have a coin, they had to buy you a beer/drink. If they had a Challenge Coin you had to buy them a beer/drink! I would collect and receive many Challenge Coins in the military and throughout my law enforcement career.

Being on flight status in the Army requires an annual flight physical. I took my annual flight physical in July of 94, always in your birth month. I had eye surgery when I was a young kid for lazy eye in my left eye. I always divulged that information, so it was nothing new. I had taken at least five previous flight physicals with this never coming up as a problem. The Army knew about my surgery when I first went in and went to Air Traffic Control School. The flight surgeon said my depth perception could be compromised especially flying night missions with night vision goggles. OK, now what? I was grounded pending a waiver for the medical issue from Fort Rucker and the Department of the Army in Washington, DC. It was not a great time to be in the military. Clinton wasn't exactly pro-military. His administration was riffing (reduction in force) all branches of the military. I left the Army with an honorable discharge and a breach of contract on their part, not being able to fly due to no fault of my own and the Army changing their stance on my known medical/eye condition. I moved back home to Sterling Hgts. with my mother and stepfather. She had seen an article on the front page of the *Detroit News* titled "Michigan State Police Hiring Troopers." The article had two old-timers/Road Dogs standing in front of their patrol car explaining how they were retiring and needed young troopers to replace them. Sweet Michigan needed a shit ton of troopers—perfect timing! I will apply to the State Police. I contacted a recruiter at the Pontiac Post, and he said they were running back-to-back academies in Lansing.

I went on unemployment for a couple months. The State of Michigan had a really good job search program for unemployed people at the time and a fast track for veterans. I was offered a job at Chrysler as an auto line worker, which I turned down. Most of my family had worked for the Big 3, Ford, GM, or Chrysler. I also had known many auto workers that went to my mother's bar growing up a young kid; great people, just not what I had my mind set on for a career. I was dating a girl at the time who was a salaried employee for Chrysler. She got in my ass when I turned the Chrysler job down. That relationship didn't last long. I was then offered a job with Central Transport, a trucking company based out of Warren, Michigan. They had a subsidiary, Central Air Freight, which dealt with freight forwarding. They treated me great at Central even knowing I was applying to the State Police. I took that job until I could get in the earliest State Police Recruit School.

CHAPTER 1: RECRUIT TO TROOP

NEWS ARTICLE: "Vacancies Open for 250 State Troopers." Thousands of people apply to become Michigan state troopers with a small percentage being accepted and even less making it through the military regimented Academy. Deciding to pull the trigger and apply to the State Police wasn't too hard of a decision. I wasn't one of those guys, "I wanted to be a State Trooper my whole life" bullshitters. From a young age I noticed something about Michigan State Troopers stood out from other law enforcement. When I was getting out of the Army my mother showed me that article above and cut it out of the newspaper for me. I figured, "What the hell! I'm fairly qualified. I'm a US Army veteran, I have a bachelor's degree in aviation from Western Michigan University, I have many life experiences; go for it!" Again easier to become a cop with an aviation degree than a pilot with a criminal justice degree and the State Police does have an aviation section, not like Sterling Hgts. PD, where I stayed with my mother and step-father when I got out of the Army.

There are three positions you can apply for when you first start the application process. state trooper, motor carrier officer, and capital security officer. State Troopers have full police powers/authority throughout the state 24/7. Motor carrier Officers only deal with commercial vehicles working mostly weekdays and no holidays with limited arrest authority and duty and off duty. Motor carrier/commercial vehicle officers can only arrest drunks or felons. Capital security officers provide security at the states' complexes/buildings. They have less authority than motor carriers. I had never heard of the two latter positions until I started the application process. I'll pass on those, there was no doubt in my mind I wanted to be a Trooper!

After contacting a recruiter at the Pontiac Post, I was given various dates to attend a pre-employment seminar. The seminar is conducted by troopers, and they give you an idea of what a career with the Michigan State Police would entail. They also showed a pretty cool video titled "Blue Diamonds." I showed Troopers in action with some old-timer from the UP (Upper Peninsula) singing the title song. I was told to arrive in business attire wearing a suit and tie. There are always the "Schmos" that show up looking like shitbags. The Troopers weren't too happy sending them home, advising that if you can't listen to simple instructions about a seminar, they will no way make it through an academy and are not trooper material. I guess that's where my military discipline helped. Basically do what they tell you or they are going to get in your ass! The Troopers also asked for our drivers licenses and vehicle information, making sure we were valid and had proper plates and insurance on our vehicles in the parking lot. Pretty slick—another way to weed out applicants. They actually went outside making sure we didn't have illegal window tint on our vehicle or any contraband in plain view. Damn, I didn't see that one coming. No worries, have fun looking in my Jeep Wrangler from when I was in the Army, Trooper!

The first step in the testing process was to take the Michigan Law Enforcement Council (MLEOTC) physical fitness test. The test consisted of a half mile shuttle run, push-ups, sit-ups, 100 lb. bag carry, 150 lb. dummy drag, grip strength, and a wall climb. The 100 lb. bag carry and dummy drag were a bitch. I was five eleven and 160 lbs. soaking wet after leaving the Army. I passed the test on the first attempt; some didn't pass and had to keep retaking it. I was probably in the best shape of my life, or so I thought. When I was in the Army we would run 10 miles at times and go on long "road marches" with 100 lb. backpacks on. The State Police Academy was harder!

I had already taken this test at Macomb Community College. The State Police didn't recognize other testing sites that conducted the physical test and written test for their process. They wanted the test administered by troopers and troopers only! It's the same if you're already a certified officer or deputy in Michigan. You still have to attend the MSP academy in Lansing to become a trooper—no lateral transfers. Some people look at it like screw that shit, I'm not going through another academy, and others look at it like they have the experience or a leg up to complete the MSP academy. Different strokes for different folks. Just like the military, the MSP had different passing standards for men and women. I always scratched my head at this policy, especially with law enforcement. Is a criminal going to use less force punching a female cop in the face or slow down in a foot pursuit because she is a female? I think not! Anyways—can't do anything about it, just bitch to yourself or other male cops. There are some badass female cops that would be able to pass the men's PT test but few and far between.

The next step in the process was taking the written exam. I bought one of those Arco career study guides at a bookstore, but it didn't help for shit. There is really no way to study for those tests because they change them constantly. There was a lot of memorization, visuals included and scenario-type questions on the test. One part was a two-page cartoon depicting a street scene with vehicles, buildings, people, etc. The test proctor gave us a long time to look at the scene and then advised us to turn the page and answer as many questions about the picture as possible. What was the license plate number on the truck parked illegally? What was the name of the street where the truck was illegally parked? Etc.

The State Police also had an affirmative action policy and were ADA-compliant (American with Disabilities Act) The feds mandated that state and local municipalities were not allowed to have maximum age restrictions or other similar restrictions. However, the feds themselves still could have a maximum age, which was 32 years of age. I never understood how they could impose that on locals but not on themselves. We had a guy in our school that was 43 years old, and he was a badass! It was said if you were a white male, you had to get a 95 percent or better on the written exam to proceed in the process. I got a 96—whew, that was close—so I could proceed. There was actually a reverse discrimination lawsuit that was filed and pending when I started in the process. A group of five white male troopers had sued the department for being constantly passed over for promotion. They ended up getting promoted and receiving back pay. I ended up working with four out of five of those gentlemen later on in my career. This lawsuit made the department change hiring and promotion practices, making it fair for everyone across the board.

Okay, I've passed the first two steps; now it was time for the background investigation. I had to complete a full disclosure of my entire life—damn, some things are better left unsaid. Just kidding; wasn't that a title of an 80s hit song? I told my background investigator about every ticket I received, the first being a speeding ticket from an Ohio Trooper down near the amusement park Cedar Point when I was 18 and was with my girlfriend. Police contacts were also included, cruising Gratiot looking for girls, an MIP (Minor in Possession) ticket when I was in the back seat with a buddy who had a beer. Trying marijuana at a high school party and of course my OWI arrest when I was in college at WMU. My background investigator was from the Richmond Post, which covered Sterling Hts. She was a badass and a looker. She called me up to come in for an interview when I was working at the air freight company on mids. I told her I had to check my work schedule, with her responding, "Who's in charge here, Mr. Bommarito?" "Uggghhh, you are, Ma'am!" She contacted friends, family, checked on tickets, arrests and work history, etc.

When I arrived for the interview with her, again I was advised to be in business attire, suit and tie. She was very stern and direct, in a sexy way. She asked questions in relation to the previous answers that I had given, changing them up, I imagine to try and jam me up changing my answer. "No do, Miss Magoo." I had participated in many interviews in the military and college, so I kept to the same principle. "KISS": Keep it simple, stupid." "Yes, Ma'am" and "No, Ma'am." I would not elaborate on any of the questions.

Once the interview was over and completed on her end, I had to wait for the supplemental background to be completed. One from Kalamazoo, where I had gone to college at Western, and the other with the New York State Police, where I was last stationed in the Army. The supplemental from Western took the longest for some reason. A Trooper from the Battle Creek Post was doing the supplemental investigation. I contacted him a couple of times to put a fire under his ass with a typical response. "I'm still working on it, Mr. Bommarito. Just keep running and doing those push-ups, Mr. Bommarito." Screw that, I was in the best shape of my life having just gotten out of the Army ready to start the Academy, and he knew that because he was a veteran too. "Get the goddamned background done, Skippy, and stop calling me Mr. Bommarito!"

I ended up getting into the 114th Trooper Recruit School. I should have made it into the 112th if the background investigator from Battle Creek had done that supplemental in a timely manner. I knew this because I became a background investigator early in my career. That supp covering a very short period of my life could have been done in about a week at most. The Governor authorized eight back-to-back recruit schools starting with the 107th through the 114th. Luckily, I made it into the 114th because there was almost a year and a half until they ran the 115th Recruit School. The United States Congress and President signed a huge crime bill in the 90s giving monies to the locals to hire city cops, deputies, and State Troopers.

After the background investigation is completed, an oral interview panel is convened with three department members and a civil service civilian within about a month, fairly fast considering the holdup with the background. The interview took place at MSP headquarters near Michigan State University's (MSU) campus on Harrison Rd. The HQ building originally belonged to MSU with them leasing it to MSP for a dollar a year until 2040 or so. Pretty cheap lease, seeing as the HQ building had been there since the 1930s. The old HQ building looked like a creepy mental hospital out of a 50s horror movie.

I stayed at a local fleabag motel in Lansing the night before so I would be fresh the following morning, and it also allowed me to drive the route to the HQ building doing a recon ahead of time. Pretty smart, eh? Don't want to be late for oral interview! I was required to wear business attire again, suit and tie—wouldn't expect anything else! The following morning I went to MSP HQ getting there at least 30 minutes early, checking in with the secretary and having a seat in the hallway of the infamous second floor. The second floor is where all the Executive Council (high-level brass) in the MSP worked. Later on in my career any issues or correspondence would henceforth be referred to the second floor. Oh shit, the second floor said we're doing this wrong. Damn it, the second floor said we have to mobilize for that! Fuck, Lt./Colonel so-and-so from the second floor is in the area, watch your p's and q's.

There were three other applicants sitting in lined-up chairs with me waiting for our interviews. We didn't say shit to each other. We just sat there waiting for out turn, keeping our mouths shut. I was finally called in for my interview, sitting in a chair with four men sitting at a table to the front, with notepads. There was an MSP Lieutenant, two Sergeants on either side, and a civilian gentleman to the far left. They asked me various questions about my past, including my drunk driving arrest from Western. "Oh shit, here we go!" I told the panel I was drunk, was of legal age to drink, but I never drove that car drunk and never crashed my car, as the Kalamazoo officer described in his report. When asked why he did what he did with the report, I replied, "I have no idea, sir." I never said one disparaging word about that officer, which I think they liked.

They asked me who the current director of the Michigan Department of State Police was, to which I replied, "Colonel Ritchie T. Davis." The Lt. in charge of the board got a pissed-off look on his face and said, "He's not the colonel! He's sitting in his office down the hall. Do you want to go ask him what his name is?" "Ugghhhh, no, sir." I had a get-out-of-jail free card. I told the board that when I attended the pre-employment seminar in Pontiac the troopers gave me a pamphlet with Colonel Davis on it showing him as the director. I took it out of my folder and showed it to them. That was my ace in the hole. At first, they thought I was a dumbass, and they had me until I put it back on the Troopers at the Pontiac Post. Ha! They then asked me If I had any relatives in the mafia. Uggghhh, I told them I did have distant relatives that had ties to the mob, but I didn't have any contact with them since my parents divorced when I was five years old. Shit, how did they find out about old Uncle Pete? Anyways, later to find out there was a Trooper Bommarito in the Michigan State Police when I was a young kid that was arrested for running cover and numbers for the Detroit mob in the 70s. As far as I knew, I had no relation to that Fredo!

They then gave me various scenario questions to respond to. I specifically remember one, asking if I was on patrol and had two vehicles speeding side by side, one a white Cadillac with an older white couple in it and the other a red Camaro with a carload of Black teenagers, which one would I stop. Shit, the Lt. in charge of the board was Black. Here we go. I answered the question fairly fast, stating I would stop the red Camaro because a carload of teenagers might be more apt to have something further going on in the vehicle, such as open intoxicants or something else. I never mentioned anything about race. Good answer, Mr. Bommarito; they appeared to like my response.

The Lt. then told me to close my eyes and tell them what items were in the room. I told him there was a picture of the governor behind him, an American flag to his right, and a Michigan flag to his left. I also described some other items in the room. Damn, that really impressed him! I then finished the interview, with them telling me I would be advised of my score in the near future. Some applicants found out their scores in the hallway after the interview. I figured those were ones that knew someone in the department, so I just left. The oral interview score was the same as the written exam, based on a 100-point scale. I scored a 96 with 5 more percentage points being added for veterans preference points, which gave me a 101. Damn, I was happy with those results.

The final step in the application process was taking a physical and psychological exam after getting a conditional offer of employment to attend the next MSP Recruit School. I also had to go see one of the department's eye specialists to examine my eyes from my being grounded from flying in the military, seeing if this would affect my performing duties required of a trooper. I passed the eye test with no problem having 20/15 vision. The military issue had to do with flying at night with night vision goggles on reducing my depth perception.

The psychological exam consisted of around 200 questions. Many of the questions were repeated with different wording. I suppose they were trying to see if you would change your answers so they could jam you up for not being consistent. You would have to be an idiot not to pick up on the tricky format! I remember a couple of questions such as "If you were in a line at a movie theater and someone took cuts, would you address it? Yes or no?" My response was yes, or hell yes, if I could have put that down. Another question was "Would you eat grapes at a grocery store without paying for them to see how they taste?" My response was no, again, hell no, if I could have put that down as an answer. They asked questions about honesty/integrity, etc. Well, I passed the psychological exam. Today's mindset would probably have the opposite answers. Don't say anything to the asshole taking cuts in the movie line, coexist and eat all the grapes you want: it's a healthy vegan thing! I was offered a position with the 114th Michigan State Police Trooper Recruit School to begin on Sunday March 10, 1996. Hot damn, it appears I'm going to be a Michigan State Trooper. Here we go, and we're off to the races!

Time to get a fresh haircut! I talked to the recruiter, and he said to get a military-style haircut shaved to the scalp. Hmm, I wonder what that entails. Again, good to be prior military! I had that done plenty of times in the Army. Not a big fan of the shaved head look, but it is what it is. I went to my regular barber, who were a bunch of old-timers up the road in Sterling Hgts. They knew I was going to the State Police Academy, so they gave me a good shaving. They also knew I'd be coming back every Saturday during the academy for a cleanup. The recruiter also told us recruits that we had to purchase "Sears-style" dungaree pants and button-down long sleeve shirts for the Academy. They were a dark blue uniform that mechanics would wear. I had to buy three sets of shirts and pants. I also had to buy and bring a pair of black shoes, no boots and no military, high-shine-style shoes. We had to bring a typewriter to use for report writing, no computers at the academy, which I found surprising. Was this 1996 or 1980? Turned out they had some computers but none for use by recruits, only staff.

Sunday March 10, 1996, my first day of Recruit School, a day never to be forgotten. My mother and stepfather also came. I was single at the time, thank god. No distractions, I love you honey, miss you, blah, blah, blah, I was so glad to be single going through the Academy. There were many recruits that were married and had a rough time leaving their spouse and/or kids every Sunday night to go back to the Academy. They had a short seminar for the families giving an idea of what to expect the next 18 weeks—yeah, 18 weeks; over the years, Academies have gotten longer and longer: 20 weeks to 22 weeks, then 24 to now 26? The higher-ups have decided to add a bunch of superfluous bullshit over the years. More administrative than meat and potatoes to be a good cop. What the fuck. They are not coming out any smarter or better troopers. In fact, most, if not all, of the millennials are lazy and dumbasses with no work ethic or motivation. Toward the end of my career they reminded me of Beavis and Butt-Head from the old Music Television (MTV) cartoon, duuhhh. They probably don't even know what MTV is. "My name is Cornholio. I need TP for my bunghole." Enough said.

The Academy staff gave us an overview of what to expect and answered any questions family might have. They then let us break for about an hour to go grab some dinner before we were to report back. I went to a burger joint with my parents really not being all that hungry, knowing what was in store. A few recruits left for dinner and never came back—what a bunch of pussies. It pissed the rest of us off because they took a spot that someone else could have had. Later I found out they called in standby applicants that night to report to the Academy the next day and start with the rest of us.

Again, boy, was I glad to be single during the Academy, no distractions. We had designated student parking to the far end of the parking lot. I parked my Jeep Wrangler in the designated student parking area, making sure I had no vehicle violations and all the proper paperwork in the glove box. I knew an inspection would be coming sometime in the near future. You better park where they tell you, or its your ass! Oh shit, they checked our vehicles after the families left. No window tint, no expired plates, better not have any contraband either, candy, soda pop, etc.! We lined up in front of the Academy, 85 or so of us with typewriters in one hand and a suitcase in the other. Yup, no iPads, Kindles, cell phones that only rich people owned, we were still old school. I used my olive drab Army C bag, which was perfect for what I needed. Not sure what the staff thought; they knew I had to be prior military, and that could be a good thing or bad thing, depending on the staff. I was lucky enough to have mostly emergency support (ES/SWAT) team members on staff. They were the badasses of the department and pretty military regimented most of them giving a little more respect to veterans. There were temporary staff that came from posts from all over the state and permanent staff that were assigned to training in Lansing and the Academy. The temp staff were more chill than the perms, who were mostly hard-ass Sergeants. We were from all around the state, the Upper Peninsula (U.P.) West Michigan, the Thumb, and Metro Detroit. What a vast group from within the same state. There were also a couple of recruits from Toledo, Ohio, moving up to Monroe, Michigan, to establish residency before starting the Academy. I had never been to the U.P. and found out they sound like the Canadians I had known in Windsor and rooted for the Green Bay Packers instead of the Detroit Lions, fellow recruits that were a bunch of cheese-heads! How could you be from Michigan and not be a Lions fan? Strange but cool at the same time.

We changed into our "Sears" dungarees after our family's left and went over administrative issues with staff. They issued us five gray T-shirts for physical training that had Michigan State Police on the front. They had stencils and black permanent markers for us to draw our names on the T-shirts. BOMMARITO on the front and back. They also gave us two pairs of shorts with MSP stitched in yellow on them at the bottom. One pair light blue and one dark blue. Why two different colors? Hmm, turned out so Academy staff could fuck with us concerning uniformity sometime in the near future. We also had two sets of generic gray hooded sweatshirts and pants that we had to put our names on. We had to buy those separately and bring them with our Sears dungarees. It was still pretty cold outside when we started the Academy in early March.

The State Police Academy located off I-96 and exit 98A is an eight-story brick building that was opened in the 70s. Two recruits to a room with the female recruits staying on the seventh floor. Every week the male recruits had to change roommates and floors. The females only had to change roommates. There is a huge MSP shield on the front top of the building looking toward the highway. The Academy has a swimming pool for water safety training and lifeguard certification ("the Tank," better not call it a pool!). There is an indoor shooting range with moving targets, multiple classrooms, and a large auditorium that we mainly used every day for classes. There were two elevators in the main lobby only used by staff. Recruits were advised to use the stairwells for all movement to the other floors. It was your ass if you were caught on the elevators. There was a full-service chow hall in the basement that included a salad bar—nice! We didn't have salad bars in Army basic training. There was a full-size gymnasium with basketball nets and multiple rope climbs. A long descending ramp led to the gym from the lower level of the Academy. This was where we lined up every morning for physical training (PT). A large square podium about four feet high was to the front of the gym, where P.T. staff could administer our physical training, which included push-ups, sit-ups, swivel hips, mountain climbers, squat thrusts, and various chair exercises.

There is a scenario house near the K-9 kennels that we trained in, with simulated ammunition (simunitions) that were small paintballs. There is also a large drive track off to the side of the Academy that's used for precision driving training and vehicle testing. The Michigan State Police and California Highway Patrol are the only two major organizations that perform yearly vehicle testing on passenger cars such as Chevrolet Caprices, Ford Crown Victorias, and Dodge Chargers; sport utility vehicles (SUVs) such as Jeep Cherokees, Chevrolet Tahoes, and Ford Explorers; motorcycles such as Harley Davidson Electra-Glides, BMW 1200s, Suzuki sport bikes, and Victory Cruisers that are used in law enforcement around the world. Having the Big 3—Ford, Chrysler, and General Motors—in your backyard helps getting vehicles for testing. For about a week of the Recruit School the drive track staff had about 15 Crown Vics lined up on the track with all kinds of emergency light configurations to replace our old-fashioned overhead bubble. There were light bars, solid red, solid blue, red and blue, V lights, and low-profile light bars. I wish I had a camera to take a picture of all the cars with the different lights on them; it was pretty cool.

After all that testing, our department kept the same old-fashioned oscillating bubble light. Staff showed us how to change that light, which was a bitch. You had to stand on either front door jamb, looking over the roof, taking a metal ring off the red bubble with a screwdriver. You then had to unscrew the bulbs, which were aircraft landing lights, take a new one out of the trunk, and screw that one in. There were two lights that rotated; usually, one went out a time, so it was best to carry at least two spare bulbs in the trunk of the patrol car. The lights were also super slow in the cold. The colder it was, the slower that bastard turned. If you punched the interior roof while the lights were on, it would make the motor go faster. Eventually the old aircraft lights were replaced with LEDs that had all kinds of different flash patterns. If these broke, the whole light would have to be replaced, not single bulbs anymore.

Going through military basic training totally prepared me for the State Police Academy. Up at the butt crack of dawn with reveille playing on the loudspeakers in the hallways, lining up on the ramp in alphabetical order to get our asses handed to us with PT. The PT staff gradually worked us into a regimented routine for the first three weeks or so, and then they dropped the hammer. We would do floor exercises, push-ups, sit-ups, etc., and then bust out the gym doors to go on distance runs. Again started slowly with short distance and then gradually picking up the pace and distance as we got better. It was pretty ugly in the beginning. A lot of the recruits, especially the females, had trouble keeping up. I had no problems with the running.

We would go back to our rooms after PT having to bust ass taking a quick shit, shower, and shave before inspection. Each floor had a community shower and toilets/sinks in the middle of the floor. The rooms surrounded the bathroom/showers, which we called the "head." Each room had two single-size beds with two military-grade blankets, a pillow, and sheets. The bedding had to be changed every morning, and the beds had to be made in the classic military style, tight where you better be able to bounce a coin of the mattress. I showed many non-prior military how to make a bed properly. Each room also had a counter with lock drawers and lighting for each recruit to secure valuables and our weapons when issued to us. The rooms also had another sink that you could use to shave or brush your teeth in if the ones in the head were all taken in the morning.

We had inspection every morning after showering before we went to chow. We would scramble trying to get our shit straight listening to the elevators going up and down to the various floors hoping the staff would pick someone else's floor before yours. Troopers and Sergeants would come off the elevator and inspect our rooms and uniforms for cleanliness. They would check for dust, properly made beds/bunks, and other violations to ding us on. We had to stand outside our room in the hallway at attention and be asked various questions by staff. They also checked our hands and finger nails for cleanliness and haircuts for tightness. As time went on, they would ask us legal questions, motor vehicle code questions, etc. When we were issued our firearms, a SIG Sauer 9 mm semi-automatic pistol and a Smith and Wesson .357 Magnum revolver for our pocket gun, we had to keep those weapons clean and ready to be inspected by staff at any time, either in the morning or any other time throughout the day.

A Trooper assigned as temporary staff to the Recruit School from various parts of the state was assigned to assist the recruits, three or four of us at a time. They were our mentors, having short meetings once a week to advise us how we were progressing and help with any other needs that came up. My trooper/mentor would end up having a unique influence on me throughout my career in various capacities as a Sergeant and Lieutenant that I would work for again.

The staff, primarily the Recruit School Commander, who was a Sergeant, selected a recruit to be class commander, rotating this position, who then selected squad commanders for the day, which gave everyone a chance to be a leader. We had four squads in our Recruit School, Adam, Baker, Charlie, and David. They put the big boys in A and B squads and the smaller recruits and females in C and D squads. I was in C squad, being a bit on the thinner side. I found out this was done for water safety and boxing. You don't want a huge corn-fed recruit in A squad from the UP boxing a female from D squad and vice versa, having a small female trying to save a big ox from A squad in water safety, someone might drown!

We would go to chow after inspection, eating as fast as we could and healthy as the staff wanted us to eat. Each squad would have three or four recruits that would have to stay after chow in the kitchen, helping the civilian workers clean off tables and dishes. Just like the military, KP (kitchen patrol) duty teaches character and humility. After chow we went to various classes, water safety in the tank and firearms classes. As time went on, early in the school we had a flag raising dedication ceremony outside for troopers that had been killed in the line of duty. It's a surreal humbling experience not realizing at that time that some of my personal friends would be added to the list of fallen troopers! Damn, I might be one of them! At the end of the week we would have one or more Friday night speakers come and address the recruits. Some were MSP personal, some were family of fallen troopers, and a couple were politicians. One MSP inspector really stuck out to us. He was an old, salty guy that probably could have retired 10 years prior. He told us many stories about his career and how we would look back toward the end and remember him saying how fast our career would fly by. You'll have 5, 10, 15, 20 years and then you're out the door—boy, was he right! He then stressed to us that family comes first. Not working overtime on holidays or volunteering to do things for the department on your own time. He told us how being too dedicated left to the divorce of his wife and his, having a very difficult time coping with his daughter being killed in a car crash. "Family comes first," that's what he kept stressing to us. We were all in tears by the end of his talk.

Among the Friday night guest speakers, we had the parents of two Troopers killed in a patrol car crash that occurred around three years before our Recruit School. They were a two-man car responding to back up an off-duty Trooper that was involved in a bar fight in Pontiac. They tried to beat a train, crossing the tracks around the gates, getting hit and killed. What a tragedy, both moms were crying and again had everyone in our school crying along with them. They stressed to us that they died not even being able to help that off-duty trooper. I would learn to apply that throughout my career. "You can't help anyone if you don't make it there, so slow down and get there in one piece!"

We had another speaker that was Lieutenant specializing in hazardous materials (hazmat). He had worked in different parts of the state, including the Detroit area. He stressed to us, "Don't be in a rush to head into chemical spills or any biological situations without assessing the situation." He said this advice could apply to basically any situation, which was true. He had us repeat the phrase over and over at least 10 times. "What do I got?" "What do I need?" You show up to a traffic crash—What do I got? Three cars, one rollover with injuries. What do I need? Dispatch, start me at least two wreckers and medical for minor injuries. You respond to a suicide scene. What do I got? Gunshot wound to the head, no suspicious circumstances. What do I need? Send me the medical examiner (ME) and another trooper to investigate the scene.

Michigan, being the Great Lakes State, has a body of water no farther than six miles from anywhere you stand. The Michigan State Police has had troopers killed in the line of duty trying to save drowning victims in the past. Water safety was a huge part of our training being completed within the first four weeks. We lost at least three or four recruits that quit the Academy during the training and before the water safety practical. I guess they didn't want to fail and get washed out. Come to find out if you tried and didn't quit, everyone was passed that tried. Try, try, try, and try again, don't quit! That was what the staff was trying to relay to us. I grew up with pools in my backyard for most of my life and considered myself a pretty good swimmer, but that water safety training still kicked my ass. It was definitely a workout and a mental challenge. The Olympic-size pool (tank) had a viewing window in the basement, which was pretty cool, so staff could watch us above and under the water. The deep end slanted down like most large training pools. There was that oh so distinctive smell of chlorine that permeated the tank area. Tables were set up toward the front of the area for classroom instruction, where we learned how to "suck, tuck, and roll" getting away from a drowning victim trying to drag you under the water while saving them. What the fuck, who would think that happens? It does. They panic and claw, punch and kick at you trying to flail in the water as you're trying to save them. Ultimately possibly having to let them go and drown rather than have them take you to the bottom also—hard concept to swallow.

They taught us how to swim with our uniforms on, taking our shoes and gun belts off, and how to make a flotation device out of our uniform shirts. Communication was huge: call Dispatch and request help or have someone call 911 if you're not by your police radio for some reason. Another part of the training was having the ability to tread water for an extended period of time. We would get in groups of five in a circle in the deep end. The staff would throw two bricks in the pool, and we would have to swim to the bottom of the deep end and come back up with those bricks. We would then have to pass those bricks around in a circle to each other while treading water. That was a son of a bitch forcing us to pass them off like a hot potato to the recruit next to you. We were also put through cold water immersion training, having to sit in a metal tub full of ice water to experience hypothermia. Holy shit, that water was cold—talk about the shivers. This allowed us to realize how fast you lose dexterity and body control functions from being in cold water too long. "Say yes to Michigan" winter wonderland. When we finally got out of the tub we had to go in the showers in the locker room, starting with cold water and then gradually moving four or so shower heads over to warmer and warmer water, with staff monitoring us the whole time for safety purposes.

Again three or four recruits quit the night before, leaving the Academy. Not me! Bring it on, boys! The water safety/lifeguard practical was a bitch! They normally did it outside at Davis Pond, which was near the Academy. Lucky for us, it was still too cold outside when it came time for our practical, so we had to do it indoors. The first part was a written exam, which sucked, not because it was too hard, but psychologically, you had to have your backs to the water having to hear other recruits get their asses handed to them in the tank during the life-saving practical. Better not turn around to look, or they would chew your ass. One of my buddies eye poked a Sgt./victim to get him to stop fighting, and the Sgt. punched him in the head. Damn, son, don't screw with the instructors— not the smart thing to do! We had to do the practical running into the tank area from the outside hallway with our dungarees on. There was a staff member in the deep end acting as if they were drowning, flailing in the water, yelling for help. There were other staff members around the outside of the tank yelling at us at the same time. "Do something, they're drowning, come on help them," all the while you're trying to take off your gun belt and shoes before you jump into action. If you don't have one of them call 911, FAIL; if you don't get your ass into the tank fast enough, FAIL; if you can't drag them over to the side of the tank and lift them out to start first aid, FAIL; if you don't perform CPR properly, FAIL. On the first attempt at reaching them they slap, punch, and flail, forcing you to suck, duck, and tuck to get away from them. You have to tell them to stop fighting, or else they won't. Everyone was ultimately given a second or third chance to pass. Don't quit! We had one recruit who was a prior Detroit police officer. He couldn't swim when we started the Academy, having to wear water wings on his arms like little kids would wear. He didn't quit, and he passed the water safety practical! Everyone that stayed and didn't quit the night before passed. Yeah! I was now a certified American Red Cross Lifeguard, and they even gave us cards to prove it! Maybe if I didn't make it through the Academy I could go out to California and get on *Bay Watch*?

Now that water safety was done, we could get onto the business of learning how to be Troopers! The classroom instruction really stepped up a notch. The first part was learning the important parts of the Michigan Motor Vehicle Code. Statutes covering every moving violation you could imagine and how to write a ticket for it. Some of the more popular violations would be speeding, improper lane use, seatbelt violations, illegal window tint, registration/plate violations, and basic speed law. Our two instructors were Sgts., both ES/SWAT badasses. They were funny as hell and brought tennis balls to the first class. "What are these for, recruits" Uggghhh? No idea, sir. "Let me show you." One of them took a ball and threw it at a recruit dozing off. "Bam, wake up, stupid!" Ha, that was some funny shit. I was pretty good about not getting sleepy, but some others were horrible. The tennis ball idea was awesome! They tried to explain the different statutes giving examples, which were funny, and telling some pretty funny stories. One of the instructors ended up being one of my Sgts. at my first post. He was a badass there too! "Do we write attitude tickets?" The brass in the department would say no. They told us, "Hell, Yeah." If you stop someone and they're an asshole, stroke 'em! They taught us a great quote, "If someone gives you sugar, treat them nice; if they're an asshole, give them spice." I really loved that portion of the training and knew I would probably be a traffic trooper/ Road Dog most of my career, which did turn out to be the case.

Another huge portion of the classroom/auditorium training was with learning the Michigan Compiled Laws. Mostly property crimes: breaking and entering (B&E), malicious destruction of property (MDOP), larceny, etc. The other major portion was crimes against persons: murder, criminal sexual conduct (CSC), armed robbery (AR), domestic assault, etc. We would receive instruction on each block and have to take a written test at the end. If you failed a written test, you were given a second chance, but fail again and you were out of the Academy. A minimum of 70 percent was required across the board for everyone. Our primary legal instructor was a Sgt. who was a perm at the Academy and he was also a lawyer. He was a great guy and always had great examples of case law and scenarios that would help us remember different laws and how to apply them so we didn't get jammed up later in our careers for violating anyone's rights. We learned about search and seizure laws, warrants, and custodial arrests, with him always stressing, "When in doubt about something, ask a supervisor or prosecutor unless it's an officer safety issue; better to be judge by twelve then buried by six." His wife was pregnant during our Recruit School, actually having the baby boy during the school. He used to bring him up all the time. "Does Luke like law? Yes, Luke loves law!" His son, that baby born during the Academy, would end up becoming a trooper and getting assigned to my post right before I retired—too funny! I failed one test, "Crimes against Persons," and had to retake it, passing it the second time, thank God! We had to pass all the legal tests and then pass a final MLEOTC test at the end of the Academy before we could become certified law enforcement officers/Troopers in Michigan.

Firearms training was fun. I was never a big gun guy even with my military weapons training. We were issued brand-new SIG Sauer 9 mm semiautomatic pistols as our primary weapon and a five-shot Smith and

Wesson .357 Magnum revolver as our backup/pocket gun. We were also trained in the use of Remington model 870 police shotguns, shooting slugs and buckshot, and H&K model 53 rifle. That H&K rifle was badass! We actually were one of the first agencies to carry rifles on patrol even before the Bank of America' robbery/shootout in Los Angeles, California. Better to have it and not need it than need it and not have it!

We pumped thousands of rounds through our various weapons up on the shooting range at the Academy. Our instructors were all older salty troopers that were all about business. No fucking around on the range, quick way to be booted out of the Recruit School! I did pretty well at shooting at first, earning the highest award of "Distinguished Expert" for our first qualification. I then took a downward spiral or had a brain cramp, probably psychological, having trouble shooting. I never shot "DE" again only making "Expert" for the rest of my career. Fuck it! I thought the Expert badge looked better on the uniform anyways. The "DE" badge was bright gold with gold lettering—you couldn't read what the hell the damn thing said. The "Expert" badge was black with white lettering, easy to read. We shot a shit ton of rounds from various positions and distances including kneeling, around barricades, and weak handed. We were also taught the "weaver" stance, standing on an angle, limiting the amount of target for bad guys to shoot at. The instructors also taught us to drop the shells on the ground with a backup "snubby" revolver, citing a California Highway Patrol incident form years prior where four CHP Officers were gunned down in a gunfight with shit-head bikers because the officers tried to empty their shells into their hands instead of letting them drop to the ground. They resorted to training that had cost them their lives. Train as you fight, and fight as you were trained was beaten into our subconscious. They also told us over and over again if you're in a gunfight, bring a long gun with you, either a rifle or shotgun. Kind of reminded me of that scene from *The Untouchables* with Sean Connery when he tells the Mafioso, "Never bring a knife to a gun fight!" Having a long gun definitely came in handy multiple times during my career including a shooting I would be involved in later on.

The Academy definitely had a thorough and realistic course of shooting. We ended up shooting that same course out the field for the majority of my career. Once we got to the field we had spring, summer, and fall shoots. The spring shoot was a warm-up, the summer shoot was for badge qualification, and the fall shoot was usually for fun with different styles of shooting. The agency that all the training fell under to be a certified officer in Michigan was MLEOTC. This later changed to MCOLES toward the end of my career.

Halfway through the Academy they sent us home to do a ride along with our home Post, where we had applied. The Richmond Post covered my home of residence in Sterling Heights. They sent A and B squads home in week eight and squads C and D in week nine. We continued our law instruction and various other courses while the other squads were home. One recruit pissed off the staff (my hot background investigator) at the Richmond Post, so we paid the price with what they called Incentive Training (IT) when they came back before we went home. IT was the staff's way of making us do push-ups, squat thrusts, and other PT for disciplinary reasons. We had an IT card that we kept in our shirt pockets. If you got stung during inspection for a dusty room, wrinkled uniforms, etc., they would administer IT to you. I had to do it once in Recruit School because my roommate at the time had his uniforms facing the wrong way on the hangers, duh dumbass! "Recruit Bommarito, it's your responsibility to check your equipment as well as your roommates." Shit, okay, I'll guess I can do push-ups for my roommate being ate the fuck up. I was never into the peer-pressure form of discipline, which was also done in the military. I always thought the dipshit, including *me*, that screws up should pay the price, not everyone around him or her. Damn it, why make things harder than they need to be?

I went home during week nine and had to report to the Richmond Post in business attire, again suit and tie, and basically do a ride-along with troopers at the post. Fuck, they stuck me with my hot background investigator/Trooper. Word spread at the Academy that she was the one who got that recruit in trouble, forcing us to do IT because she didn't like his demeanor during his stay there. I did everything I could to kiss her ass! "Yes, Ma'am, No Ma'am!" "Do you want me to take your boots off and rub your feet, Ma'am?" "Just keeeeding!" It was not my intention to do worse that the last guy and have everyone at the Academy think I was a piece of shit. It actually went pretty well, and she smelled nice. We went to a domestic with another female Trooper, where the male suspect started cocking off at the mouth. I stood back and watched as they knocked his ass to the ground placing him into custody instantly. Damn, I was impressed. They didn't put up with his bullshit! They actually gave me a quote that I used throughout my career, "Don't start no shit, won't be no shit"!

We would stop by her house daily for the entire week to let her dogs out. Weird, no kids, and her husband had left, disappearing years prior, nowhere to be found? She would stop some cars in between calls, write some tickets, and have me fill out some paperwork for experience. We also went to the shooting range and shot for the spring shoot. That was pretty cool shooting with real Road Troopers.

The PT staff had told us not to do PT while at home, telling us to take a break. I didn't listen, as Napoleon Dynamite would say, "Idiot!" Halfway through the week, I went on a run and pulled a groin muscle. Fuck, I had that injury all the way through the rest of Recruit School. Grin and bear it, there was no way I was going to wash out for a bullshit injury.

Besides the groin injury, I made it back to the Academy in one piece without pissing off my hot female Trooper I was assigned to even though she was the hard-ass that jammed up the last recruit that rode with her!

It was time to get back to the grind of Recruit School life. We still had a lot of legal to learn, first aid training and certification, patrol techniques practicing traffic stops, and patrol car precision drive track training.

Legal classes really stepped up, requiring a lot of studying at night. There was a legal book written by a retired MSP member, "Steffel," with excerpts from our instructor and an inspector in our department. The law book/bible for police in Michigan was referred to as "Steffel." It was laid out in a simple, easy to learn manner. I referred to that same book throughout my career. An updated version came out later we were issued, but I always referred back to the original "Steffel" we were issued. There are always legal updates that constantly come out concerning new case law etc., most being minor changes. I passed all the law classes minus "Crimes against Persons," which I had to retake. You are only allowed one fail, so if you can't pass it the second time, they wash you out due to academic deficiencies.

We then had first aid training. That was a bitch, as it should be. Being able to tend to injured citizens or your partner is definitely a priority in law enforcement. Being first responders, we beat EMS and Fire to the scene most of the time. Probably because we drive faster! We had to learn and become certified in CPR and how to treat all kinds of injuries from broken bones to gunshot wounds. "Head tilt, chin lift." I had to say that 50 times to remember proper cardiopulmonary resuscitation (CPR) techniques. The staff incorporated first aid into patrols with simulated traffic crashes and other scenarios. It was actually pretty cool simulating different types of incidents that you might come in contact with as a trooper. We lost a couple recruits that could not pass the first aid training be it tests or CPR. See ya!

Drive track training was a really fun part of the Recruit School. The precision drive track was right on Academy grounds. The drive track staff consisted of four full-time Sergeants and one Lieutenant. We used

Caprice Classics with the LT1 Corvette engine—man, they were fast!—and slower, more unstable Ford Crown Victorias. The Chevy was a far better patrol car. I-96 went right by the Academy and track, and citizens would sometimes stop on the freeway shoulders to watch us driving around the track with our lights and sirens on. There were different variants of degree turns and stop simulating the road conditions we would encounter in the field as troopers. There was also a skid pad where they would turn on a huge sprinkler system that sprayed water onto the slick blacktop and across your windshield as you were spinning out of control in circles. We learned how to do high-speed driving, braking, and patrol car handling during various conditions. The staff set up a coned-off course in the center of the track where you had to accelerate forward and then backward for a set time without knocking down cones. Every cone you knocked over took time of the clock. There was a female recruit in my squad that was having trouble with this exercise. I helped her telling to line up the rear deck light on the patrol car with the cones as she was backing up and drive a straight line with that light and the cones. She passed—whew, that was close. We had a couple recruits that failed driving and were washed out. See ya! The staff then took us out onto the Lansing area freeway system, four recruits to a car with an instructor simulating traffic stops. They would have other staff drive around in department unmarked cars. We would initiate the stops with lights and sirens and use proper approach techniques (not getting your ass run over) to get a feel of what it would be like once we graduated and hit the streets. Pretty cool and fun. During the off-site training the staff let us stop by a gas station so we could get a soda and some snacks, which was a cool break from academy food.

Boxing, what can I say about boxing. They tried to match us up with other recruits of comparable stature. Each fight consisted of three two-minute rounds. I was paired up with a shorter, stocky recruit that cleaned my clock in the second round. Bam, bam, down for the count. I actually went unconscious for a second, so I had to go to Sparrow

Hospital in Lansing to get checked out. No concussion, just a slight headache. I felt like a pussy, but what are you going to do. I asked to fight again the next day but was told no by staff. This experience definitely helped with scuffles I would have later in my career. It taught me not to let someone get the better of me. Basically if someone takes a swing at you, duck faster! We didn't lose anybody for boxing, thank God! My ass would have been hitting the highway. As long as you put in the effort, you passed. I guess getting knocked out was considered good effort!

All the recruits would line up in the stairwell, waiting for class or to go to chow. One day an instructor yelled out my name, "Recruit Bommarito, front and center." I bust my ass down the stairs. "Sir, yes sir." I have a subpoena here with your name on it for a felony case and jury trial. "Uh, sir, I have no idea what that is in reference to. I have never been a police officer prior to coming to the State Police Academy." Come to find out there was another Christopher Bommarito who was a civilian in the crime lab in Lansing. WTF? I met him after I graduated, stopping by the lab to introduce myself. He was a blood specimen and matter splatter specialist. We looked nothing like each other but were both originally from the east side of Michigan. For about the first 10 years in the department I would receive calls for him and vice versa. Human resources put things in his file meant for me, and I had things in my personnel file from him. He finally left the State Police for private practice before I retired, thank god!

Patrols training was fun. Staff would take our squad out to the scenario house where they had a beat-up civilian car and a beat-up Chevy Caprice goose. We would go through different traffic stop techniques with staff acting like bad guys. It was a realistic as you could get in a sterile environment. They might not do anything and comply or jump out of the car and start shooting simunitions (small paintballs) at you forcing you to take cover and fire back. One of my patrol instructors who I would later troop with at the Rockford Post was a badass. He was a behemoth of a Black man that spoke with vigor and demanded respect. He reminded me of my Senior Drill Sergeant when I was in basic training in the Army at Fort Knox, Kentucky. Both badasses. He told us recruits the most important part of police work is going home at the end of your shift. He also gave us the "ask 'em, tell 'em, take 'em" quote when dealing with a subject on traffic stops. Ask them politely for their driver's license, tell them to provide it if no response, then drag their ass out the vent window if they refuse. He had worked in Detroit for years and didn't fuck around when it came to officer safety and going home at the end of his shift!

The end of the Recruit School was nearing—yeah! As we got closer to finishing, probably three weeks out, the staff let us wear our actual Michigan State Police uniforms instead of the Sears dungarees. The uniform pants actually had a sap pocket that would later be used to put our big Mag flashlights in. Saps were a leather handheld tool filled with lead that were used in the day to knock somebody on their ass during an arrest or confrontation. The department quit using or allowing saps to be used on patrol years prior. When I got to the field there were some really old-timers that still had and carried their department-issued saps! There was one time we pissed them off as a class so they made us wear the dungarees the whole next day, part of the program, I think. Positive and negative motivation are always part of military regimented-style training. When we went to PT in the morning, the staff brought in a boom box and played motivational music including Stevie Wonder and Queen; it was actually fun doing PT to music. When we left the gym to go on our runs, up to 10 miles by now, staff would allow prior military to call out cadence during the runs. I called cadence a couple of times enjoying it during the runs. We were so close to graduating I could taste it. The Academy staff was actually treating us like human beings.

We received our post assignments the Friday prior to the last three weeks. There are seven districts in the Michigan State Police. The first district covers the Lansing area, where headquarters is located. The second district covers Metro Detroit. The third district covers the thumb. There used to be a fourth district, but they got rid of it years prior. The fifth district covers lower West Michigan. The sixth district covers the second-largest city in Michigan, Grand Rapids. The seventh district covers Northern mid-Michigan to the UP, and the eighth district covers the Upper Peninsula (UP). When we were half way through the school we submitted the top three posts in the state to our mentors that we would like to start out our careers at. I put Traverse City as my number one, Paw Paw near WMU, where I went to college, as my number two, and Bay City as my third choice. Bay City Rollers was a cool band. Rumor had it if you were a fuck-up and they wanted to get rid of you during field training (FT), they would send you to one of the harder posts with ball-busting field training officers (FTOs), which were well known at the time as Ypsilanti, Richmond, Flint, and Bridgeport. They had a 100-mile rule at the time where you had to go to a post that was at least 100 miles away from your post of application, so getting posted to Richmond was a wash.

We were told to stop by our new posts over the weekend and introduce ourselves letting them know we would be coming soon. They already knew who we were. We received our post assignments in the auditorium. The Recruit School Commander called us down alphabetically. "Recruit Bommarito, you are being assigned to the Jonesville Post." WTF, I went down there, got a piece of paper with Jonesville (Post #19) collar brass on it. The number 19 stood for the ninth post in the first district. I had never heard of Jonesville in my life, had no idea where it was, and probably had the "deer in the headlight" expression on my face. Then I was advised I would be going there by myself, fuck! The Battle Creek Post got five cubs, Flint five, Ypsilanti six, and I have to go it alone. Just like my Army assignment, I had no luck. One of my buddies in Recruit School used to be a Hillsdale County Deputy. Jonesville is the "Maybury" of Hillsdale County, literally! He pulled me aside and told me a little about Jonesville when we went up to our rooms. Jonesville was located in Hillsdale County, which is known for Hillsdale College, which is an extremely conservative private University. He reassured me that Hillsdale County was a cool place to work with two state lines at the south end of the county, Ohio and Indiana. I was still apprehensive but felt a little better after talking to Joe.

That Saturday, I drove my happy ass out to Hillsdale County to stop by the Jonesville Post. I was being assigned there by myself with most other posts having two or more recruits being assigned to them. Flint might have five, Battle Creek five, Paw Paw three, etc. It kind of sucked going there myself but, whatever, it is what it is! I got a map and took US-12 from Ypsilanti through the Irish Hills into Jonesville. The post was located right on US-12, Michigan Ave across from a 76 gas station. I went into the front door of the post in suit and tie again and introduced myself as Recruit Bommarito out of the 114th Recruit School, shortly to be coming to the post. There was a salty Desk Sergeant with his feet up on the counter reading a newspaper. Oh shit, here comes the ball-busting. "I don't give a shit who you are." Have a seat, and I will call a Trooper up to show you around. A female Trooper came to the front desk from the squad room introducing herself. She was very nice and not a dick, like the desk Sergeant. The Jonesville Post was an old two-story "Works Program" post that was built with monies from the federal government under President Franklin Roosevelt in the early 30s. Classic brick with a large limestone Michigan State Police script on the front facade. Oscar G. Olander was the director of the State Police when all those posts were built, so they were called Oscar G. Posts. Plenty of cancer-causing lead paint and asbestos! The basement had water damage with that musty, old smell. Reminded me of a couple houses I lived in as a young kid in Detroit. There was a tiny single-car garage attached to the rear of the post, and of all things, a cemetery directly behind the post. Fuck, I'm superstitious, especially after hearing that a Trooper had recently killed himself in the basement of the "Bad Ax" post with a shotgun, which was also an old "Oscar G." Post. Creepy in a small way! I left the post and checked a couple of apartment complexes in Hillsdale to live in since I was a single young man at the time. I found a single-bedroom apartment at the Hillsdale Apts. and signed a lease ready to move in after I graduated the Academy on July 12.

The last two weeks during the morning wake-up they played the song "Highway Patrol" by Junior Brown instead of the usual military revile on the loudspeakers. Another positive motivational moment letting us know we were almost to the end. Ah, but a couple of female recruits tested the waters by coming down to formation wearing makeup. Nope, get back to your rooms, and take that shit off!

The last week of Recruit School was the most fun, and the staff made it that way. We really came together as a class, and it showed. Everyone was on step and excited to become a Michigan state trooper. We had a nice steak dinner with family the night before graduation at the Academy cafeteria, and then there was a party even with alcohol at a Holiday Inn in Lansing the night before graduation. We were told to behave within reason being advised, "Your ass can still be kicked out one day before graduation; it's happened in the past." Ha, they weren't going to get me on that one, there were definitely some recruits that drank too much the night before! We actually stayed at the hotel, and myself and some other single recruits called it an early night. The married recruits and ones with girlfriends or boyfriends, they were the partiers. Not I, McFly!

We had to get up and get back to the Academy the next day. I think I set three alarm clocks and had the hotel call my room for a wake-up call. Can you imagine sleeping in and missing the graduation? Hell no! Graduation day we mustered in the auditorium in the Academy where they actually gave us real bullets for our duty weapons. Wow, that was a true sign we were about to become State Troopers. They also finally let the female recruits wear makeup. Wow! We were put on buses and then taken to the Lansing Center for the graduation ceremony. One point in my life when I was finally happy to be on a shitbox bus. The ceremony was really nice with family and friends present. They had a patrol car/ blue goose and a Harley Davidson motorcycle in the lobby when you walked in. We marched in wearing our summer uniforms and garrison hats and were sat down in alphabetical order for the oath of office and presentation of badges. I was skinny as a bean pole, I had lost around 30 lbs. during the Academy but still in the best shape of my life.

We had the Director of the United States Secret Service as our guest speaker. He was a badass! Governor Engler had hired so many Troopers they had gotten close to running out of badges. They had to make some more in the 1700 and 1800 series. The recruit before me was given the badge number 1740. I was called up and given the badge number 1741, and the next recruit received 1742, etc. Some received their dad's or family member's if available or a badge that coincided with a post assignment; for example, Richmond (Post 24) might get a badge 241, Rockford (Post 61) might get a badge 611, etc. I was the first one in the department's history to be issued the badge number 1741 brand-new from the manufacturer. Pretty cool to have that honor. We took some pictures after the ceremony and then had to go back to the Academy to get the rest of our gear, clothes, and uniforms. The staff allowed our families to help us clear our rooms, kind of surreal; I felt like I had accomplished something bigger than I could ever imagine. Wow, I was really a Michigan state trooper! I went from being a recruit to a cub. Newbie Troopers were called "cubs" in reference to the babies of momma bears (smoky bears).

There was a recruit, who turned out to be one of my career-long buddies, in my school that had started three Academies. He failed a law test getting washed out in the 112th, got injured during the 113th, and finally made it through ours, the 114th Trooper Recruit School—what a glutton for punishment. If you got washed out and weren't a broke dick or on the staffs shit list, they would normally make you an offer to come back to the next Recruit School to try again.

The 114th Michigan State Police Trooper Recruit School started with 85 recruits and ended up graduating 72 Troopers. Ten of those quit or got fired during Field Officer Training (FTO) and around 10 more would leave the department for various reasons during my career. There were around 50 of us around when I retired in 2019. Even though I lost many personal friends during my career, thankfully no one out of my Recruit School was lost in the line of duty over that span.

CHAPTER 2: JONESVILLE?

NEWS ARTICLE: "Jonesville State Police Post Welcomes New Trooper." What can I say about Jonesville, great place to start and great place to retire! Jonesville is located in Hillsdale County, which is an extremely conservative county. When I received my post assignment I had never heard of Jonesville, Michigan, and didn't even know where the hell it was. I think I had a duh look on my face when I was told where I would be starting out my career! A fellow recruit who was a Hillsdale County deputy gave me a bit of information about the Jonesville Post. A prominent conservative school, Hillsdale College, is located in Hillsdale County and is known worldwide as an elite, private, conservative college. New Troopers fresh out of the Academy are referred to as "cubs." State Troopers are known as full-grown bears,ramp rangers and blue bellies, county deputies as county mounties, shit shirts, or brown clowns, and city officers as city kitties. Hence "cubs," the babies/newbies of the full-grown bears. We graduated from the Academy on Friday and had to report on the following Monday! I was advised I would be working the day shift, which meant a 6 a.m. start time. There we go again having to get up at 5 a.m. again. Screw it, I had no choice in the matter and was used to it, I guess! There were three shifts at that time at all posts in the Michigan State Police. Days, 6 a.m.–2 p.m., afternoons 2 p.m.–10 p.m., and midnights 10 p.m.–6 a.m. I was the only trooper sent to Jonesville from the 114th Recruit School. Everything I learned I had to do on my own. I didn't have anybody to study with or compare notes with. I didn't have anyone to bitch to about the training to follow! Some other posts were sent from two to five recruits, lucky bastards.

They had fellow recruits they could learn and grow with, not me! I'll do what I have to do and get over to Metro Detroit as fast as possible.

A field training officer (FTO) manual, which we called the Rook book, was issued to each new Trooper with specific assignments that had to be completed during different phases and weeks of the FTO program. The department had "official orders" that addressed and dealt with every aspect of law enforcement that the MSP could come up with or think of. Reminded me of Articles when I was in the Army. Basically the way government covers its ass! Each new cub had to attend an autopsy, skirted that one somehow, process/fingerprint a crime scene, issue traffic citations for various offenses, etc. The purpose of the manual was to make us well rounded Troopers before we were allowed to patrol on our own. Those assignments had to be discussed and signed off with your assigned FTO. The FTO program was broken down into four phases over 17 weeks, three phases with an FTO rating you progressively, and then the last phase four, called the shadow phase. During shadow, you drove the patrol car and answered all calls and worked throughout the day as if you were alone in the car and on complaints. Your FTO rode shotgun, only observing, not saying anything unless required because you stepped on your dick hard; they then would intercede and take over the situation. Your shadow FTO is always your first phase FTO. They get to see how you've progressed over the FTO period deciding if any refresher training is needed and or termination for a multitude of reasons.

Monday morning came fast. I showed up and put my gear and uniforms in a locker room that had 10 lockers on either side of a walkway that didn't even have enough room to bump butts while changing. I went into the squad room with my FTO, a 20-year salty Trooper mustache in all arguing with a 10-year female Trooper telling her to fuck off and leave him alone. "Fuck," I thought to myself, "I'm in a world of shit; what a way to start my first day." They both told the cub (me) to step out of the squad room and go upstairs by the front desk while they had it out! I looked up at the board in the lobby, and there was a cut-out picture of my face on a cheerleader jumping through the air titled "The Jonesville State Police Post Welcomes New Trooper Vinny Bommarito."

I was now known and until I left Jonesville as Vinny in reference to Vinny Barbarino, John Travolta's character from the TV show *Welcome Back, Kotter*. I guess there are worse nicknames to be stuck with! Ha, I'll take Vinny. "Vinny, load the patrol car with two long guns and study your Rook Book." "Sir, yes sir." My first day on the job was fairly routine. We made some traffic stops, wrote some tickets, and responded to a few complaints. We were dispatched to a felony complaint concerning a larceny of a hunting trailer. The trailer was worth more than a $1000 bucks, so that made it a felony. Most of the property crimes in Michigan all had the same dollar amount. Anything over a grand made it a felony, easy enough to remember. The complainant, or person reporting the crime, happened to be Black. That's worth mentioning because I worked in Hillsdale County for just under two years and saw maybe two Black people the whole time and knew of no Black residents in Jonesville. I grew up in Detroit, so no big deal to me. My first complaint involved a victim from Detroit, where I was from? I could relate to the victim and not the suspect. The suspect was a simpleton that thought he had done nothing wrong. The victim had left the hunting trailer on the suspect's property having a land lease agreement with him. He had not corresponded with him for a couple years and not been over to Hillsdale to hunt. The suspect ended up selling the trailer for cash, not getting permission to sell it by the victim. The incident was borderline civil because there was no written contract, only verbal. We took a report for larceny by conversion and turned it over to the Hillsdale prosecutor for review. They issued a felony warrant for the suspect a couple weeks later.

The rest of the week we investigated various complaints and worked traffic. I was only allowed to stop vehicles for non-speed unless I pace-clocked the vehicles with my speedometer for at least a one-fourth of a mile. Our speedometers on our patrol cars were calibrated for accuracy so we could testify in court that our speed matched the violators for a steady distance. We were advised to look for non-speed violations such as seatbelt, lane use, stop sign, and window tint. I would drive one day and then switch with my FTO, letting him drive. If we issued a citation, they were all handwritten and allowed for three different violations to be put on the same ticket. My handwriting was horrible with me getting my balls busted for it for years. It definitely looked like a doctor's writing. I told people I have a bachelor's degree of science and can't go back to elementary school to learn how to print better, sorry!

My first FTO wrote a decent amount of tickets and liked to work traffic, so he was assigned a "slick top" patrol car with no overhead/bubble on the roof. It was still MSP blue with all the other markings. The 1994 Chevy Caprice we had and all the others had Corvette LT1 engines in them. They were fast as hell but had shitty brakes unable to handle the high speeds reached. There were many instances in the Chevy when we were running hot (full speed) to a call or in pursuits, by the time it ended, the brakes would actually catch on fire! Half the cars at the post were Chevys and half were 1996 Ford Crown Vics. The Fords looked stupid because they had black front and rear bumpers, which didn't match. They were slow and had shitty rear end suspensions that would actually float at high speeds. If you are running lights and sirens to a call or during a pursuit and you feel that rear end float, it's enough to make have a "code brown" or shit your pants before you crash. That first FTO and the Desk Sergeant below instilled a great work ethic that I carried and applied the rest of my career. My second and third phase FTOs stressed complaints, work more, solving crime, and closing cases, which was fine but not what I wanted to pursue later in my career. I loved working traffic and was damn good at it! There was a stop sign on either side of railroad tracks he took me to show where to write some dookers/tickets when I got off FTO. We were sitting tucked behind some trees right next to the tracks. Most people would slow to around 15 or 20 mph and go through the stop sign. Bam, some schmo runs that stop at 55 to 60 mph. Damn, Shazam, here we go to initiate a traffic stop. We could go careless driving or the stop sign ticket, which are both three points on your license, one-fourth of the way to losing your license at 12 points in Michigan. My first FTO also showed me some great spots to run radar on US-12. We didn't have any lasers at Jonesville, no need for one, not enough traffic.

One of my Recruit School instructors was promoted from Trooper to Jonesville as a Desk Sergeant. We didn't have a holding cell for prisoners at the post; all there was for securing a prisoner was a pipe in the vestibule across from the front desk. A Trooper had brought in a prisoner, some young kid for driving while suspended, possession of dope, and a couple warrants for his arrest. He was handcuffed by the Trooper that arrested him to the pipe by the front door. The newly promoted Desk Sergeant stepped away for a second when dumbass slipped his cuff and ran out the front door. Oh shit, things are about to go south real quick. He was caught a few hours later and brought back to the post. The sergeant took him into the copy room, closed the shades, and threw him on the floor with his boot in his throat, telling him in uncertain words, "If you ever try and escape from the state police again, I'll smoke your ass!" He never said one word to me, knowing I knew to keep my mouth shut.

Justice in Hillsdale County was fast and furious. Back to that first case I took that first Monday out of Recruit School, the larceny of the hunting trailer. The defendant didn't want to take a plea from the prosecutor's office, so the case went to trial. The case was in circuit court due to the value of the trailer being over $1,000. The circuit court judge in Hillsdale County had a unique nickname, "Hang 'em Harvey." Oh shit, here we go. They picked an all-white jury for the trial, and a Hillsdale County deputy/jailer was picked as one of the jurors. He actually showed up for jury duty and the trial in uniform and sat on the jury in uniform. "Holy Shit, Is this normal? I thought. I was a new trooper having little knowledge at the time of what the process was. The defendant reminded me of Forest Gump, a simpleton white, married man with a two young children. "Take the plea, take the plea," I kept thinking to myself. He had a court-appointed attorney and wouldn't take the plea. The rest of the jurors, not surprisingly, picked the uniformed deputy to be jury foreman. Needless to say, after testimony the defendant was found guilty and received three to five years in the state prison system on top of having to pay restitution to the victim for the cost of the trailer. Even the Black victim seemed surprised. During small talk he knew that I was from Detroit. We looked at each other in amazement. We both knew that shit would never fly in Detroit! Wow, case closed, onto the next one?

News article: "Police Investigate Driving Incident." Troopers from the Michigan State Police Jonesville Post investigated a possible drive by shooting involving a black and tan Chevrolet El Camino as the suspect vehicle. The complainant's side window had been blown out and he thought somebody had shot at him. I also believed it could have been a stray bullet from someone shooting at a nearby range, case closed after 30 days. I also had windows of my patrol cars explode three times throughout my career. The first time it scared the hell out of me but come to find out its fairly common with stress fractures in the glass.

I spent just under two years at the Jonesville Post. Again, great place to start and great place to retire. One of my FTOs took me to the south end of the county where there is a historical marker/rock where Michigan, Indiana, and Ohio actually meet. It was dark out, and he asked if I had to piss. I did, so I was able to stand on the rock and piss in three different states at the same time. I guess it's a guy thing; working mids, we would always find an empty field or go behind a closed business and piss behind a dumpster. Not too many places open with a bathroom at 3 a.m., especially in Hillsdale County.

I was single during FT, having a lot of free time on my hands. I asked the FTO Sergeant, who was a U-Per (from the Upper Peninsula in Michigan), if I could do some VOT (voluntary overtime) ride-alongs with some of the other Troops at the post. I stayed after from a day shift to ride with one of the other young Troops at the post who was a Recruit School ahead of me. We were at the post when Dispatch advised there was an active breaking and entering (B&E) of a residence on the west end of the county. I jumped into a shitbox Crown Vic with a Troop two schools ahead of me and another Trooper one school ahead of me in a Chevrolet Caprice, far better patrol car than the Ford. It might be hard to believe, but Hillsdale County has a lot of Hills. We were flying lights and sirens one behind the other when we crest a hill and there is a pickup turning left with no cut out for passing traffic to the right. The Trooper ahead of us in the Chevy passed on the shoulder in gravel at about 90 mph with no problem. Our only option in the shitty Crown Vic was to rear end the pickup or hit the gravel. Ugh, hit the gravel on the right. and the next thing you know we're doing 360s across both lanes of travel; we crashed in the opposite ditch almost hitting a huge oak tree with my passenger door. The driver, with a year on more than I, kept saying, "Fuck. Fuck. Sarge is gonna be pissed. Three flat tires, and he almost killed the fucking new guy (FNG)." When we were spinning around I kept seeing us get closer to that oak tree, "Fuck!" It was like being on the "Tilta-Whirl" at an amusement park. We violated the golden rule of emergency driving: "You can't help anyone if you don't make it there." We were out of the call; the other Trooper had to respond by himself after he checked on us to make sure we were okay and busting our balls. Hey Skippy, you're in a Chevy; we're in a piece of shit Ford. U-Per Sergeant came to the scene, "You guys, okay?" "Ya, Sarge." "Okay, Vinny, no more VOT ride-alongs, you're bad luck." Shit that didn't last long.

I made it through FTO training with no major issues even though it sucked doing it by myself when most of my classmates went to a post with multiple cubs. Each FTO has a different personality with different issues they address and different pet peeves. The FTO program we used worked great giving training and experience all the way through the program. The last phase, called "Shadow," was the best. You are put back with your first-phase FTO so they can see how you have progressed and see if you have any deficiencies that need to be addressed before you are allowed to go on patrol by yourself. I did pretty well only getting my balls busted for minor issues. My handwriting sucked, so my FTO downgraded me on penmanship when issuing citations, saying I needed to work on writing the tickets more clearly. Before we were given the green light to go on solo patrol all the cubs in the district had to go to District Headquarters in Lansing for an interview with the district commander. My first-phase FTO drove me to Lansing. We were not allowed to drive a patrol car by ourselves until we passed our district interview. I couldn't even go across the street on US-12 to gas a patrol car by myself. It was a rite of passage. The district interview involved the more critical aspects of the job. Use of force, pursuit driving, knowing key official orders that mandate procedure and protocol for the Michigan State Police. The District Captain was not available for the interview, so the second in charge, the Inspector, stood in for the Cap. The Inspector was cool as shit not busting my balls too bad. He was in Lansing, originally from Detroit; maybe it helped me being form Detroit also. I passed and was given the go-ahead to patrol on my own after returning to the post.

When I left the post for the first time on my own on day shift, my senior FTOs and desk Sergeant said I would probably get an arrest on my first traffic stop. At 6 a.m., I doubt it! I loaded my patrol car, 19-05 the slick top with my duty bag, an H&K rifle, and a Remington 870 shotgun. We did not have gun racks, so our long guns were kept in cases with extra ammunition. I put my shotgun on the passenger floor board to the right of me, and my rifle was seat-belted directly behind me on the rear passenger seat. I pulled out slowly, stopping at the end of driveway near US-12, and turned on my hood light. "STOP State Police" clearly lit up in the morning darkness. Wow, I couldn't believe I was actually driving a Blue Goose by myself getting ready to go on patrol. I turned my hood light off and made a right turn onto US-12. About two miles down the road I stopped a pickup truck with a cracked windshield and loud exhaust. Upon making contact with the driver he could not produce a driver's license. Shit, now what? Okay, sir, can you please step from the vehicle and place your hands behind your back. He complied, cuffs out, zip one cuff on, zip second cuff on. One in custody to dispatch. Two of my FTOs left the post to back me up. "Damn, Vinny, we were only joking about you getting an arrest right out of the shoot." I parked the gentleman's pickup for him, saving him a tow bill, and transported him to the Hillsdale County Jail for lodging. Basically, everybody went to jail in Hillsdale, even for traffic. The jail had plenty of room, and everybody there was conservative as hell. They encouraged us to lodge everyone possible.

Four of us troopers went to a residence, "out county." Anything out of the City of Hillsdale or any city with their own police department was considered "out county." My FTO and two other Troopers were on day shift when we were advised by the desk Sergeant there was a felony warrant for a man/grandpa who had molested his grand-children. He told us to go arrest him at his residence. As we were going up the front sidewalk, we heard a single gunshot! Fuck. We ran for cover when his wife came out of the house yelling and screaming that her husband had just shot himself. Damn, better him than us. We cleared the residence and called for the Medical Examiner's Office to respond. My prior FTO actually made me fingerprint the man after he killed himself for identification purposes, even though we knew who he was. My guess is my FTO was just screwing with me making me fingerprint stiff fingers on a dead CSC (criminal sexual conduct) suspect. It appeared the suspect decided he didn't want to face justice and took the easy way out? Damn, I'm off FTO, and the FTO is still bossing me around; sucks to be the FNG ("fucking new guy")!

I was still posted at Jonesville when the infamous "Detroit Red Wing" limousine crash occurred. A majority of the hockey players had gone on a golf outing after winning the Stanley Cup. Most of the players had been drinking alcohol, which is not out of the ordinary. They had left the golf course being driven by a man who had a suspended license and who also had marijuana is his blood. He supposedly fell asleep at the wheel, causing the crash on Woodward Ave. I worked the state fair that year and was able to drink beer out of the Stanley Cup at the hospitality room at the hotel where all us Troopers were staying. We talked the "Cup keeper" into bringing it up to our room, which was not a big deal at the time. The crash also put a fire under the state legislators' ass to pass a "Repeat Offender Law" that turned out to be a moot point for years to come. Anytime we stopped a repeat offender we had to seize their license plate and put a paper plate in the back window. I don't know, showing they are a shitty driver, I guess? It wasn't going to keep them from driving, duh!

I was on day shift for the rest of the time I was on probation, which was a year anniversary date from when we started the Academy. Every time I checked in for service with Dispatch, I would have to go take a delayed B&E (breaking and entering) or larceny from a vehicle. BORING! Our call signs went by what patrol car we were driving at the time: 19-05. Post 19 and car number 5, the slick top. "Nineteen-oh-five, you need to respond to this delayed call or that delayed call." We had a Central Dispatch Center in Hillsdale that dispatched us, the county Deputies and city officers. If the Deputies didn't like the call, they would literally not answer the radio depending on where the call was. Dispatch finally got smart and polled cars for their location to send the closest car. Fuck. senior Troops would have Dispatch hold those calls for the FNG (fucking new guy) to check in. In the short time I was at the Jonesville Post, I took a shit ton of felony complaints that took so much time with investigation and follow-up. Great experience, but not my cup of tea. I liked working traffic much more. I kept a list of all my complaint numbers on a folder, never able to keep up. When I closed out a case either through arrest or due to no investigative leads, I would cross out the incident number with a dark black marker. The cases that were left open for whatever reason were marked with a red marker.

Our patrol cars did not have car stereos in them. The department actually paid Ford, Chevrolet, and Chrysler to remove the radios. What the fuck was that all about? My FTO had a small battery-operated portable radio that he bungeed to the front radar to listen to music. I bought one for myself and used it when I went out on my own. There were no decent radio stations in Hillsdale, so I had to try and pick up reception from Jackson to the North or Toledo, Ohio, to the South. The Command in Lansing thought having car stereos was too much of a distraction to listen over the police radios. We had a state radio low band with the big whip antennas and a low band county radio to listen to the local agencies on. We could hear and talk to them on their radios, but they couldn't hear or talk to us on ours.

Michigan International Speedway (M.I.S.) was located in the first district. I worked my first NASCAR race a month into the department. It was a great detail, most shifts usually working for a 24-hour period all on overtime. Show me the money. We would start our shift at 4 a.m., have to be over to a scale house on US-12 for briefing by 5 a.m., and finished getting everyone out of the area by 4 a.m. the next morning. No biggie, I was still used to getting up early for the day shift I was on and early rising in the Academy. The detail usually involved around 75–100 Troopers in two-man cars. Most of us were assigned to traffic points at various locations around the track. If you had a lull in time before being on point, you could go down to Pit Row and check out the race cars. I met the actor Paul Newman at a PPG/Indy Race once. Pretty cool guy and down to earth. We would work two NASCAR races and one INDY/PPG race every season. The NASCAR race fans were mostly good ol' boys; they were mostly fine before the race, but some became flaming drunk assholes after the race. We would have drunk driving crashes, fights, and other issues after the race. Alcohol is always good in moderation; too much and bad things happen. We were told to use extreme discretion with open intoxicants as long as they were of age and had plastic cups. The INDY/PPG race fans were the wine drinkers that were more refined. Definitely no glass bottles that don't feel too good when you're hit upside the head with one! I always had a good time working the MIS races. I was at the Jonesville Post, which out onto US-12 with a gas station directly across the street. The NASCAR semitrucks with cars and equipment would drive by our post later in the evening, after the race was over. I was at the front desk when a NASCAR semitruck drove by the post. The driver of the semi activated his "Jake" brake, which is a safety brake that makes a shit load of noise and actually shook the windows of the post as he drove by. I later learned throughout my career that semi drivers would activate those brakes as a sign of contempt as they drive by police, be it a post or on a traffic stop on the freeway. My U-Per Sergeant again, shouted out, "Vinny, go write that asshole a ticket for excessive noise!" "On it, sarge." I jumped in a patrol car, flew out of the post, and stopped him in downtown Jonesville. He knew exactly what was up and took his ticket without no reply, just shaking his head. I can't remember what NASCAR driver he drove for, but I really didn't care. Could have been Jeff Gordon or Dale Earnhardt Jr. Who gives a shit. You wanted our attention? You got it!

Being the one and only trooper out of my Recruit School to go to Jonesville, I was stuck on days and always got screwed when it came to getting assigned complaints. There were four Troopers ahead of me from previous schools with less than a year seniority over, but I still got screwed. Calls went to the FNG with the least seniority. I would check into service, try and catch up previous complaints, and get sent to FIA (Family Independence Agency) Social Services to take a CSC usually involving young children and family members. Being a State Trooper is different than being a City Officer or Deputy. They have detectives that they turn all their complaints over to for follow up only gathering initial information. We investigate ours all the way through unless there is a homicide that our post detective (Dick) Sergeant would look at or want to be bothered with. The whole time I was at Jonesville I had no idea what our post detective did; nice guy, but clueless on where he went every day? He went to lunch with our female motor carrier officer every day, hmm?

One CSC I took involved a young boy around four years old where the suspect was his father. Mom and Dad were separated, and he had come home from visiting Dad with some strange bruises and marks on his bum. Dad had claimed they were a rash and Mom thought he was being sexually abused. I'm not a doctor. The social worker I dealt with said the health clinic in town said the examination was inconclusive. Okay, now what? I asked the suspect if he would be willing to take a polygraph exam, to which he said yes. I set up the exam with a D/Sgt. in Jackson. The polygraph examiner was a character. He told me to wait in a separate room, where I could watch the exam. The Dick/Sgt. asked him various questions about his son and then asked him if he had ever had any out-of-the-ordinary sexual encounters in his life. The suspect thought about the question and then stated, "Once I was down on my luck and gave a guy a blow job for some extra cash." "Okay," said the Dick Sgt., "that's understandable, you needed some quick cash." He then asked him if there was anything else that might be construed as a strange sexual encounter. The suspect thought about it again, hesitating and then stated, "I once worked on a dairy farm when I was younger, got liquored up, and had sex with a cow" WTF? The Dick/Sgt. kept a straight face, told the suspect he would be right back, and then came into my room laughing his ass off, telling me he passed his polygraph.

"It doesn't appear that he molested his boy." Wow, okay. I submitted the results to the Hillsdale prosecutor for review. Ultimately a warrant was not authorized due to lack of evidence. I contacted the mother of the child in person to advise her no further action would be taken and to obviously keep an eye on her son, contacting us if any other issues arose. She was a looker and around my age. I went to leave when she asked me, "Excuse me, Trooper Bommarito. I was wondering if you'd like to go out with me for a cup of coffee." Holy shit, I couldn't get it out of my head that her ex-husband had admitted to screwing a cow! "Ugghh, I appreciate the offer, but that would be a conflict of interest. Take care, Ma'am!"

Two Michigan State Troopers die in shooting. Wow, what happened? What did I get myself into? This being a trooper shit is dangerous! Robbery in progress? Traffic stop gone bad? No, not what you would think. Two capital security officers, not TROOPERS, got into a gun-fight across the hood of their patrol car shooting each other at the Collins state building in Lansing. WTF?! How does that happen? One male and one female that supposedly had little use for each other. The Vatican (MSP Lansing HQ) tried to get rid of that story as fast as possible. Don't force two people to work with each other when they don't like each other? Definitely made me happy I didn't work in the Lansing area and never would!

Due to lack of seniority I got bounced to fill in on midnights with a 24-year salty Trooper we called "Pops." He was funny as shit and had a wealth of knowledge. Law enforcement is weird in the way that the median seniority troops screw with the new guys and senior guys. We always kept our lockers open in the locker room. One night, Pops came to work to get changed in the closet / locker room we had. I was sitting in the squad room when I heard Pops yelling, "You mother fuckers." He came running out of the locker room with his pepper spray out. Someone had put a snapping turtle in his locker so when he opened the door, the reptile—and a big one at that—came out chomping! "Chomp, snap, chomp." Boy, was he pissed. We all ran. I went for the basement where it was dark. I told him, "Pops, I wouldn't have the balls to pull that shit on you, not your temporary midnight partner Vinny!" He knew it wasn't me, but that shit was pretty funny. Pops ended up going to the Hillsdale Clinic having chest pains after I left Jonesville transferring to Metro. They sent him home instead of doing further tests or sending him to a better hospital. He ended up crashing his car into a swampy ditch on his way home from the health clinic and dying. The department fought with his widow for years denying his death was duty related. I think this was a critical point for me deciding to take the union leader route instead of sucking ass route to become a command officer. That really affected me, the department always preaching how much of a family we were and then trying to fuck Pops' family out of his pension!

Jonesville and Hillsdale County were again very rural. There were three or four families of shitheads that the Sheriff's Department and we dealt with on a regular basis. The first pursuit I had by myself involved a "Wood Tick" from one of those families. "Wood Ticks" are rural criminals and "Hood Rats" are urban criminals. Chasing a shithead down a dirt road is like the movie *Days of Thunder*; when all the race cars bust through a crash, you can't see shit—you just hope you don't hit something or crash! I lost him down some unknown dingy dirt road in the middle of nowhere where he bailed on foot, crashing his pickup truck in a ditch. The truck smelled rank of beer, go figure. Dispatch send me a hook (tow truck) to tow this shitbox.

I would get into two more pursuits with two of the same shithead brothers, once going across the state line into Indiana after they feloniously assaulted some guy with a tire iron. I left the post on mids with another Trooper toward the end of the shift with no prep radio and no flashlight. We chased those turds into Indiana, advising Lansing

ELOP we were pursuing the suspects across the state line for a felony assault. No big deal. The lieutenant in charge just advised to let them know when we came back. The shitheads bailed on foot just across the state line. My partner pursued the driver, and I went after the passenger, tussled with him a bit, pepper spraying his ass in the process, no such thing as tasers then. We turned their stupid drunk asses over to Steuban County deputies in Indiana, pending extradition. They charged the driver with drunk driving and both brothers with resist and obstruct police. Not a fun ride back to Michigan and the post with pepper spray lingering in the patrol car with all windows down. That was my first experience questioning if it was worth pepper spraying the dumbass. I guess it was, he was resisting arrest, but it sure does suck when you get hit with that juice also.

Suicides: Besides the grandpa that shot himself when we went to arrest him, in the short time I was at the Jonesville Post I responded to various suicides. One involved a motor vehicle where a wife and husband were arguing when the wife opened the passenger door and jumped from the vehicle at 55 mph. She didn't fare too well hitting the concrete at that speed. We interviewed the husband and investigated to make sure he didn't open the door and push her out; you never know. Her death was ultimately ruled a suicide.

Another Trooper and I were dispatched to the south end of the county where there was a significant Amish population. A man had gone behind his barn and put a high-powered rifle in his mouth, pulling the trigger—what a mess. It appeared he killed himself over financial reasons. We arrived on scene with EMS on standby for safety, immediately calling for the medical examiner (ME). There were a couple of Amish women and kids standing on fence looking toward the barn when my partner mentioned one of the women was wearing a thong. WTF, are Amish women allowed to wear thongs? Cops have a weird sense of humor; we must, to maintain our sanity. I would see Amish men driving pickup trucks to the local Walmart and wonder, "Hmm? Are they supposed to be driving pickup trucks?"

When I was working mids with Pops we always hit the 7-Eleven in Hillsdale for our first cup of coffee. Most gas stations and stores give police free coffee or soft drinks as a professional courtesy, especially on midnights as a deterrent to keep shitheads from robbing them. The cashier was a young dude in his late teens. We always had friendly small talk with him while we were at the store. Pops and I were dispatched to another suicide only to find it was our cashier from the 7-Eleven. Fuck! When we went into the house, his parents were in shock and crying uncontrollably. He had shot himself in the mouth with a 12-gauge shotgun, again basically exploding his brains all over his bedroom walls. He also had shot multiple rounds into his water bed before killing himself. Another huge mess. He left a note for his parents stating, "I'm sorry I couldn't get those classes at JCC [Jackson Community College] and that I am such a disappointment." Wow, not getting classes is worth killing yourself and in such a horrific way? Was he trying to send a message to his parents? Only he knew!

I was single when I graduated from the Academy, which helped me to stay focused on my training. I was at the Hillsdale County Fair when one of the troopers set me up with a retired trooper's daughter who was an elementary school teacher in Hillsdale. Nice girl, but I had no intentions of staying at the Jonesville Post or getting into a serious relationship. I was biding my time waiting for transfers to Metro Detroit to open up so I could get closer to home. I went to dinner at her apartment once, when she asked why I was not making any moves on her/ trying to get in her pants. "Uhhh, I am on probation and your dad is a retired Trooper, which means I do not have a death wish." That was probably not the best answer I could give; needless to say, we didn't date much longer.

We had an annual physical fitness test, which was the same as the MLEOTC (Michigan Law Enforcement Officers Training Council) test. We were taking the test in the fall of 1997 at Hillsdale College when a Sergeant told us whoever had the fastest run on the PT test could go work the Michigan State Fair in Detroit for two weeks. Well, shit, I was in great shape and busted everyone's ass with the run except for my senior FTO. He was 20 years older than me and most of the other troops at the post, but ran like a gazelle. I came in second place, but he didn't want to work the fair, so I was able to go. I took a patrol car over to the eastside for the state fair detail and parked the car at Fraser PD when I was off duty. I did a couple ride-alongs with Fraser before joining the State Police, and one of their officers was a good friend of the family. I had a great time at the state fair detail solidifying my wanting to transfer to Metro Detroit. There were at least 100 troopers from all over the state that came to work the fair. We were always doubled up for officer safety because number one, you're in Detroit and during the afternoon, which was the shift I worked, and number two, most of the Hood Rats would come to the fair looking for trouble late afternoon into the night, with the Fair closing at 10 p.m. Detroit PD (DPD) handled everything off Fairground/state property, and we handled everything inside.

The Pirate Ride was always the hot spot where most of the shitheads hung out looking for trouble. MSP State Fair Command would send at least four to six Troops over there every night as a visible deterrence to avoid trouble. The arrest policy was pretty liberal the first time I worked the fair detail. We had a great Lieutenant from Detroit that was old school. If some shithead needs to go to jail, they go—period. Maintaining public order was the number one priority.

The majority of Troops on afternoons were assigned to the Pirate Ride or Band Shell detail every night, which took most of the concerts to the end of the night when the fair closed at around 10 p.m. Throughout the 14-day fair, there would be all kinds of concerts, Kid Rock, Beach Boys, and others, a good mix of various music genres. We were working the James Brown concert one night, which was primarily attended by Black people. Come on, James Brown. Who's more hip? There were at least 5,000 people at the concert, which is significant for a state fair band shell. My partner and I were enjoying the show when we were notified by a young Black mother and her daughter that a drunk older Black man had sat in their reserved seats close to the stage and would not move, causing a disturbance. We went to contact him when he jumped up and ran up the aisle behind us. There were two female Troops walking down the aisle toward us; he ran right through them knocking one over. We caught up to him tackling him to the ground with him trying to fight us, resisting arrest. There were two times in my career that I was visibly and mentally afraid I was going to die; this was one of them! As we were wrestling with this asshole, I remember looking up and seeing all kinds of people hovering around us. Holy shit, we were about to get our asses handed to us by a mob. Luckily James kept on singing and didn't stop the show for us! We got him in cuffs and scooted his ass over to the command post expeditiously. After processing numbnuts, turned out he was a higher-ranking member of the Detroit Fire Department. Dumbass. He was still lodged for drunken disorderly and resisting and obstructing police!

The Michigan State Fair was a great detail for a young Trooper who grew up in the Detroit area and worked in Jonesville. Damn, I definitely knew I needed to get back to Metro Detroit. My feet were killing me after all the walking we did, but we received a fairly large stipend for meals working out of our post areas. It was like an extra $500 at the end of the fair, thank you very much! This was also a year the Red Wings won the Stanley Cup. They had a public relations gig at the state fair with some dude known as the "Cup keeper" traveling around the area with the Cup. As I previously mentioned, we talked him into bringing that beast of a trophy up to our hotel hospitality (drinking) room. I got to drink beer out of the Stanley Cup, can you say bucket list? We also dressed the Cup up as a Michigan Troop!

Back to Jonesville, working on afternoons the remainder of my time there. I stopped a lady out in rural Hillsdale County, can't remember for what, probably speeding because it was dark. I approached her vehicle and asked for her driver's license with her responding, "How do I know you are a Police Officer?" What the fuck, lady? I have that stupid red bubble on the top of my patrol car spinning in circles, I am in full uniform, duh, okay, stand by, don't go anywhere, and I'll be back with ya! I called my favorite desk Sergeant at the post, who was the instructor at the Academy that would hit recruits in the head with tennis balls when they nodded off, advising him of the situation, with him advising me what to do over the radio, again no cell phones at this time, "Show her your State Police Identification Card you are required to carry. Then advise her again you are a REAL State Trooper and if she does not give you her REAL driver's license, advise her you'll arrest her and take her to the REAL Hillsdale County jail, where she can sit overnight, then ask the Hillsdale County judge in the morning if he is a REAL judge!" After that dissertation, she was more than willing to hand over her driver's license and receive a citation in return!

Dead bodies have a distinct, almost unbearable smell to them. I never experienced that in the military, but I did at the Jonesville Post. We had a tip that a gentlemen connected to some Michigan militia assholes had executed him and buried his body in the southern part of the county, near the Ohio border. This guy supposedly knew Timothy McVeigh, who blew up the federal building in Oklahoma City a couple years earlier. They found his body and took his clothes back to the post leaving them in the garage, which is attached to the post. Whoa, that was one of the worst smells I had ever smelled in my life. They should have left that shit with his remains and taken it to the medical examiners in Toledo, Ohio. Hillsdale County didn't have an ME's office, too small. Bodies had to go to Toledo, which was closer than the next one in Michigan. Weird, go to another state for autopsy's. Okay.

My Post Commander(PC) at Jonesville was cool as shit. I went to this house looking for some dude with a warrant for his arrest. His mother was a flaming bitch, "Get off my property" etc. She called the Post to complain about me. The PC holds a post level interview about the contact with me and the Post Rep. At the end of the interview she turns off the tape recorder and said, "Fuck that Bitch Vinny, I tried to have her come in multiple times to give a statement and she won't. Your'e all set, keep up the great work!"

Our district union Rep for the first district, which covered Jonesville and Lansing, where the "Vatican" was, was a badass. He was known for pinning upper commands' balls against the wall when it came to defending and looking out for troopers and rights under union rules. There were stories that mid-level troopers told us cubs about him. One story was he and his partner were sent by Lansing Operations (ELOP) to Columbus, Ohio, to pick up a prisoner but doing something with Big Balls before the pickup. He and his partner drove around Ohio State University's Campus in a Michigan State Police "Blue Goose," with the overhead red bubble swirling around singing the U of M fight song, "Hail to the Victors" on the PA system of the patrol car, pissing off Ohio State students and faculty! Ha, take that to the bank, bitches! Another story was told of that same Trooper when he worked at the Detroit Post on midnights driving again with his partner to the Upper Peninsula of Michigan and back at Mach 1. When they did it, all the posts throughout the state at the time actually had gas pumps. You couldn't go to a random gas station and use a fleet card to get gas like today. The only reason they got caught is they had to stop at a post up north, raising a red flag to the post commander. "Why is there an MSP Detroit Car getting gas at our post?" Oh well, busted!

Domestic assaults: When we attended the State Police Academy as recruits we were taught that to arrest a suspect for domestic assault the couple had to reside together, formerly reside together, or have a child in common. As time went on they kept adding more and more stipulations for domestics in Lansing. If you went to the movies with someone and shared popcorn, you could get arrested for domestic assault! Just kidding, but actually there are a lot of stupid stipulations now. It's funny that liberal activists think it would be a great idea to send an unarmed social worker to a domestic instead of a police officer. A large number of Troopers, Deputies, and Police Officers are assaulted and/or killed responding to domestic incidents. They often involve alcohol and/or drugs, weapons, and heated emotions. That's why we were told you always respond to a domestic with at least two Troopers, never alone! Maybe they should pick a liberal city (Seattle, New York, Austin) and try their proposed experiment. Send unarmed social workers to domestic assault complaints and see how that pans out!

Dispatch call: "Female Driver passed out behind the wheel in minor crash." I was dispatched to investigate a woman who was intoxicated and passed out behind the wheel. It was at seven o'clock in the afternoon on a hot summer day. She was in a convertible and actually crashed in a ditch in front of the house trying to pull up in the wrong driveway of the wrong house about a half a mile from her house. I arrived on scene, woke her up, had an ambulance on standby, and then had her step from the vehicle to perform sobrieties and give her a PBT (preliminary breath test). She was clearly intoxicated and placed into custody without incident going to the Hillsdale County Jail for DUI (driving under the influence). Months later she requested a jury trial for the DUI arrest. I was thinking what's her defense gonna be. Her and the defense attorney came up with the defense that she was so upset at being at the wrong house and putting her car in the ditch upset her so much that she had a pint of whiskey hidden in the convertible top that she drank after the minor crash! Really? That's the best defense you can come up with? After hearing the bullshit testimony/perjury the jury (Hillsdale County, conservative) came back from deliberations in about 30 minutes finding her guilty!

Every State Police Recruit School goes back to Lansing. the state cap-ital, on their one-year anniversary from joining the department for two weeks of additional training before getting off probation. They call this "Re-Tread." The Mighty 114th Trooper Recruit School graduated 72 out of 85 starters and were down to approximately 65 headed to Lansing. Seven or eight probationary Troopers had quit or been fired during FT. One female Troop had quit after getting pregnant. Her hus-band was a Troop and didn't want her working anymore. Only a year and she quits; what a crock—she took a spot from someone else that might have been more committed. Just saying! Another probationary trooper got drunk at a house party and pulled a knife on a dude, not his department handgun, I guess would have been worse; anyways, he was fired. We lost another at Flint for pistol-whipping some cat after a foot pursuit; can't do that! Then there were others that couldn't cut the mustard in the field unable to deal with real-life police work. I actu-ally thrived with the real-world shit more than the Academy, maybe growing up in a divorced family in Detroit? We got radar training and other schooling on advance police topics not learned in the field. They wouldn't let us run radar while on probation because they wanted us to learn how to stop vehicles for other violations, such as, seatbelt, equip-ment, careless or reckless driving, instead of relying on a radar as a crutch. We stayed at the Academy if possible while at Re-Tread unless there is no room due to a Recruit School being run at the time. We had a smaller class so they sent us all to Re-Tread together, which was sweet. Other previous Recruit Schools such as the 112th and 113th were split because they were too large. Re-Tread was basically a 10-day class reunion where we drank way too much after class showing up hung over for morning class. Some morons, not me, actually slept in and had to be rousted out of bed by Academy staff. I met an MSU (Michigan State University) graduate student at a bar the second night we were there and basically spent every night with her at her apartment. She would drive to the Academy, pick me up after class every day. I'd spend the night at her place and then she would drive me to the Academy early in the morning before breakfast and class. I had taken a patrol car from Jonesville, not knowing I wouldn't need transportation. I never expected to hook up with a coed the whole time. All my classmates, including the women, thought I was a player; nope, it was just all about timing—okay, maybe a little bit of a player! The department had such a hard time with returning cubs and drinking at Re-Tread they proposed being able to give students a PBT (preliminary breath test) each morning to hung over Troops if suspected of being intoxicated! Damn, that's pretty crazy; how'd it get to this point? Anyways, most of us had a great time at our first Re-Tread. We went for one week the next four years again on our anniversary date, but those could never top those first two weeks!

I stayed at Jonesville for another couple months until transfers opened up for the Metro Area, which was in November 1997. Jonesville was a great place to start and a great place to retire, not in between. Peace out. See ya, Jonesville and Hillsdale County!

CHAPTER 3: METRO NORTH, METRO SOUTH, OR DETROIT?

THE DETROIT/METRO Area had three state police posts, which primarily covered the Detroit Freeway system dealing mainly with traffic, which is why they were called "traffic posts." Originally, I wanted to go to the Metro North Post 21 in Oak Park, which covered the north end suburbs of Detroit in Oakland and Macomb Counties. I had missed being able to transfer there by one spot in seniority. God damn it. I really wanted to go work where I grew up. Okay, now I had to choose between Metro South, which was downriver in Taylor and covered all of Wayne County except for Detroit, or the Detroit Post, which Troopers, I was told, had to pay city taxes for working there.

I rode with two Troops from Detroit when I was still at Jonesville to get a taste of the work there. One of them went to Jonesville out of the Recruit School ahead of me. He was the one that took the shoulder in the Chevy when we crashed in the ditch in the Ford. The other, Trooper Fred Hardy, would later die on a traffic stop on I-96 after getting hit by a drunk driver. The Detroit Post was located at 6th and Howard in the old State Building downtown. If you went to Detroit as a Trooper, you were strictly working the Detroit Freeway system, which was fucked during rush hour. The command also discouraged troopers there from working top side (off the freeways) in the city to avoid getting caught up in a shit sandwich, which was the fun part of patrolling in the city. The Detroit Post was also kind of a shithole being old and run down. Rats in the parking lot bigger than cats. Hmm, I was a little familiar with

Out-Wayne County, otherwise known as "Downriver" near the Detroit River. I ended up going to Metro South in Taylor. The City of Taylor was known as "Taylor-Tuckey" with a large population of Wood Ticks and good ol' boys living there and in the surrounding area. It was almost like a larger version of Jonesville with interstates and a bigger population. Dueling banjos could be heard late at night in the summertime. The Metro Posts and Richmond Posts were both newly built buildings with state-of-the-art equipment built by the same contractor. We had two holding cells for prisoners, which were nice because we are not allowed to lodge at posts per state law. We have to take our prisoners to county or city jails for lodging. Taylor was different because a lot of the local police departments would lodge our prisoners for us as long as the court officers took care of them first thing after being arrested. The Wayne County Jail on Dickerson in Detroit was a pain in the ass to lodge prisoners just as Detroit precincts were. Gotta do this, gotta do that, fill out this paperwork. Fuck off, do your own paperwork. If I lodged a prisoner at Taylor PD, all they required is we write the perp's name and date of birth on a log hanging on the wall. Our post also had its own computerized fingerprint machine and an OWI Breathalyzer machine. The Detroit Post didn't have any of the new equipment we had.

Drunk driving/OUIL (operating under the influence of liquor) /OWI (operating while intoxicated), whatever Lansing wants to call it, kept changing throughout my career. I called them Slushies, and the Slushie arrests really ramped up when I transferred from Jonesville to Metro Detroit. We were taught the basics when I was in the Academy and learned more out in the field with real drunk driving arrests. The paperwork was pretty simple when I first started filling out a two-page quick form checking all the boxes. Toward the end of my career an OWI report was a bitch. I always used the same sobriety tests for my drunk investigations: three physical and two verbal. I always started by asking them if they had any medical conditions that would preclude them from participating. The one-legged stand. Hold one leg up and count from 1 to 30. If they were skunked they would wander and keep putting their foot down. The finger to nose touch test. Touch the tip of your nose with either index finger in this order: left, right, right, left. Again if drunk, they would miss the tip or switch the order given. The last physical test I demonstrated was the finger touch test, where you count from one to four and then back to one starting with the thumb to the pinky. They would miss fingers or count the wrong numbers if drunk. The first verbal sobriety test I gave was to ask them to pick a number between 16 and 14. They would say 12 or pick the wrong number while standing there thinking hard about what I had told them. The next verbal test (and last test) I asked was for them to count backwards from 20 to 12. Easy enough, right? Oh, hell no; they would miss numbers in-between and keep going past the number 12 to 0. I used these same tests throughout my entire career, which made it easy to testify in court. Next step if they failed the sobriety test was to get the PBT (preliminary breath test), which was not admissible in court in Michigan but a great tool to help us determine if they were getting arrested or not. If they refused all the tests, that made it simple to take them to the local hospital and get a search warrant for their blood. Michigan was an implied consent state like most.

There were at least 10 Troops that transferred to Metro South when I did. The rest had already been assigned there when the Flat Rock Post was closed. All of us were young troops that came in from different parts of the state ready to spit fire and piss vinegar with most of us being originally from the Metro Detroit area. We had 52 troopers assigned to the post when I went there. The department did a study trying to determine how many troopers each post throughout the state needed in able to provide adequate police services to that community, be it in a rural area or urban area. It was called the Patrol Allocated Model (PAM). The Detroit Post was 120 Troops, the Metro North Post was 65 troops, and my old starting post, Jonesville, was 15 Troops. The Metro South was 50, which meant we were two Troops over PAM. The PAM staffing model appeared to be the best with other models/studies being adopted throughout the years.

The department would spend hundreds of thousands of dollars to have some company or university do these studies every time there was a new governor or major regime change at the top. There was Community Problem Solving Model (CAPRA) adopted by one of our directors/colonels because he was buddies with the director of the Royal Canadian Mounted Police. Its main goal was to promote discussion with employees, "the cops," and citizens. They wanted us to talk to people and have coffee with them more often instead of writing tickets and arresting shitheads. One of my sergeants put it well with the stance of the department. He said it was like going to "Baskin-Robbins" 31 flavors and asking what the flavor of the week is. One week they bust your balls for not writing enough tickets, and the next week they want you to dick the dog and have coffee with people you don't know or wanna know for half of your shift. I was never the kind of trooper to sit at a coffee shop or gas station during my shift. I wanna be out there "shakin' and bakin." That's what I'm supposed to do, right? "BPI" Best Practice Institute, Bullshit People Interested, who knows, who cares, etc. They did so many stupid studies I couldn't keep track of them. What a fucking waste of money. If it ain't broke, don't fix it, you morons! I think that's why I never wanted anything to do with Lansing because they were always fucking shit up, and the longer I was in the department, the worse it seemed to get. When I first joined the state police the district captains throughout the state pretty much ran their district, and post commanders ran their posts. Lansing would usually stay out of shit and mainly deal with the politicians and their bullshit at the capital.

When I transferred to Metro South we had four motorcycle Troopers on Harley Davidsons at the post. I told myself ,"That's badass!" You get paid to ride around on a Harley all day and write tickets—what a sweet gig! I knew someday I would be on that unit. We had thirty or so patrol cars pretty much one for every Road Trooper. Ten of the Troops at the post were in administrative positions. We called them "admin pukes." They didn't want to work the road, so they became court officers, abandoned vehicle officers, detective troopers, or community service Troopers (DARE) that pass out teddy bears and balloons to little kids. Everybody brings something different to the table, right? Fuck that! I joined the state police to work the road and look for bad guys.

We had three shifts at that time. Days 6 a.m.–2 p.m., noons 2 p.m.–10 p.m., and mids 10 p.m.–6 a.m. There were different weekly shifts that were always tried out and used until the troops started bitching too much, and then they would try something else. Per our Michigan State Police Troopers Association (MSPTA) the department had to give us at least one Saturday/Sunday weekend off per month. We worked every third weekend off, then 10 on straight with a four-day weekend off, which blew balls, and then later on the department went to extended work shifts on 10s and 12s. At first, they fought it tooth and nail because on an extended shift the troops would get more days off. "We can't have Troopers getting more time off than us," most command thought, and then we kept losing Troopers due to staffing cuts; it benefited them for better coverage of the road.

Most of us young troopers chose to work noons or mids. The old-timers with more seniority were all on days. We had so many troopers working when we would check into service that we had to fight on the radio for check in with Dispatch or to run file and status checks on people or vehicles. It was a crazy cool time to be a Trooper in Metro Detroit. We were running around with our hair on fire stopping everything that moved that needed to be stopped. A trooper would get a suspended driver and two or three of us would go lights and sirens to back them up, surprised we didn't have more crashes driving hot all over the place. Working in Metro Detroit was such a target rich environment, we would never go out of business. Careless and reckless drivers all over the place, armed robberies from businesses, carjackings up the ass, shootings, etc. The biggest priority would be and remain to make sure you go home at the end of your shift! I had a lot of friends that didn't make it home—so sad!

All of us young, single Troopers that transferred to Metro from all around the state were introduced to the rest area detail. We had two rest areas in our post area: one in Canton Twp. on I-275 just north of Detroit Metropolitan Airport and one in Van Buren Twp. on I-94 just west of the airport. Rest areas were built by the State of Michigan for travelers on the highway/freeway system to stop and rest, use the bathroom, or get snacks from vending machines. The State Police Post was constantly getting complaints from citizens that they would stop to use the bathroom or take their child inside being exposed to men masturbating out in the open areas and worse. The rest areas were also known for a meeting place for gay men to hook up. Most of us new Troops worked afternoons from 2 p.m. till 10 p.m. A sergeant asked, "Hey, anybody want to make some overtime after work tonight?" All of us were like, "Hell, yeah." We all had short, high and tight haircuts, clean shaven, wearing T-shirts and shorts. Sarge gave us the rundown: "Okay, tonight we're going to work the rest area on I-275. We'll have two female Troops doing the paperwork, and you guys will be the decoys for the 'Johns' soliciting you for sex and actually having sex with each other." Gross, okay, what the fuck. We're getting paid time and a half; fuck it!"

Per our afternoon Sarge, who appeared to a pro at soliciting gay men, all you had to do was go in the rest area bathroom, wash your hands while looking in the mirror, and they will open the stall door and beat off in front of you! Show your badge and advise them to put their junk away and that they are under arrest for disorderly conduct. He also told us to take our wrist watches off and ask someone what time it was and that was their cue to do their thing/expose themselves. Most of the "Johns" were local residents also. What are you doing hanging out at a state rest area when you live five minutes from there; again for travelers on the freeway, not locals. We were also advised while on patrol in uniform to perform property inspections and advise local residents per the Wayne County Prosecutor's Office that if they were local residents loitering/hanging out in the rest area, they were trespassing on state property. The county also instituted a nuisance abatement policy called "Push Off." This was applied to rest area issues, drag racing, prostitution, and any drug-related crimes. If a suspect was charged with any of the mentioned crimes, the complaining witness/Trooper, deputy, or city officers would complete a one-page report "Push Off" sheet and tow the defendants vehicle at a cost of $1,000.00 plus the towing fee. Holy Shit, $1,200.00 or roundabout to get your vehicle out of impound—talk about a deterrent! We very rarely took anybody to jail for disorderly, just issue them an appearance citation with a court date and towed their rides. To see the look on their faces when you gave them a piece of paper saying they had to pay over a grand to get their car out of impound and then dispute it in court was priceless. We arrested men from all walks of life at the rest area including doctors, cops, and clergy. One time we had to go to the parking lot and advise a woman and her kids they had to step out of their minivan and call for a ride because her husband was arrested inside the open area of the bathroom for masturbating in public / disorderly. She started crying profusely and yelling and swearing at him—don't blame her!

For some reason, I was constantly asked by desk Sergeants to take ride-alongs on patrol. Desk Sergeants didn't work the road. Only Troopers worked the road at this point in my career. They would have another sergeant or trooper cover the desk so they could run to McDonalds to get a Happy Meal. This was even before I became an FTO (field training officer). I was a hard-charging Road Dog that liked to tear it up, write tickets, and arrest people that needed to go to jail. Our department had a policy that ride-alongs had to wear business professional clothing and a bulletproof vest under a button-down shirt with a tie. This was relayed to them before they participated in the ride-along. If they showed up looking like a shitbag, they were sent home. I had a college intern in the patrol car with me one day, good kid who had a sincere interest in law enforcement. After giving him the pre-patrol speech we cleared the post and head north on Telegraph Rd to I-94. I look to the left at the entrance to a Blockbuster video store and see a two-car T-bone crash with smoke coming from the scene. I immediately let Dispatch know and advise them to let Taylor PD and Fire know to send units to assist. I rolled up and removed a female from the passenger side after removing a male subject and putting him on the grass. The female driver was unconscious and not breathing, so I started CPR with the assistance of the intern. As I'm doing CPR, I look up and see a desk Sergeant from my post drive by the crash scene in a Blue Goose. We looked at each other eye to eye. As I'm doing CPR, I'm thinking to myself, "Hmm, WTF, sarge, are you gonna stop and help?" That woman ended up dying with us trying our best to revive her. Shit, he could have at least stopped and assisted with traffic. Taylor PD ended up taking the fatal crash in their city, so I went back to the post and got in the Sergeant's ass. "Why didn't you stop, you drove right by us?" "Sorry, Bomber." That's all your gonna say? What a disappointment!

I actually thought about going to the Old Man (PC) about the incident but figured, they are out of the same Recruit School and both are retiring in less than a year; they'll just give me the big blow off.

Another incident with the same desk Sergeant. One of our troopers stopped at Subway near that Blockbuster to grab a sandwich on the way to work. I'm at the post and hear radio traffic at the front desk on the Taylor PD radio there's an off-duty Trooper needs assistance at the Subway on Telegraph. Shit, I'm headed that way. I got stuck by a train, so I couldn't make it there, but Taylor PD called out they had two subjects in custody. Trooper Dave, who is a full-blooded American Indian, had this State Police varsity jacket that he wore everywhere. Other troops use to bust his balls, he was advertising for trouble with shitheads that don't like cops! He's in line at Subway behind these two Wood Ticks that are hassling the staff and not wanting to pay for their food. He tells them to cut their shit and pay, with them commenting on his jacket and him identifying himself as a state trooper. "Wham, bham, pow" fights on. Dave's getting the best of the two shitheads before Taylor PD gets on scene. They drop the Wood Ticks off at the State Police Post where they are put in the holding cells. I get back to the post and check on Dave, who had some cuts and bruises and was visibly pissed. I go back to the holding area, knock on the glass, telling those turds, "You mess with the bull, get the horns, mother fuckers." Oh shit, the desk Sergeant comes around the corner and tells me, "Bomber, stop chewing their ass, it's not worth risking your career." Really, Sarge? Fuck this, put me down sick. I'm going home. Asked Dave if he wanted to have a couple beers later; he bowed out saying he had to do in-custody paper and go to the hospital per command for a medical clearance.

"S.P.I.T.E." (State Police Interdiction Team Enforcement) was a new concept already tried in the past, which involved criminal drug interdiction on the freeway/highway systems. I along with other young troopers attended all the training we could even going out of State to South Carolina for interdiction training. We had training with a Maryland State Trooper who years later was arrested for skimming monies of the stops he made—can you say "dumbass"? The best training I had was with a Louisiana State Trooper who was blind from getting shot in the face with a shotgun during a traffic stop. What a great man and great speaker. The takeaway I got from his presentation was how fast things can change in the blink of an eye. Having lunch with fellow troops and deputies at a diner, then being ambushed and left disabled the rest of his life. Stay on guard, never take things for granted, family comes first. All great information he gave us that I applied throughout my career as a road trooper. I stayed on the "S.P.I.T.E." team for about six months and then went back to regular patrol. The training was not feasible in the Metro Detroit area. Other state interdiction teams also had K-9 police dogs assigned to the teams for instant vehicle clearing;

our department didn't want to do that at this time. Too much traffic to look for indicators such as nervousness, pulling away from you, having no luggage traveling far, and a carload of fast food wrappers. Just like anything else, criminal shit bags adapt and look for ways to avoid being caught. We would have to sit in the freeway median for the whole shift specifically looking for dopers. BORING. Some trainers even recommended bringing a Gatorade bottle to piss in so you don't have to leave the freeway to go take a piss. fuck that! Not my cup of tea. We definitely had some Troops that were great at sniffing out shithead dopers. I wasn't one of them. I liked working regular traffic and taking drunk drivers off the road.

Detroit Officer Shawn Bandy, 23 years old, was shot and killed in the line in December 1998. I volunteered to assist with traffic control, shutting down ramps for his funeral detail. This was the first police officer killed in the line of duty funeral I had assisted with and attended. Shawn's dad was a retired DPD officer. What a shit sandwich having to bury your 23-year old son that did the same duty as you. I can't even imagine! Rest in peace, Shawn!

Michigan State Trooper Frederick Hardy, 36 years old, struck and killed by a drunk driver while on traffic stop. Every year on the Fourth of July they sent a shitload of troopers to Detroit to assist DPD with traffic and crowd control. There had been shootings, stabbings, and other critical incidents in the past. I worked the 1998 Fourth of July detail with Trooper Fred Hardy. Fred was a great man who was also a captain in the Marine Corps. He had a funny, jovial personality and reminded me of Eddie Murphy. I had a great time working with Fred that night and was working the night of November 6, 1999, when Fred was hit and killed by a hit and run drunk driver. His partner was screaming on the radio when Fred got hit. That was my first horrible experience where my heart sank to the floor while working on patrol. We went to the scene and helped looked for that prick that killed Fred. Detroit

PD was able to track him down that night; thanks, DPD! They actually found Fred's handcuffs impaled on the hood of the Slushies car! Little bit of damning evidence.

The Troopers Association asked myself and other Troops to assist with fellow State Troopers from around the country that came to the funeral to honor Fred. I had the privilege of helping those outstate Troops including a Minnesota State Trooper. He was a character with his Minnesota accent, eh! We were in the funeral procession with our police lights on when these little turds threw a football over our patrol car. The brakes were slammed and a stern talking was given to the kids. I told my partner to keep the football, but he said we better not, we didn't want to get charged with larceny by the Wayne County prosecutor. The funeral for Fred was the first funeral I had ever been for a fellow Trooper and a Black man. There were nurses in the old-school white uniforms with the paper hats on their heads passing out tissues to everyone, balling like something out of the 50s. Over 1000 people and officers attended his funeral with Troopers coming to pay their respect from all over the country, including Texas, California, and even officers from Canada since Detroit is right across the river from Windsor. Rest in peace, Trooper Fred Hardy!

The cool thing about belonging to a large police organization such as the State Police is there are so many specialty details and assignments you can apply for. Everyone knows the most important job in the department is Road Troopers, ha! Undercover drug teams, fugitive teams, surveillance teams (later disbanded because of budget cuts), violent crime task force teams, aviation, dive/underwater recovery team, motor unit, canine unit, and emergency support (ES) team, basically our SWAT team, the badasses of the department. After five years you could try and get promoted to sergeant moving up the ladder joining Command (the administrators). Once you had two years as a uniformed Road Trooper, you could apply for the above specialty positions.

Canine Unit, having a police dog, sounded cool. The first step to the Canine Unit was passing a long-distance run near the Academy. Cool, I'm in pretty good shape. The Canine run was a bitch. We had to wear boots, no tennis shoes, and fatigues. As soon as I started the run for time we had to run through a swamp where I was running on a log and fell into waist-deep water. Okay, at this point I was fucked! My uniform was soaked, my boots were soaked, and I finished the run but not in a fast-enough time to get an interview to continue in the process. I guess I won't be in the Canine Unit. I'll try something else.

Michigan State Police Trooper Rick Johnson, 35 years old, killed in the line of duty by a distracted driver while on a traffic stop. The lady that killed Rick was eating fast food not paying attention when she left the roadway, striking his State Police SUV as he was walking in between the vehicles to get back in his Goose. She pinned him in between and then flew him underneath the SUV, causing traumatic injuries. WTF, lady? This young trooper was married with young kids. Your ignorance killed one of our best! On the day before his death, Trooper Johnson had talked a suicidal subject from jumping from an overpass to his death close to where this same incident had occurred! We went to the funeral for Trooper Johnson near his post area in Paw Paw. We left early in the morning and had a caravan of about 10 to 12 fully marked "Gooses." On the way there a moron in a black Chevrolet Impala was in the left lane and wouldn't move over to the right. I was the second car back in the caravan riding shotgun with one of our buds to the front. He came right up on the ass of the black Chevy hitting his siren and airhorn for the guy to move. I shined my spotlight on his car with him finally vacating the lane and moving to the right. (Improper lane use on his part under Michigan law.) We get up next to his car, I looked over at, and it's a command officer driving an unmarked detective car. He picks up his garrison cap and points at it like we're supposed to be impressed. I did the right thing, flipped him a salute, and continued on our way to the funeral of one of our fellow troopers. Boy, was he pissed; he called our PC after the funeral, copying down our license plates on our cars, bitching up a storm. Kind of weird he waited till we got back to the post three hours later, also? "If I could have found those Troopers at the funeral, I would have written them a reckless driving ticket." Really? Our PC, who just happened to be out of the same Recruit School as this joker, laughed at him, busting his balls, stating, next time get the hell out of the left lane when you see a Blue Goose" behind you. You know better. Our Lieutenant who was an old-school Troopers Lieutenant, verbally counseled us, "Boys, I know you technically didn't do anything wrong besides tail-gating or speeding a bit; just don't do that again." "Okay, sir." That command officer didn't have the balls to approach us at the funeral because he knew he would look like a dink! Rest in peace, Trooper Rick Johnson!

The "Tower of Terror." That was the title of the article on the front page of the *Detroit Free Press*. Kind of sounds like a Disneyland ride. There was a senior citizen high-rise apartment building on Fort St. in Lincoln Park, which falls in the Metro South Post area. We would always back up the local PDs on serious incidents such as shootings or robberies. They were mostly always glad to see us show up, some not so happy to see us. Fuck it, we're State Troopers, we can go where we want and enforce the laws anywhere in the state 24/7; some were just jealous. Most of the downriver agencies had formed a "Downriver SWAT team" years prior. Our ES/SWAT guys would rally like they did; problem is we didn't have too many ES guys in the Metro Area because the locals had their own teams. Needless to say, it took them awhile for them to get to the scene of the murders. Some shithead was hanging out the window waving a rifle after murdering two people and wounding another. He was pissed off that fellow residents complained about his lewd behavior and inappropriate comments he would make. A sniper could have easily taken his ass out from across the street. He ended up giving up to negotiators—what a coward! Our post ended up assisting Lincoln Park PD with the investigation. The PC picked one of my buddies who was built like a brick shithouse and looked like Arnold Schwarzenegger and another Trooper to escort shithead to his arraignment.

Detroit Officer Michael Scanlon, 35 years old, shot and killed during traffic stop. I was working in a patrol car in the City of Dearborn when a call went out on the local radio. "Officer down." Dispatch advised a Detroit PD officer was shot and his patrol car was stolen. They advised he was working in an all-white semi-marked patrol car, and the shithead that stole the car was a white male in his early 20s, per a witness. As you can imagine, every cop, deputy, and Trooper working was headed that way. The shithead had been shot through the arm when he was assaulting the officer to get his gun from him and drove himself to St. Mary's Hospital in Livonia. A Livonia police officer and a Redford police officer crashed into each other running hot trying to catch that cocksucker. I went by the scene of the shooting where other DPD officers had scooped up Officer Scanlon to rush him to the hospital. It was later learned that Officer Scanlon stopped the shithead and got him out of the car for driving while suspended. The shithead assaulted Officer Scanlon, fighting over his duty weapon. Shithead was shot through the forearm as they struggled for the weapon with the shithead winning and executing Officer Scanlon. Officer Scanlon died from his wounds. I had the honor of participating in his funeral detail days later. Rest in peace, Officer Scanlon!

I was on my way work from Sterling Heights driving down I-75 freeway when I see police lights on a Troy PD patrol car on the right shoulder of the freeway with a car stopped in front of it. I slow down and see a Troy police officer in uniform fighting with the driver shithead number one in the right ditch. Oh shit, I pull my privately owned vehicle (POV) to the shoulder and notice shithead number two is sitting in the passenger seat of a car the Troy officer had pulled over. I jumped out of my car and ran over to the front right side of shitheads' car drawing down on the passenger holding him at gunpoint. Shithead number one stops fighting with the Troy officer with both of them now looking up at me with my gun out. At first, the Troy officer had a "oh shit" look on his face, so I identified myself, "State police." Once I identified myself as a state trooper, the Troy officer seemed relieved. Shithead number one stopped fighting the Troy officer, which allowed him to place the suspect into custody. Shithead number two complied with my commands and didn't move until additional Troy officers arrived. Both men were wanted for retail fraud over $1,000, which is a felony, from the Oakland Mall nearby. Bam, two shitheads in custody en route to jail. I was later given an award from the City of Troy for stopping at the scene and assisting their officer, remembering Officer Scanlon from DPD that had no help when that shithead was able to wrestle his gun away from him to kill him with his own duty weapon.

State Police in full force over holiday weekend: The Michigan State Police, Indiana State Police, and Ohio Highway Patrol joined together for the "Care Weekends" primarily focusing on traffic enforcement for travelers and OWI arrests. We were always told to put everything else on the back burner during "Care Weekends." No follow-up on complaint investigation unless they were emergencies. Sucked for the troopers at complaint posts because they never had enough time for follow-up. The "Care Weekends" included the three major holidays during the summer months. Memorial Day, the Fourth of July, and Labor Day. For the first five years or so, the department would actually beef up patrols on holiday weekends and issue a directive to all posts throughout the state to strictly enforce traffic laws as part of a multi-state "Care Weekend." Over the years following Democratic control in Lansing it was all fluff and circumstance. They should have changed the title to "We Don't Care Weekend"! They put out the same press release and left us bare-bones staffing, which was a huge disservice to the motoring public and the citizens in general of Michigan. I had a reporter do a ride-along from the *News Herald* when I first arrived at the Metro Post. Ten people were killed throughout the State of Michigan with none dying on Wayne County freeways. Seven people were arrested for drunk driving over the weekend with other various citations issued for speed, running red lights, etc. Forty-five citations were issued for no seatbelt use and child restraint violations. I was quoted in the paper as saying, "There is no reason a child should be in a car and not belted properly." She actually took pics of me issuing tickets that were in the newspaper article. Super star, Booyah, take that, no holiday fatalities in our post area for the weekend, Lansing bean counters like that! Lansing Headquarters, mainly the second floor, where all the big dogs worked, was always referred to as the "Vatican" after the Roman Catholic Headquarters in Rome, Italy. Very fitting especially coming from a Catholic background. I spent most of my career trying to stay away from the Vatican, others mostly ass kissers thrived at the Academy and near MSP HQ, the Vatican.

Trooper Chris Bommarito of the Michigan State Police Metro South Post in Taylor talks with a driver during a recent patrol along Interstate 75. More police patrols will be out looking for drunken drivers over the July 4 holiday.

Working as Trooper in Metro Detroit was cool because we were constantly working a shit ton of different details that could be worked mostly on overtime. We did details on our own including "Wolf Packs," doing speed enforcement and fugitive sweeps looking for shitheads that had outstanding warrants for their arrest. We did other details with city officers, sheriff's deputies, and the feds, including the Secret Service, FBI, ATF, and Border Patrol, being close to Canada. NASCAR races at the Michigan International Speedway. The Detroit Grand Prix and fireworks. The "Woodward Dream Cruise" with all the classic cars. There were many task forces that Troopers could also work on. The Violent Crimes task force looking for the violent hardcore shitheads wanted for murder, rape, carjackings, etc. There was a surveillance team that only did surveillance, duh. Many drug teams looking to arrest dopers, which were plentiful in Metro Detroit. There was an Auto Theft task force, which tried to reduce vehicle theft. I loved being a Road Dog uniformed trooper and never worked any of the other details. I was offered different positions and turned them down respectfully. "Thanks for the offer, but I'm all set." There was one thing I really wanted to do, which was totally cool: join the MSP Motor Unit and ride a Harley Davidson on patrol. We had four motor Troopers at our post, and I used to get a chubby when I would see them leave the post to go on patrol in the Metro.

Our main responsibility at the Metro Post was traffic. Sure we would have rolling domestics on the freeway or road rage shootings and crashes. I had a slick top Chevy Caprice when I was at the Jonesville Post and loved those cars for traffic enforcement. When I initially transferred to Metro, the PC didn't like slick tops because he thought they were dangerous. We had one slick top that he actually had a bubble put on. What the fuck, Lt.? We're a traffic post and you have four Harley Davidson police bikes—you don't think those are dangerous? He retired shortly after arriving there and when we got a new Lt., I was able to talk her into getting us some traffic cars since we were a traffic post. When she came to the post she actually had a meeting with all the troopers in the conference room giving us her expectations. At the end of the meeting she said, "The State of Michigan gives you a badge and a gun and pays you to fuck with people. I want you to fuck with people." She obviously was referring to aggressively dealing with shitheads/criminals that had to be dealt with. We looked at each other saying, "Holy shit, did she just say that?" She was a badass that didn't fuck around with bullshit, and she didn't hold any punches; we loved working for her! She got us traffic cars and any equipment we needed to improve our activity. We only had a couple Chevy Caprices with the Corvette LT1 engine when I transferred there. We had mostly shitty Ford Crown Vics with the black bumpers that were dangerous as hell. The rear end/suspension was shitty and would actually float at high speeds, and they were slow as shit also only topping out at around 129 mph. The Chevys topped out at about 146. Big difference. There was so much traffic in the Metro area we had to use lasers for speed enforcement. It was hard to use radar with the traffic congestion making it hard to pick out and single out speeders. The lasers were very vehicle specific, accurate within an inch on the front or rear bumper. Radar units threw out a beam, picking up many vehicles that would be hard to pick out at times. I would give speeders 15 mph over the speed limit before I would pull them over. Eighty-six or faster on the freeways, 71 or faster on secondary roads, and all other roads 16 over and faster. Most people speed including myself so that's why I gave people 15 over, which is fair. Sometimes I would stop for lower speeds if there was some other violation, such as seatbelt or window tint. Working in the Metro area I could go out on patrol and stop car after car all the time. It was like shooting fish in a barrel. All of us young troopers had a great time; the job was actually fun.

News article: "I-94 crash kills 4 after game." When I was at Jonesville I took one fatal car crash where a lady supposedly jumped from a moving vehicle. No biggie, sucks that she died, just had to make sure it wasn't a domestic dispute gone bad making sure the male driver didn't push her out of the car. I took a shitload of fatal car crashes when I transferred to Metro. It was my birthday in 1998, I was close to the end of my shift working days so I could go to a birthday function my family was putting on for me over on the east side. There were at least 10 of us road troopers working that day at Metro South, a nice sunny day, which also happened to be the last baseball game at the old Tiger Stadium on Michigan Ave. in Detroit before they moved to the new stadium at Comerica Park. Metro Dispatch advised there was a single SUV crash on I -94 W/B near the Big Tire. There is a huge Uniroyal Tire that is on the south side of Interstate 94 that was actually a Ferris Wheel from the World's Fair years past. An SUV full of young people were on their way home from that last Tigers game when the driver swerved onto the left shoulder hitting a broke down fuel tanker. That tanker cut through that SUV like hot butter. I arrived on scene first being the closest car and found a fucking mess with dead bodies everywhere. The driver was decapitated with an open beer can between his legs, bodies were ejected, and one was trapped underneath the vehicle. One of the victims was from Massachusetts, so we had the Mass State Police do a death notification to the family. There was a strong smell of alcohol in the vehicle with beer cans all over the place. Holy shit, my first real "What do I got? What do I need?" Send me more troopers for traffic, an accident investigator, and a reconstructionist, Fire/EMS, and the medical examiner (ME). Turned out the front seat passenger was hanging out the passenger window trying to take a picture of the Big Tire over the roof of the SUV when the driver reached over to grab him causing the vehicle to swerve left into that disabled fuel truck. The fuel truck was well off the road with hazards on and triangles out required by Michigan law. The passenger was thrown from the SUV and was the only survivor of the crash. Hey Mom, I won't be able to make that birthday party you guys are throwing for me! Our abandoned vehicle officer at the post that was assigned by the PC to assist with all fatal car crashes wanted to submit a warrant for that passenger for negligent homicide. Really?

The kid hanging out the window taking a picture has to live his whole life with knowing all his friends from that day are dead! WTF? I totally disagreed with that and let my opinion be known!

Rosa Parks, a legendary icon, passed away at the age of 92. Again being Motor Men, we were tasked and had the honor of escorting her body during her funeral. We were also tasked with escorting dignitaries prior to the funeral. I was assigned to the Henry Ford museum with a Wayne County deputy for a special dinner being held the night prior. Michigan Senator Levin approached my patrol car asking, "Hello, Trooper, can you tell me where the dinner is?" "Yes, sir, right over in that building." He asked me and not the deputy. Good man! I was sitting side by side next to the deputy when all of a sudden, the prior First Lady, Slick Hillary Clinton, and the Governor, Jenny on the block, were walking between buildings right across my bow. I saw them coming from a distance away and put my finger on the air horn ready to hit it when they walked by. "Come on, Bomber, push the button, don't be a Puss." Well, I puss'ed out thinking about it too much, shit, knowing their personalities, they'll bitch, and I'll get kicked off the motor unit! After they walked by but too late to have them jump out their ass I could have just knocked by clipboard onto the button, saying, "Sorry 'bout that, ladies!" Ms. Parks' funeral escort was a pretty long distance. The funeral home had a cavalcade of horses leading the front running at a fast pace on the roadway bordering animal abuse. The horses were actually foaming at the mouth by the time we made it to the cemetery. If PETA would have been there, they would have been pissed! When we were driving by the crowds of people, being on a motorcycle gives you a widened scope of sensory abilities. I.e., shitheads smoking marijuana/dope along the parade route being pretty easy to smell. Really? Some turds have no couth! I just shook my head, gave them a stern eye, and kept rolling along. Rest in peace, Rosa Parks!

That same Governor that almost got hit with the air horn was receiving threats to her and her family when she was Governor-elect. She lived in our post area and was the state prior Attorney General. She was a great Attorney General, supporting the Troops in various ways during her tenure, bringing home baked cookies to the Troopers at the Detroit Post in the same state building she worked at times. That shit changed when she became Governor. Why? Who knows? Only she knows! We were told to do property inspections on her home until she took office and moved to Lansing. A couple of our midnight Troops went by her house around 2 a.m. with her garage door being wide open; okay, that's not normal. They knocked on her door to check on her family's safety and to make sure everything was okay. Her response shocked the Troopers. Instead of saying, "Thanks, guys, appreciate it," she chewed their asses and told them never to knock on her door that late in the night again, slamming the door in their face. That right there told me we were fucked for the next eight years having her as Governor.

NTC, the National Troopers Coalition, represents State Troopers and Highway Patrol officers throughout the US. We were told about the NTC when we were in the Academy when the Troopers Association president and vice president came to speak to us to become full-time members, which most Troops and Sergeants are or associate members that pay a reduced monthly due but have the same benefits. At the time I think there were four or five Troopers out of 1500 Troopers and Sergeants throughout the department that were anti-union and were fair share members.

The NTC had yearly meetings and picnics usually in the fall. A group of us Troopers and Sergeants went to these Trooper picnics in New England from 1999 to 2001. They were held in New Hampshire twice and Maine once. You had to be an active State Trooper or retired and show identification to get into the picnic. One of the guys at the post had a contact at a local camper sales showroom (another retired Trooper) who gave us a great price on a rental camper. The first year we went, our driver, a 20-year Trooper, was pulled over by a New York State Trooper for speeding. Once he found out we were a bunch of Troops from Michigan he kicked us loose telling us to have fun!

The Trooper picnics had sporting contests, raffles, all-you-can-eat lobster, and plenty of tables and tents with SWAG (shit wild ass gear) you could buy from other states. I was collecting 1/64 scale police cars at the time, so I was able to buy all the ones I could never find elsewhere. They also had beer trucks with four or five tappers on the sides of the trucks. Man, I thought I could pound them when I was in the Army! Good times were had by all, and many people and friends were made.

Another cool thing about the picnics was there were high-ranking command officers from other departments drinking beer with us. My buddy and I drank a beer with the director/colonel of the New York State Police. Our upper command would never go to an NTC picnic because they would have to remove a huge stick out of their ass! A captain from Massachusetts kept asking, "How many scout cars do you have?" "Sorry, sir, what was that again?" Awesome accent, we were also talking about getting pulled over by that New York troop on the way, and his response was, "When you work in a pencil factory, you should get some free fucking pencils!" Forgetta bout it!

The first two NTC picnics we went to were a blast, but the one in 2001 was the following week after the 9/11 attacks; it was a really somber mood, with shitty weather/rain during the whole picnic, which is mainly outdoors. Oh well, we tried to make the best of it!

I learned fast as a young Trooper that I was going to take the path of the union and fight for troopers and sergeants becoming an MSPTA (Michigan State Police Troopers Association) representative. It was also a pain in the ass sometimes because you come to learn about stupid shit that your coworkers do and you have to defend them like a good defense attorney would. Sometimes hard to do when you have a strong work ethic but a positive because Command respects you and your opinion because of that same ethic they know you have.

We had shift Sergeants at every State Police Post throughout the state. We also had shift Sergeants at Metro Dispatch down in Detroit, which was above the Greyhound Bus Station that covered the whole Metro Detroit area. The running joke was if you wanted an easy promotion to Sergeant just promote to Dispatch in Detroit because you had to supervise civilian dispatchers that were a pain in the ass and nobody wanted to go work there. Stay at Dispatch a couple years, then transfer back to a post when you get a chance. The department had to re-post promotion positions constantly for Dispatch because it was a shitty place to get promoted. I was a four-year Troop working on I-75 when a six-month Troop advised that Dearborn Heights PD was pursuing a suspect involved in a hit and run fatality (K) crash that occurred on Michigan Ave. That young troop helping Dearborn Hts. sounded scared on the radio. I advised Metro Dispatch I was headed that way because the pursuit jumped onto I-94 headed toward the airport. We had a senior Trooper that was sitting desk as an acting Sergeant that got on the radio busting my balls for leaving my beat area. I got in a spat with him over the radio, and when I went back to the post about not leaving a young Trooper by himself in a serious pursuit and reminded him what officer safety was about. The Metro Dispatch sergeant who was buddies with the trooper at the post wrote a memo trying to jam me up, which backfired on him because my PC scolded them for busting my balls for doing my job. I tended to have confrontations like this throughout my career, which probably led me to being a union rep for most of my career instead of trying to promote my way up the ladder being a kiss-ass. I always tried to do right by the Troops and not throw them under the bus.

I was asked by the MSPTA and had the honor in 2000 of attending the funeral of Oklahoma Trooper Matthew Evans, 24 years old. Every time a Trooper is killed in the line of duty our union, not the department, sends a trooper or two to attend that funeral to pay respect to the fallen Trooper, their families, and fellow law enforcement. He was killed along with Officer Jeffery Rominger, age 42, of the Oklahoma City Police Department during a pursuit with armed robbery suspects. Both Trooper Evans' and Officer Rominger's funerals were held together at the same church. The funeral was very touching and sad. While we were outside before the service a bunch of Troopers were hitting their key fobs on their patrol cars turning off alarms. I asked a Troop why alarms were going off in the lot. He explained most of their Troopers have taken home cars and they have alarms because sometimes dirtbags try to steal their patrol cars! Holy shit, that's crazy. They had Ford Mustangs, Crown Vics, Chevy Camaros, and other vehicles. Some fully marked, others slick tops with no lights on top. They actually let Academy graduates pick what kind of patrol car they want depending on where they are assigned and what they like to do. Damn, that's badass, I would take a slick top semi-marked Camaro. I could really kick ass in Metro Detroit with one of those. During the procession they had patrol cars blocking the medians with all police lights on—what a moving moment. My escort Trooper said they had "crash" cars out with me asking, "Do they respond to traffic crashes during the procession?" "No," he said, "they crash into some asshole if they try and interfere with the escort." Wow!

I had flown out to Oklahoma for the funeral and had my Sig .40 semi-auto handgun on my hip. I only had to sign in on a log and meet the pilots flying the aircraft so they knew I had my weapon on me and where I was sitting on the aircraft. Before 9/11 obviously different then than now but maybe shouldn't be. Imagine if I or any other police officer had their gun on them when the terrorists took over those planes on that fateful day, just saying! Rest in peace Trooper Evans and Officer Rominger

We had an assistant prosecutor in Wayne County that also happened to be the head APA at the out-county office that was like a lot of the prosecutors today, woke and on the side of criminals more that the police. He would only authorize a warrant for resist and obstruct police if you were injured and had to be admitted to the hospital. No, that's assault on a police officer you dumbass! The Michigan statute had nothing in it about having to go to the hospital. Our court officer at the post was constantly arguing with his ass about warrants getting denied. Guess the job must have been too hard on him because the dude committed suicide by suffocating himself with a plastic bag in his car. Northville PD officers found him in the parking lot of a Meijer grocery store in their city. No foul play uncovered; shit, he always let criminals go so why would they be mad at him or want pay back? Come to find out he had a child with a debilitating disease that he couldn't deal with anymore; what a coward! My brother died from muscular dystrophy and had the best life he could with us while we had him for the short 15 years of his life!

"Hey Bomber, do you want go to Field Training Officer (FTO) school in Lansing?" Four years in the department, I'm still wet behind the ears. "Ughh, sure, I guess I'll go." The department was currently running the 119th Recruit School with close to 200 recruits. The FTO school was three weeks long leading up the graduation of the 119th so we could attend the graduation, which I did and meet our cubs that would be coming to our post. We had five FNGs (fucking new guys) that were assigned to our post. The post commander and four of his classmates retired at the same time. Five retire and five start fresh; we'll take it. The FTO school was fairly easy and fun to attend having cool instructors. One challenge was taking cubs to a traffic post knowing that they would not have the knowledge and experience of a complaint post dealing with various incidents and crimes you just don't see at a traffic post, such as murder, CSC (rapes), B&Es, arson, and domestic assaults. We worked it out and tried to show them as much as possible sometimes responding to calls with local PDs for training. I believed and would stand by it throughout my whole career any Trooper can go to small posts and survive the FTO program, but go to a busy traffic post, and you get your ass handed to you even though you're primarily dealing with traffic. When outstate troopers came to the Metro and Detroit Posts they were always dumfounded. Holy Shit, you guys are busy and definitely earn your money! You also have to learn how to become a badass driver. As a trooper working in Metro you had to drive offensively, not defensively. If you drive like a pussy, they'll run your ass over. My first cub was ate the fuck up. I thought to myself, "Was I that ate the fuck up?" I don't think so, but I did go to Jonesville by myself where he had four classmates that I could compare him to. My buddy who had transferred from the Ypsilanti Post to Metro had him for phase 3 before shadow and tried to get him fired. The PC stopped that from happening giving him some additional extended training. As Napoleon Dynamite would say, "LUCKY." Later in his career he got his shit together and actually turned out to be a decent trooper. He called me years later thanking me for the training I gave him since he was an

FTO, now saying, "Damn, sir, was I that fucked up?" and my response was, "Yes!" I trained many young troopers/cubs remaining an FTO for the next 15 years. The only thing we got for the extra effort was a pin for our uniform. It was enjoyable and rewarding having past cubs call me throughout their careers thanking me for pointers I had given them.

Working in Metro Detroit was very unique compared to other parts of the state and probably other parts of the country as a state trooper. We had Detroit Troopers sniped at on the freeway assisting a female motorist whose car had broken down. Jesus Christ, are we in a fucking hostile combat zone or major metropolitan area in the US? It's a constant battle with these cocksuckers who obviously hate the police and everything we stand for. The summer of 2001 just prior to September 11, "911" was extremely busy for us. We had multiple pursuits with violent felons that were ending up with Trooper-involved shootings where the suspects were killed at the end of the pursuits for trying to kill troopers and run them down. The last incident involved a Black male suspect with two Black male troopers. They tried to arrest him, and he put the vehicle in drive trying to run them down. Our district captain, who also happened to be a Black male, held a meeting with all the troopers in the Second District, which was extremely rare, advising we needed to revert back to Recruit School training and stop running up on cars after pursuits putting ourselves in harm's way where shitheads can run us down hence having to use deadly force on those same shitheads. "You guys are doing a great job out there. We need to curtail being put in a position where we have to use deadly force on these Idiots." We all looked at each other and said, "Okay, Cap, we can do that." End of meeting, get back to work, and stay safe out there.

The 2000 US election was one of the most contentious in American history. With the chads down in Florida, the US Supreme Court getting involved, and the candidates running, it was a crazy whirlwind with motorcades all over constantly. Michigan was a huge swing state for the election, which also kept us busy. There was one day before the election where we were running four separate motorcades in the Metro Detroit area at the same time for both presidential and vice presidential candidates. One thing that made it even more confusing and funny as shit that day was our PC, whose name was Bolling, and the sheriff's Lt. named Burger. The radio traffic was slightly confusing to say the least! "Burger to Bolling, Bolling to Burger" Ha that's some funny shit all day long on the multi-jurisdiction radio channel. "Bolling to Burger and Burger to Bolling." We had a Troop that was a peach. He jumped out of his patrol car on Telegraph Rd., took out his rifle pointing it at traffic for cars to stop! Can you say felonious assault? The PC was so pissed off he sent that Trooper home for the day, paid; only seen that once in my career. We were doing four simultaneous motorcades at the same time, never been done before!

Same Troop came across a car deer crash where a man was gutting/dressing the deer on the shoulder of the freeway. The Troop called out priority screaming for backup on the radio saying he had some kind of satanic ritual going on. He held the dude at gunpoint with a shotgun until backup arrived and toned down the situation. A desk Sergeant asked him what kind of deer it was referring to, a buck or a doe, and he said it was the type with wood on its heads. Baaaah, that's some funny shit.

News Article: "Woman Takes Command of Trooper Post." Our former assistant post commander who had left to run the Monroe Post for a spell came back to Metro for a transfer. She was one of the best PC's I ever worked for. No bullshit, she always took care of her road troops unless they were stepping on their dick/ovaries. Her first meeting at the post all of us gathered in the post conference room, where she told us what her expectations were. Easy-peasy: do you job, and there won't be any problems.

CHAPTER 4: ATTACK ON AMERICA "9/11"

NEWS ARTICLE: "Attack on America." Sitting at the Livonia Court with multiple traffic cases including an Arab American Man who was issued a speeding ticket. His wife was with him at court, not with him during the traffic stop, and acting like a flaming bitch in court. I actually advised her if she didn't calm down and stop causing a scene, I would take her in front of one of the judges for causing a disturbance. The hearing was in front of the magistrate, who cannot find people in contempt. He did tune her up as much as he could. Her husband was found responsible with her cocking off all the way out of the court building. I'm standing in the lobby talking to other troopers and Livonia officers when the court clerks advised we were under attack. Holy shit, all of us ran out to our patrol cars where Dispatch advised to "Signal 3" to the Post, in other words, get your ass back to the post ASAP! I turned my lights and sirens on and flew back as fast as possible where we were stood by at the post and were advised to help shut down Detroit Metro Airport with the Wayne County Airport Police and Romulus Police. Everybody was in shock, not really understanding the gravity of what had just happened. Being a US Army veteran and pilot, I wasn't naïve as to what was going seeing the commercial aircraft strike the World Trade Center and the Pentagon, but it still sucked. Man, I thought about all my buds in the Army that would be getting into this fight. Fuck to only be there with them. Hey, at least I could do my part in law enforcement as a Michigan state trooper.

Wow, the Vatican actually had stickers made advising us to put them on the patrol cars. Lansing normally would have never authorized anything to be put on the patrol cars. "We're the State Police, we don't do that!" "United We Stand" with crossed American flags. The post commander bought us a bunch of flags to go in the rear windows and flap in the wind. Everybody double up, two-man cars and patrol in Dearborn, which has the highest Muslim population in America. Show those colors and be proud, and we sure as hell were!

Everything changed after 9/11! Besides having to deal with and worry about your normal run-of-the-mill shitheads, now you had to be on the lookout for Islamic extremists/terrorists that want to destroy the American/Western way of life. Fuck that. Not gonna happen. We were sent to Islamic Terrorist Training at the State Police Academy, which was awesome training explaining the mindset of these monsters and why they believe in Jihad and destroying the infidels. The instructor, who was Muslim American, was great. He explained the disputes between the Shiites and Sunnis and their mindset, which was extremely useful. We definitely could use that training in Metro Detroit. One thing that stuck in my head was timing with these extremists. They could wait 50 years to win as long as they win, way different than impatient Westerners.

We were advised by the Feds the hijackers entered the US through various cities as part of a group of two or three. They experienced international travel prior to their trip to the US. Many of the hijackers traveled to and from Afghanistan at least once. After arriving in the US, the hijackers obtained driver's licenses, state ID cards, and other forms of identification.

The hijackers adopted Western-style dress and grooming habits frequenting Western-style restaurants and stores. The hijackers committed no serious crimes while in the US. The hijackers used common methods of communication while in the US, such as calling cards, cell phones, pay phones, and publicly accessible computers for Internet and email.

At least 9 of the 19 hijackers used Post Office boxes to receive mail. The hijackers stayed in small groups, and the pilots were the most proficient English speakers. They were typically the ones who rented vehicles, made hotel reservations, rented apartments, etc. Several hijackers kept themselves physically fit by joining local gyms.

America was as united toward one goal/enemy as I had seen or experienced in my entire life. I contacted a recruiter with the US Air Force at Selfridge Air National Guard base to see about going back in the military to do my part with something in Aviation. Former US Army Air Traffic Controller, left seat Navigator/Observer OH-58 Helicopter, Aviation degree from Western, Michigan state trooper for five years. "Thanks, but no thanks, you are too old, Mr. Bommarito." What the fuck? I was 32 years old and all washed up, at least I tried. We had some younger troops that were in the reserves or National Guard that all went to Afghanistan or Iraq. I felt a little left out but did my part by organizing "Care Package" donation boxes to send overseas to the troops in my old Cav Unit.

The Feds came out with a directive to patrol the US-Canadian border to make sure Al- Qaeda or other terrorists weren't trying to infiltrate from the northern border. Prior to that 9/11 attack we had a US Border Patrol Station in the city of Wood Haven, just south of our post with approximately 20 agents. After the attack they beefed up the station to over 100 agents. Shit, within a year we saw Border Patrol agents all over the place. Damn, for a while I thought I was near the California-Mexico border at San Diego/Tijuana. If we stopped an illegal alien, we would call Border Patrol, who would show up within 10 minutes, verify they were here illegally, and transport them downtown Detroit to the US Customs station at Atwater and Bridge to be deported out of Metro Airport within the week. "Operation Stone Garden" was instituted to have the Feds (mainly Border Patrol), State Police, deputies, and city officers patrol the border on midnights. We were in two-man cars, usually an SUV for comfort, making unlimited overtime to make sure our country was safe. That was probably some of the easiest overtime I ever made during my career. We wore fatigues for the first year instead of our pretty trooper uniforms until some command officer out of district HQ found out and threw a fit about not looking professional. We are on midnights in the dark, having no contact with the general public. Why not be comfortable, just saying, common sense. Leave it up to some command officer with a stick up their ass to spoil the party. Pay me time and a half, and I'll wear a clown costume if you want me to.

We would also do daytime patrol in boats with the locals up and down the Detroit River. We would wear swim suits under khaki shorts with our SIG Sauer 9 mm in a paddle holster, handcuffs in our back, and a small flashlight in our pocket. Of course we had a bulletproof vest on with our badge in a necklace holder hanging from our neck. It would have been asinine to wear heavy cotton pants and full-duty gear if the boat goes down for whatever reason; even with a life vest on, you're fucked! If that command officer out of district HQ knew we were doing that detail with khaki shorts on she would probably have stroked out! Our post commander was cool with it, might as well be comfortable out on the water. We weren't issued any Coast Guard uniforms to wear, so you have to adapt and improvise to get the job done.

Everything changed after the attacks on 9/11. We were all on edge for at least the rest of 2001 going into 2002. We saw a ton more US Border Patrol agents on active patrol in our post area. If there was a pursuit, shooting, or other critical incident, they would back us and the locals up.

One of our young Troops stopped an old crappy school bus that was loaded deep with illegal aliens, all Hispanic, near a business district on Eureka Rd. in the city of Taylor. He contacted the driver and realized crime was afoot, so he called the Border Patrol to assist. As soon as the Border Patrol Tahoe pulled up, people started running from the bus and climbing out windows to get away. They were running in the roadway almost getting struck by cars, running down the freeway ramps onto the freeway and over to businesses trying to hide. They estimated at least 60–75 illegals took off on foot. The young Trooper caught two and handcuffed them to the front door of an Art Van furniture store. An off-duty State Police Lieutenant was driving by and stopped to help keep the people off the freeway so nobody got hurt. They were able to take around 10 into custody and the rest got away. Oh well, you catch some and lose some!

The Michigan State Police, just like the Feds, came out with Emergency Management positions in each district to deal with terrorist issues and other emergency issues throughout the state. Each district had an Emergency Management Lt. that would come up with plans for county and local municipalities. Hey, eight more command officer positions, which needs a captain and inspector to supervise those Lt's. The Troopers and Sergeants had a term we used more and more as time went on. "Too many chiefs and not enough Indians" The chiefs were command officers and the Indians were Sergeants and Troopers. If you throw civilian employees in the mix our department was way top heavy with not enough road troopers serving and protecting the citizens of Michigan. The time after 9/11 I spent working in Metro Detroit I was always mindful that a terrorist attack could occur, so we had to always stay vigilant. I enjoyed working with the Feds and locals on terror-related issues.

The State Police purchased a huge camper-looking mobile command post that had the latest/greatest technology to take to large events for command and control purposes. It was used at football games, NASCAR races, and other events including the Woodward Dream Cruise, Detroit Grand Prix, etc.

I was nominated by my girlfriend, later to become my wife, and chosen by General Motors to attend the annual Thanksgiving Parade in downtown Detroit. General Motors was sponsoring the parade and put together a Patriotic Salute to honor Police, Firefighters, and Military in the parade. There were also two Sergeants from my department, one being my mentor during the Academy and future Motor Sergeant . We carried a 30-by-60-foot garrison-style US flag with other public safety personnel including firefighters and paramedics down the parade route on Woodward Ave. by the iconic Fox Theater. What an honor. I was able to meet the mayor of Detroit, Dennis Archer, who was a great man, always trying the make the city a better place to raise a family. I also got to meet the new mayor-elect who was a turd that ended up being arrested years down the road for various federal felonies ultimately going to federal prison. I knew when I met him he was hanky and no good, had the "Spidey" sense feeling!

I worked on patrol that day; big mistake with my head not in the game and having to be in downtown Detroit at 5 a.m. for the parade. I was in

Dearborn with a Ford Motor Company security pickup truck in front of me coming up to a traffic light. I thought it was the weekend because of Thanksgiving assuming the light would be a flashing yellow, which it was not. The guy in front of me slammed on his brakes when the light turned yellow, probably nervous with me behind him. I swerved to the left trying to avoid hitting him; no good, slammed into the rear left of the pickup demolishing the front of my Goose. The air bags deployed, breaking my sunglasses and smashing my duty bag on the front passenger seat. Fuck. I got out of my patrol and check on him. "I'm okay, sir. How are you?" I had minor air bag burns but I was okay for the most part. What a dumbass! Now I had to call Sarge to the scene for an at-fault crash. I was so pissed at myself I asked sarge if I could take the rest of the day off on sick time, which you never do on holidays.

For a few years after the 9/11 attacks it was awesome being a police officer/firefighter. We love you guys, you run into burning buildings to save people when others are running out! Blah, blah, blah from the politicians and upper command officers. After the accolades bled off, the taking of benefits started to come from Police and Fire across all spectrums. More concessions were given by our unions. Every three or so years we got fucked in contract talks getting lower pay raises and having to pay more into health care and our pensions. It didn't matter who the politicians were, Democrat or Republican, they both screwed Public Safety across the board. We'll give you a 5 percent pay raise, but you have to pay 5 percent into your pension and 3 percent into health care. What the fuck? I wasn't the greatest in math, but I knew we were ending up on the short end of the stick. Gradually over the years we had to pay more and more into our health care and pension.

After 9/11 every detail we worked was beefed up huge with extra security and protocols. This included extra Troopers at the U of M football games at the "Big House," NASCAR races at MIS (Michigan International Speedway), professional sporting events including Detroit Lions, Tigers, Red Wings, and Pistons games. People were advised they could no longer bring large purses or bags into most venues. Our troopers would assist the local and federal agencies with a multitude of details. Prior to 9/11 we mainly dealt with your typical shitbag criminals; now we have to also focus on terrorist threats—damn, it really stepped up a notch. National terrorist attacks both domestic and foreign were constantly popping up as a reminder of what could possibly happen in our neck of the woods. Detroit is a huge security threat with major automotive manufacturing and an international border with Canada to the north.

One politician, the Speaker of the House in fact, in Lansing whose dad was actually a retired command officer had the balls to say, "We appreciate what you do, but you guys are no different than other state employees." Wow, what a fucking idiot! How did someone like him get elected to office at the state capital in Lansing. Corrections officers in the prison system deal with shitheads on a daily basis but in a controlled environment. I can't remember the last time a legislator or other state employee walked up on a car and was shot in the head by some turd with a suspended license! Many brave Troopers and Sergeants have given their lives serving and protecting our citizens, and for him to say that during contract talks is a huge insult, and he should be ashamed of himself, especially growing up in an MSP family. Washington, DC, the Nation's capital has a police memorial, "Police Week," service every year in May near Mother's Day, where law enforcement killed in the line of duty the previous year are put on the wall and other officers throughout history that research has determined that were also killed in the line of duty but were never recognized as such. The first year I went to DC for Police Week was in 2002, the year after the 9/11 attacks on the US. NYPD must have had 1000-plus officers to honor those heroes that gave the ultimate sacrifice the year prior. From the first time I went in 2002 I had gone at least six more times, usually when we lost one of troopers to be put on the wall. We would get a group and troops to go usually with some local cops and deputies also. We flew twice and drove the other times. Flying was a pain in the ass after 9/11 because we had to get special TSA locks to put on a lock box in check baggage, which is a crapshoot if your shit ends up missing.

We had to get a letter of introduction by the Colonel to travel out-state with our uniforms and firearms. President George W. Bush was the keynote speaker at the main ceremony at the US capital. This was probably the most positive time when I was a trooper, and I would almost say in history, where there was an enormous amount of support for law enforcement, firefighters, and the Military! "Thank you so much for what you do" was relayed constantly. "Can I buy you lunch?" "Hug a cop," etc.

The National FOP (Fraternal Order of Police) set up a huge tent city on the street where they were located. It was roped off, and you had to have a police ID to get into the area. The area was surrounded with smaller tents on the outside where vendors were selling everything from police badges, T-shirts, and all kinds of other swag. I had six years on the job, so I was still in the John Wayne mode. Holy shit, this was amazing. The center of the zone had a huge wraparound bar with DC cops selling can beer and other food areas set up. It totally reminded me of the trooper picnics held every fall out east but way better because there were cops from everywhere! NYPD, LAPD, troops from all around the US, English bobbies, Australian and New Zealand cops. Wow, pretty impressive. I would recommend any law enforcement officer to attend National Police Week at least once in their lifetime, definitely a bucket list item. We met a good ol' boy West Virginia State Trooper who went to college in the UP in Michigan and married a Michigander! Damn he brought some great apple cider moonshine to Police Week!

Miranda: Every Tom, Dick, and Harry in law enforcement knows what Miranda is and when it should be used. When I was at Jonesville and had a larceny or a breaking and entering with possible suspects sure I would call them into the post and Mirandize them. We were given Miranda cards in Recruit School and told to keep them in our uniform shirt pocket and read verbatim from that card, not from memory, when dealing with arrest. Custodial interrogation was a critical part of Miranda. If they are not in custody, you don't have to Mirandize their ass! When I transferred to Metro primarily dealing with traffic only, I never Mirandized anybody, no need to. Most of the crimes I dealt with, felony flee and elude, reckless driving, assaults were always committed in my presence. Once they were placed into custody, I would only ask administrative questions. If there was an arrest such as an OWI (operate while intoxicated), I would ask them the question before placing them into custody.

Dearborn, Michigan, has the highest Muslim population in the United States. The city is also the home of Ford Motor Company's headquarters. We have always had a great working relationship with the Dearborn Police Department. There were no significant issues that arose after 9/11 in the Metro Detroit area concerning terrorism. The Iraqi soccer team had won a national title, so there was a peaceful celebration. Dearborn called us for assistance with crowd/traffic control, and we were down huge in staffing, thanks Jenny on the block! I suggested mobilizing troopers from area posts but was shot down by a desk sergeant. Pretty embarrassing being the State Police and not providing assistance to another agency when requested; that's what we are supposed to do, right?

CHAPTER 5: MOTOR SCHOOL/MOTOR MAN

THE MICHIGAN State Police had patrol motorcycles early on in the department's history until approximately 1944 using Harley Davidson and Indian motorcycles. The powers to be got rid of the motorcycles because too many Troopers were getting killed on the bikes in traffic crashes back in the day. With a 50-year break the department brought the motorcycles back in 1994 using Harley Davidsons again and putting the first bikes revisited in the Michigan State Police at the Detroit Post. The bikes had only been back two years when I joined the department. They had an MSP Harley and a Blue Goose on static display at the Lansing center when we graduated. I remember seeing that hog as I was marching by in the front lobby, saying to myself, "I'm gonna ride one of those Hogs as a Trooper in the very near future." Okay, it took me six years to get on the motor unit, not as soon as I had wanted.

I had some experience riding motorcycles when I was a young man. My uncle John, who joined the Navy, left his 1970 Honda 125 cc at my dad's house in Detroit. I suppose you can't take your personal motorcycle on ships with you? My parents divorced when I was a young kid (I was five), our dad staying in Detroit and our mother moving to the suburbs in Sterling Heights. My older brother James and I would take the motorcycle out riding on the streets of Detroit. I also had that "Jawa" moped I used for a year before I was able to drive a car. Our dad owned a collision shop on Harper in the hood, so when he left for work we would go cruising on the Honda. He would come home and bitch at us for riding Uncle John's motorcycle all around while he was gone. "Sorry, Dad." Our uncle John came back from the Military and picked his motorcycle up; damn it, that sucked. We talked our mother into getting us a Chaparral dirt bike that we could ride in the field behind her house in Sterling Heights.

Some experience riding a street bike and dirt bike. "What the hell. I'll put in for the motor unit." I purchased a Suzuki Katana 600 in 2001 and rode that sled all over Metro Detroit, going on some long-distance rides with some other trooper buds that also had crotch rockets. Okay, time to put in for the motor unit.

We had four Michigan State Police Harleys at the Metro South Post, where I worked. The Metro North Post in Oak Park also had four bikes, and the Detroit Post had, give or take, ten to twelve bikes including a Motor sergeant who ran the whole motor unit from the Detroit Post.

I put in for the bikes in 2001 having five years as a Road Dog after 9/11, and my PC at the time screwed me. He would not recommend me for the bikes because I did not have pursuit experience on police motorcycles! What the fuck, Lieutenant, I have a bike for the last year driving that thing all over the place, rode street bikes and dirt bikes when I was a young kid, and obtained my motorcycle endorsement on my own. I heard stories of applicants getting picked for Motor School not even having their cycle endorsement at least having it by the time the school started. I also would park it in the post garage so he could see I had been riding, with him seeing it and only bitching about us parking our personal bikes next to police bikes. Our department also had a no-pursuit policy with the police bikes for safety purposes, which I agreed with. All it takes is a shithead side-swiping you during a pursuit or spiking the brakes, and you're roadkill! He didn't even know we couldn't pursue on the bikes! No biggie; he was soon to retire.

The PC, Old Man, retired with four of his Academy classmates with our post getting five cubs from the latest Academy to replace the five retirees. Our previous assistant post commander came back to the post to replace him. She was a great PC. I busted my ass working for her, and she appreciated it giving me a great referral for Motor School. In 2002 I was able to slide into a Motor Man position where I had enough seniority to actually stay at the post I was at. I had fellow classmates at the Metro North Post and Detroit Post asking me what I was going to do. I had first pick, and I decided to stay at the Metro South Post.

The Michigan State Police Motor School was one of the best and hardest in the country, probably next comparable the California Highway Patrol. Both of our agencies have extensive police vehicle testing including police motorcycles. Our Motor School took place over three weeks, Monday through Friday with weekends off. We started our Motor School in mid-July being hot as hell driving a Harley on hot sticky blacktop sweating our balls, later to be known as "Swamp ass." The first two weeks of Motor School was learning inside drive track, slow cone maneuvering, braking, and high-speed driving on the outside perimeter off the drive track. The third week involved leaving the Academy grounds and making traffic stops on motor instructors who were in unmarked MSP cars in the Lansing area. The third week also included going to the shooting range to practice shooting from the bikes if needed during traffic stops and using the motors for cover and concealment. We also took the bikes and went on ride-outs to different parts of the state including Metro Detroit, mid-Michigan, and West Michigan.

They put us up at the Academy, so I brought my own television with a built-in VHS player to watch movies after training. Back to three weeks of eating Academy food, and dreading sleeping on the shitty Academy beds, ugh! I had always dreaded going to the Academy even during Motor School. Call it Academy PTSD, remembering the days of being a recruit, I don't know, I just knew I always dreaded going back to the Vatican and the Academy!

We went through Motor School in July, hot as hell riding on black top. The instructors start off first thing Monday morning with a hearty welcome by drive track staff and classroom training showing us what to expect for the next three weeks. There were eight of us men in this Motor School, including six troopers and two city officers, one from Birmingham and one from Traverse City. We trained on MSP Harleys each of us being assigned our own motor, just like we would back at our home sites on patrol. I had heard that a female trooper had gone through Motor School in the late 90s but couldn't pass the third week and dropped out. I had never seen a woman motor cop till later in my career. They said you had to be nuts to be a cop and even crazier to be a cop on a motorcycle.

We were told to bring blue jeans, work boots, leather gloves, sun glasses, and white T-shirts. We had to wear white drive track helmets on the motors, which were the same used in the patrol cars for recruits and trainees. We looked like Q-tips riding around the track on the Harleys!

The first exercise we did was the cone weave, damn harder than it looks with that big ol' Hog! We must have dropped that bitch at least 20 times the first day. Brake, throttle, clutch, that's what the instructors kept saying. Too much throttle, not enough brake, you're gonna burn the clutch out, Bomber, you dumbass! Those Harleys are a son of a bitch to lift back up. You have to put the stand down and use your legs and back to heave that motor back up to plop back on the stand. Harley Davidson Electra Glides with all the police gear weigh approximately 850 lbs. and with a rider, over 1000 lbs. The next exercise was the offset where you had to weave back and forth like half figure eights; seems pretty simple but is not! They taught us everything to progress to the next harder maneuver. By the end of the first day we were all spent. Our shoulders hurt like a bitch from continually lifting that heavy-ass Harley off the hot-ass blacktop, knees and egos were equally bruised, whatever, it was still fun, time to go have a beer. I went through a lot of Ben Gay muscle ache cream during Motor School!

Dinner at the Academy, yeah, tuna boats, chicken, or various other meals that were so bland, a slight tad better than military chow I had eaten in the Army. One of my Motor School buddies, Bill, known as the "Big Bag of Chips," liked to drink beer. "Bomber, let's go to the pub and have a boomba." "Damn it, Bill, we're in Motor School, this shit's serious." "Okay, let's go, but only one boomba!" We did that shit the whole time through the rest of Motor School. Did it help? Who knows, but it was nice to get away from the Academy and have a brew for stress relief.

The rest of the first week was slow cone exercises, which were the easiest to perform. In and out of cones in the hot sun all day. Fuck, this shit ain't easy! There was an intersection that simulates having to turn left and right, U-turns etc. I had trouble with the intersection exercise during Motor and for years to come at Motor refresher every spring. Then comes the "key hole," probably the hardest exercise for any person going through the Northwestern Police Motor School. You had to drive the motor into a semicircle, crank the forks all the way over, and whip that bitch back out of the same hole you went into. I learned a little trick that I used to pass and used for all my future refreshers. I would hit that first cone going in (the sacrificial cone), which would allow me to whip that bike back out the hole. Cheating? Not really, to pass the course you were allowed to hit so many cones in a certain amount of time. I think in the 15 years I was on the motor unit, I only aced the course once. The next exercise was the "180 Decel"(deceleration exercise), where you accelerate to around 40 mph, jam on the brakes, and then weave through more cones, left, right, left, right, then back out of the exercise; damn easy to get dizzy. Then to the outside of the drive track for the "30 mph cone weave." Two cones are set up side by side then spaced out ahead where you weave through five or six sets trying not to knock any cones down. If you kept the bike in second gear with higher rpms on the engine, this exercise was pretty easy to do. "The Brake and Escape" would simulate a hard-braking action to avoid an object or vehicle. You accelerate to approximately 40 mph, jamming on the brake and then swerving left or right, your choice, to avoid crashing. Not bad practice, and confidence helped with this one. The "Bump and Go" was tricky especially with the heavy Harleys. You pulled up to a cone doing a controlled stop hard on rear brake (not front, you'd go over the handle bars), go around left or right, come to stop with foot down the go toward another cone same hard controlled stop, and then swerve around continuing on with other exercises. I dropped my Harley on this exercise plenty of times with it just falling over sideways, "Oh no, here we go over like a sack of potatoes." We went through Motor School with early late 1998/99 Harleys, which had no ABS brakes. If you locked those brakes, you were going down. Ass over elbows. Harley Davidson came out with ABS brakes for their police bikes around 2005/2006.

The second week of Motor School involved high-speed driving around the outside of the drive track. It also included practicing over and over all the exercises before we had to pass the "Northwestern" Police Motorcycle certification. The State Police added additional standards above the Northwestern standards making it harder than other Motor Schools. Michigan State University put on a Police Motor School, blah! The only requirement was that the instructors had to be trained by Northwestern to teach future motor officers. The State Police also added a third week for motorcade training and off Academy group/formation driving that other Northwestern Schools did not offer, again making MSP's more thorough. We were taught staggered, side-by-side, and leapfrog training with 20 or more motors riding in tandem. Badass, to say the least.

We all passed the Northwestern Motorcycle School and finished the third week with no major issues. One of my classmates actually fractured his foot the first two weeks during slow cones and gutted through the rest of the school.

The drive track staff took us all out for a steak dinner at some bar/restaurant near the State Police Academy. The lieutenant invited all us to a new fraternity that few would ever be part of. He said being a trooper or cop is dangerous enough, but doing the job on two wheels is far more dangerous and an individual has to be a little crazy to want to do it! We all sat in a private room enjoying each other's company eating steak and drinking beer with each one of us getting our motor officer pins. They even gave the Traverse City and Birmingham cops a motor pin. From that day on for the rest of my life I would proudly be referred to as a "Motor Man." Whoa, wait a minute, that sounds sexist! Word is there was one female trooper that was chosen to attend Motor School back in the day but washed out during the school for an unknown reason.

I spent 15 years, the majority and best of my career, as a State Trooper on the motor unit. The Motor Men had nicknames like military fighter pilots; my nickname was "Bomber" of course with a sticker on the back of my helmet. The guys had some pretty cool nicknames. Tram Dog, Wrinkles, Pretty-Pretty, Cha Chi, Coco, Kerby, Big Bag of Chips, Sweet Chuck and too many others to list!

We performed many details for the State Police on the motor unit. NASCAR races at the Michigan International Speedway, all the classic car cruises in Metro Detroit including the Woodward Dream Cruise, Gratiot Cruise, and Downriver Cruise. We escorted dignitaries including the president of the United States (POTUS). I was involved with motorcades for five presidents including Clinton, Bush, Obama, and Trump. Clinton had a huge head always having a cigar in his mouth. Bush was cool, taking a picture on our MSP Harley just before the 9/11 attacks on America. After 9/11, the Secret Service would not let anyone including cops to get anywhere near POTUS.

The Harleys we drove were slow as hell and had shitty emergency/police lighting. My first bike, a 2000 Harley Electra Glide, was a hand-me-down from another Trooper that had left the Unit the previous year. Max speed 90 mph, 95 mph if you reached up and pulled the windshield back (not too safe). Each trooper was assigned their own specific motor, we did not share motors like troopers sharing patrol cars. The bikes have different seat settings, shock settings, and a feel that each Troop would try and tweak to their own needs and liking. The new Motor Men also had to borrow helmets, boots, and breaches from troops already on the Unit until our gear came in from Lansing. There was a lag time in ordering new gear for new Motor Men to make sure they passed the course and weren't stuck with new gear and no trooper. One of my buddies loaned me a pair of horse boots with strings. Supposedly horse boots were originally used but were not that great because the soles on the horse boots were extremely slippery. I borrowed a helmet and a pair of breaches from other troops. Some of my classmates wore straight legs, regular trooper pants while waiting to get our gear. Fuck that, I refused to go on patrol with straight legs looking like a dork on a Harley!

Every spring for 15 years I and other Motor Men had to go to the Academy in Lansing for Motor Refresher! It was usually the first three days in April. Sometimes it was nice; most of the time it was still freezing and there might even still be snow on the ground. For the first five years I still had trouble with slow cones and passing my cumulative test at the end of refresher. I guess just like being a Trooper getting to the five-year mark allowed some comfort, being a Motor Trooper was the same time period for comfort, that magic five-year mark.

I would end up staying on the MSP Motor Unit for the next 15 years of my career, the second longest in the history of the Unit. I started on a 2000 Harley Davidson Electra Glide in blue, slow as hell, with shit police lights strobes and shit brakes and finished on a 2016 BMW RTP 1200 with much more speed, LED lighting, and ABS brakes all the way around—what a difference! When we transitioned to BMWs from Harley's there was a lot of flack from Harley and many citizens we came in contact with. My last Harley was a 2006 with ABS brakes, great LED light, and 10 mph faster than my original 2000 max speed 95 mph if you held the windshield back. The 2006 also had a cool exhaust rumble that sounded tough. If you ride a Harley, you know what I'm talking about. I bitched about the BMW and resisted the transition until the transition. We had a retired MSP sergeant that started and brought back the original Motor School in 1994. He loved the Harley like most of us until he hit a deer with his personal bike. He switched to a BMW for his personal bike and still had a huge influence over the drive track issues even being retired from MSP. He was on drive track staff for years and determined what vehicles we used for patrol including patrol cars, SUVs, and motorcycles. His word was gospel when it came to police vehicle testing and use. Remember there were only two agencies in the world that did yearly police vehicle pursuit testing, the Michigan State Police (duh the Big 3 headquartered in Michigan, Ford, GM, and Chrysler) and the California Highway Patrol.

One of the first motorcades I participated in was with Governor George W. Bush and Dick Cheney. My post commander knew I was in the US Army at the time when Dick Cheney was the Secretary of Defense in the first Gulf War. I had received a Joint Service Achievement Medal signed by a colonel on behalf of the Secretary of Defense. Dick Cheney signed my medal for me, which was pretty badass. I was also able to meet Senator John McCain, a true honor meeting a true American hero! I was still a Straight Leg (not a motor cop) at the time not getting on the bikes for another two years.

I had two years on the bikes when the 2004 election rolled around, which was crazy as hell. We did at least 50 motorcades that fall with multiple times in the Detroit area running four simultaneous motorcades with all four candidates. This was where "Eat, sleep, and repeat" came to be a well-known slogan. It's not the best idea to ride a motor when you're tired, but we knew that for the most part all the routes would be shut down by the Straight Legs. We had enough down time on a motorcade in Detroit, I had time to stop and get a haircut at Gus's Barber Shop!"

The longest motorcade was a bus tour by the Democratic candidate Senator John Kerry when he ran against President Bush; go figure! He's gonna save the world from climate change and used the most gas during our longest motorcade I've done in 15 years, hmm? He is a Vietnam combat Navy veteran, so I did thank him for his service! We picked him up from the Ohio Highway Patrol in Toledo. We're leapfrogging by their tour bus with one of the guys singing, "Living on a Prayer" every time he passes the bus; now that's some funny shit! We took him to Macomb Community College (my hometown college). John had Jon on the tour bus with him. Jon Bon Jovi gave an acoustic concert at Macomb while we were there. A bunch of us Motor Men snuck around the curtain to listen to the concert. The Motor Sergeant sees us and chews our ass quietly with a smile on his face. "Hey, you guys, you're supposed to be outside standing by your motors, not in here listening to Bon Jovi!" Ha, Motor Men getting scolded like a bunch of little kids. We left Macomb and headed west to the Grand Rapids area, which was covered by the Rockford Post. By the time we turned him over to the Rockford troops we had been on those Harleys for 19 hours. Fuck, your ass is killing you, tired as hell and ready to call it a day. Twenty motors three hours back to Detroit at full speed at 2 a.m., which was stupid, we were at 22 hours. Holy shit, that was one of the most dangerous details we ever did due to fatigue. When I finally got home and hit the sack I slept like a little baby.

Other dangerous motorcades would be where you get caught in shitty weather, including downpour rain and sometimes even blowing snow. You hit a "tar snake" on a Harley at 95 mph and during a motorcade, and you come close to shitting yourself. A "tar snake" are the squiggly lines in the pavement that work crews use to fill cracks in the pavement. Those things are slippery as hell when wet or hot!

Having spent 15 years on the Michigan State Police Motor Unit was amazing, two-thirds of my career as a Trooper. This would include 14 years of going back to Lansing for spring Motor Refresher for three days. I hated going back to the Academy, too many bad memories. I had weird feelings going back there even my last day in the department when I turned all my shit in. Every time we went to Motor Refresher we did the slow cones, high-speed driving, and cumulative exercises. The Motor Men called it a Motor Refresher, which is what it was, not a Motor recertification like some of the drive track staff would like to call it. Once you passed the "Northwestern" motor officer course you were certified, period! We would ride bikes during the day in rain, snow, or blistering heat. Over 15 years I experienced every kind of weather you could imagine. We had a tradition the first night we would go to Hooters in Lansing to see Hooters, drink beer, and eat wings. After riding motorcycles all day we had to get our drink on as a motor unit, great times! Someone came up with a game called credit card shuffle, where the bar tab would be given to a poor schmuck whose credit card was drawn out of a baseball hat by the waitress. I lost that game twice during my tenor on the motors. It sucked getting hit with a $200 bar tab; whatever, it's only money! Most of the time we had to stay in the shitty/uncomfortable Academy rooms, but every once in a while, there would be a Recruit School running, so the department had to put us up in hotels. Then it got to the point where we would fuck with staff so bad they put us up in hotels to get rid of us, ha. Some Motor Men might not go out drinking for various reasons so they would get the "donkey kick" on their door at 2 a.m. You do a reverse kick on the steel doors, which is loud as shit, sounds like a bomb going off. I had it happen to me a couple times when I was a more senior Motor Man. Another thing we would do is put shaving cream on the door handles and block the doors with laundry carts so you had to move and clean all that shit when you woke up before going to the track to ride motors. The first five years were a bitch for me and some of the other Motor Men doing slow cones, the last 10 years, no problem! I had that sacrificial first cone I would knock over in the key hole exercise to be able to bust back out with no problem. The worst Motor Refresher we went to was in 2016, the year after Chad Wolf was killed on his motor by that old fart. We were sad as expected and spent a lot of time just talking and reflecting on his death. But we always got back in the saddle and took care of business, like Motor Men do. Our Motor Lieutenant Mario, who was my Recruit School mentor as a Trooper, also did an outstanding job keeping us grounded.

Riding a police motorcycle was the best time of my career, and I wouldn't give it back for anything. Are you kidding? I got paid to ride around on patrol on a Harley for eight years and a BMW for seven years. What a blast! We started with the high Chippewa leather boots (women loved them), the breeches with puffy hips and standard DOT-approved open-face helmets wearing Ray Ban sunglasses and then switching to a different uniform with the BMW motorcycles, including closed helmets with a tinted visor, straight leg, too tight, Moto pants with Kevlar, and polo shirts with no ties. Our helmets were the same sweet MSP blue and then were switched to a metallic silver helmet that looked stupid. I received that stupid silver helmet my last year and wore it once switching back to my blue helmet for my last year on the bikes. Nobody said shit to me about wearing the blue helmet; being the senior Motor Man, they knew not to fuck with me and also gave me some leeway the younger Motor Men didn't earn yet.

I decided to put the deaths of two of my friends and fellow Motor Men in this chapter even though they occurred later in my career. They died in the line of duty on their MSP motors after we transitioned from the Harleys to the BMWs, which were supposed to be safer?

Trooper Chad Wolf "Wolf Man," 38 years old, was killed on his MSP motor on August 28, 2015. He was on patrol near I-75 when an old-timer changed lanes from left to right trying to get on the freeway at the last second, striking Trooper Wolf and then dragging his limp body that got hung up on the trailer in tow up I-75 for approximately five miles. Citizens were driving next to the old coot beeping their horns, trying to get his attention, seeing Chad being dragged up the freeway like a roadkill animal. The coot then pulled into a rest area, where he exited his vehicle and tried to change a flat on the trailer, doing nothing about Chad, no first aid, no call to 911, nothing. Witnesses stopped to help, doing as much as they could. His motor partner found him behind the trailer and called an ambulance, and he was transported to a hospital in Flint, requiring immediate surgery for the trauma he had gone through. The Rockford MSP Motor Men and all the other Motor Men from various State Police Posts went to the Hospital in Flint and were there when Chad passed. That was one of the hardest things I've ever had to deal with and be a part of. Chad was married with four little ones, two boys and two girls who will never be able to experience the many things life has to offer thanks to that old coot. The old man never admitted to doing anything wrong and didn't even try to help Chad at the scene, just change his flat tire. May you rot in hell when you finally kick the bucket! Chad would probably still be alive today if he would have stopped when he first hit him! Many Motor Troops were skittish and trailered their bikes to the funeral. I rode mine over from Rockford believing it best to get back in the saddle. I had the honor of escorting my friend and fellow Motor Man to his final resting place. Rest in peace, fellow Motor Man Trooper Chad Wolf! "Wolf Man." Our motor unit went to Washington, DC, to honor Wolf Man and see his name put on the National Law Enforcement Memorial Wall.

Trooper Timothy O'Neill "Gator," 28 years old, killed in the line of duty on his MSP motor on September 20, 2017. I had just finished working midnights in a Blue Goose with Tim's roommate, Ron Balls. We were off duty at 6 a.m. but left the post early because we were pissed that night knowing our Director/Colonel Kibbles and Bits had instituted a very limited pursuit policy that night, imposing a department-induced dereliction of duty on Road Troopers and Sergeants. I was pissed about the new pursuit policy leaving work about an hour early, not seeing Tim when he checked in on that day shift. There was a slight drizzle/rain, and if I would have seen him, I would have told him not to ride and he would have listened, I believe. He was my motor replacement when I got off the bikes after 15 years to start my last two years in the department. I went to midnights to build up my FAC (final average compensation) pension, and you can't ride motor on mids. I went home and went to bed like I always did after working mids, which I hated when my phone was blowing up. My wife kept calling when I called her at work; she said Tim had been in a serious crash by our house to get up to the scene. Shit, the crash was one mile from my house on the beltline. Still half asleep, I went to the crash scene, and a Sergeant told me to get to Butterworth Hospital ASAP because Tim was in serious condition. I went down there as fast as I could, trying to get information as I went. When I arrived there were many troops there. They said he hit the back of a pickup truck that stopped suddenly at the traffic signal, was thrown from his motor, and hit a utility pole head first. As before with Chad Wolf, waiting at the hospital we were there when the doctors came out and said they tried everything they could but couldn't save Tim! Fuck, here we go again, we lose one of our Motor Brothers on the operating table. Second most horrible experience I've had been involved in. MSP upper command showed up from Lansing, I can't remember who, but I told someone of higher rank to keep them away from me. Tim was engaged and due to get married within two weeks. Troops from the Flint Post transported his fiancée Carli to the hospital. How horrible. I left the hospital and had a parking ticket on my vehicle (MSPTA sticker on rear window), what a dick, writing us parking tickets when we lost our friend and they knew it, fucking meter maids. I paid the ticket and put a note in the back of my head, better hope and pray I don't stop one of the bastards for anything. I had the honor of being requested to be a pall bearer for Gator's funeral, which was an honor! I went in a Blue Goose with some other Motor Men, and my good friend Gracey took my family with him in his Goose. Rest in peace, fellow Motor Man Trooper Tim O'Neill, "Gator."

The Michigan State Police Command decided to disband the Motor Unit in 2023 after saying the Unit was too dangerous five years after my friend and motor replacement Tim died. The ES team is dangerous, Kevin Marshal was killed in the line of duty trying to arrest a barricaded militia idiot. "Hey, let's get rid of the ES team; too dangerous." Trooper Butterfield was shot in head while approaching a vehicle on traffic stop. Hey, making traffic stops is too dangerous, no more traffic stops. Undercover detective/sergeant is shot while placing GPS tracker on doper's vehicle in the city of Detroit. Nope that's too dangerous, let's get rid of our drug teams? What a joke! They could have at least waited until 2024 after having the Unit back for 30 years and spend a million dollars on some stupid study explaining why we shouldn't have a motor unit? They told 20-plus Motor Men to turn in their bikes, never having a meeting or discussion about their intent in Lansing. Typical, Feckless Cowards at the top as Administrators, not Leaders! They would never have the balls to do what we did or could do what we did! One of my good friends, senior Motor Man Reebs blindsided by the decision said it well. "We chose to do what **most** other officers are afraid to do. No more Presidential motorcades,

Woodward Dream Cruise, and other Cruises, funeral escorts, static displays for the public, Make a Wish rides, and umpteen other details that we did that made the department shine. The Motors were also great traffic tools not like the "tools" that decided to get rid of them! The morons that made this decision to disband the Michigan State Police Motor Unit should be ashamed but will never be because they are cowards! The upper command should reference the hood sign on the cars, **"Stop State Police"** making stupid decisions that degrade the history and luster of the MSP!

CHAPTER 6: THE JOHN WAYNE SYNDROME

A FAMOUS John Wayne quote: "Life is tough, but it is tougher when you're stupid!" The five-year mark is a milestone in any law enforcement officer's career. Many of the senior Troopers remind the younger ones by busting their balls and ovaries for being too arrogant thinking they know it all, been there, done that after five years on the job.

I was no different. I became a field training officer at four years, worked at two different work sites, a Motor Man at five and a half, the 9/11 attacks occurred at my five-year mark; damn, I was ready to take on the world. Slow down, little buddy, before you step on your dick.

Working in Metro Detroit was a cool experience, having at least 30 different district courts and three circuit courts that we could work in: 36th Detroit, 16th Livonia, 19th Dearborn, 23rd Taylor, 3rd Circuit, etc. Some judges were more hard-asses than others that might be more liberal, which kind of dictated where we would work or write more tickets. Sweet thing about being a trooper, if one judge was a moron and dismissed a lot of tickets or cases, we would just go work somewhere else. We never had ticket or arrest quotas in the State Police, but if I wrote 10 seatbelt tickets in one city and not the other a secondary by-product of those tickets would be a portion of $650 to that city, just saying!

Speaking of seatbelt tickets, I had an informal hearing in front of a district court judge in my post area where the defendant who lost the hearing used profanity as he exited the courtroom, slamming the door. "This is bullshit." Oh no, you didn't. The judge directed me to bring that gentleman back into the courtroom. "You are in contempt, sir. Your $65 ticket just jumped to $200. Any other comments, sir?" Well you might be surprised to hear he did have other comments with more profanity! "Ten days in jail. Any other comments?" Trooper, place that man in handcuffs. Bailiff, take custody of that man from the trooper and place him in a holding cell." Wow, some people don't know when to shut up and take their lumps. A $65 seatbelt civil infraction ticket turned into 10 days in jail. Note to self, don't piss the judge off!

Lincoln Park was a small city in our post area that borders the city of Detroit. They had a decent police department we got along with pretty well. The city of Detroit has had problems with for years of illegal street drag racing, where shitheads knew they could street race with little or no ramifications. Illegal drag racing in Michigan is a six-point misdemeanor, which is an arrestable offense; this means you can be lodged in jail and given a bond for release. On a brisk October night, four Lincoln Park officers in two patrol cars were watching a drag race from their city limits across into the city of Detroit. A moron driving a Ford Mustang lost control, crashing into a crowd, killing a woman who was a spectator. It was reported that the Lincoln Park officers were in their patrol cars blaring music over the public address (PA) system and taunting the racers. They advised they had tried to call Detroit PD multiple times about the racing in the past with no response from DPD, not a surprise. A newly elected Wayne County prosecutor ended up charging those four Lincoln Park cops with dereliction of duty and participating in the drag race by playing music over their loudspeakers. Wow, what a stretch. The department had already disciplined all four cops for conduct unbecoming, which is reasonable, but to criminally charge them was bullshit! There is the "Rod Rule" in Michigan, which gives a city or county approximately a fourth of a mile distance outside of their jurisdiction to make an arrest. I'm sure the four Lincoln Park cops were not aware of the Rod Rule, but even if they were, they still would have probably not taken any enforcement action. If they did, DPD brass would bitch about it surely! Damned if you do, damned if you don't!

Restaurants? More important, who offers 5-0? Five-O is 50 percent off our meal bill. Some even gave us 100 percent off, yeah, totally free. We would only go to those places periodically not taking advantage of them, realizing they had to make a living too! Sure they had some lieutenant give us an ethics class in the Academy. "You better not do this, you better not do that!" "Is taking a free cup of coffee an ethics issue" "You bet it is." Really, get real, Lieutenant! That was one of the first things I learned as a cub at the Jonesville Post after the Academy by my training officers and Senior Troops, the restaurants to go to with great food and the restaurants that "were on the plan." Shit, many times throughout my career citizens that were eating while we were would pick up our entire bill, thanking us for our service. When I was at Jonesville I would meet Troops from neighboring posts like Jackson, Adrian, or Coldwater for a bite to eat. We all went to places that were on the plan! After transferring to Metro Detroit, then Grand Rapids later, there were a bazillion restaurants to choose from. We stayed away from fast food joints because a lot of the employees had not so pleasant contacts with the law or were just plain shitheads that didn't like the po-po much. We would mainly go to sit-down joints sometimes getting carry out, especially when we were on mileage restrictions. Always sit at a table, never a booth (pinched in can't get your weapon out of the holster easily) and always have at least two of you watching the door in case some mental anti-cop shithead comes in raging! Happened to four uniformed city officers in Washington State on a coffee break. Horrible tragedy, all four of them got smoked with only one able to draw and pop off some rounds at the monster! Back to the good stuff, family-owned, Italian, Chinese, Greek, Arabic, Mexican, and last but not least the fave, Coney Islands. You name it, the Metro Areas had everything to choose from. That was always a priority for shift, we would call other Troops on the radio, "25-10 from 25-16 where's lunch?" "Down River Coney," then other troops would chirp up, "25-40 will be en route also." We had 30 minutes for lunch but would usually stay longer adding our two fifteen-minute breaks we were allowed per shift. The only stipulation was we could not eat within the first or last hour of our shift. I had one Lt. at the post that kept busting our balls about eating during rush hour usually Mon-Fri, 3 p.m. till 6 p.m. Most Troops would wait till after rush hour because it was the right thing to do, but some senior salty troops would eat when they wanted, pissing the Lt. off. Sorry, Lt., they are not violating any department or contractual policy. The post was okay with three or four Troops eating together as long as we had the same about still on the road to cover calls. We were fat at the time with staffing putting out 8–10 afternoon cars most days in the Metro. The Jonesville Post was lighter in staffing being a rural area only having around three or four Troops on afternoons, which was considered "fat." One of our senior troopers at Metro left his police prep radio at a local Coney Island one day. The restaurant owner grabs the prep, "Hello Mr. Police, Hello Mr. Police. You left your radio at the Coney Island." Holy shit, everyone working, "Who the fuck is that?" Oh shit, troop boogies ass back to the Coney Island to get that prep. Ha, nice job, dumbass! Even senior troopers can have brain farts.

Mental hospitals? Many in Michigan and across the US were closed in the early 90s to save money and make Liberals happy, who think putting someone in a mental hospital equates to "cruel and unusual punishment." A huge negative side effect to this is they close the doors, send the patients home to families to give them their medication three times a day to tell the patients themselves to self-medicate. That's all good until they say, "I don't think I'm going to take my medication today." Also a large portion of the released from mental hospitals become homeless, living on the streets, forcing law enforcement and citizens to deal with their mental issues. I would occasionally have to petition someone into a regular hospital that had a mental ward. Myself and other troopers had to deal with many EDPs (emotionally disturbed people) throughout my career. The only time I would petition them is if they were suicidal, wanting to hurt themselves, or someone else. The petition form was fairly easy to fill out, only one page. You had to articulate to the hospital staff and or doctors that the EDP had to be admitted and examined by a doctor. One example of this might be someone hanging over a freeway overpass threatening to kill themselves, which wouldn't be good for them or the vehicle down below that might have the unfortunate experience of running a human body over!

RIF (reduction in force) proposed by same governor (Jenny on the block) that put us on mileage restrictions three times and proposed laying Troopers off. It was the first time and only time done while I was in the State Police. I'm a road Trooper with enough seniority that it didn't affect me getting transferred, but I did get bumped to midnights with 15 years on. It was still a crock of shit! The RIF mostly affected Sergeants and Troopers in the MSPTA. Let's not reduce the do-nothing command officer positions; they might get upset. Mainly Sergeants were getting demoted to trooper to cover the layoffs of Troopers. One sergeant was a polygraph examiner at district HQ when he got demoted to Trooper and forced to work the road. Oh shit, was he pissed. He wouldn't make any traffic stops, not like you could on mileage restrictions anyways. He wouldn't answer up for calls. The lieutenants finally pulled me aside as the post rep giving me a heads-up he needed to get his shit together. Did it suck he was demoted, absolutely. There were plenty of other people in the same boat. I pulled him aside to talk to him trying to smooth it over, "You'll get your stripes back, just be patient, the moron Governor can't do this forever; she's term limited out soon." His response was not what I expected. "Fuck this, Bomber, I got fucked and I ain't gonna put up with this shit." "I'll nuke this mother fucker." Uhhh, nuke what? The post, me, the Lts.? He needs to talk to a shrink more than me. He ended up quitting the department a short time later, having lined up a six-figure job making much more than he did as a Sergeant in the polygraph unit.

Death notifications are extremely difficult to do as a police officer. I had probably taken over 20 fatal car crashes throughout my career, all of them horrible in their own way. If I was busy at a crash scene, I would send other Troops or locals to notify the family and then follow up with them later. Sometime we would get notified to do a death notification by another agency in Michigan including other posts or even other State Police or Highway Patrol Agencies around the Country. When I took the Big Tire crash at Metro one of the victims was from Peabody, Massachusetts, so we had the Massachusetts State Police do the death notification, which I'm sure sucked just as much for the Mass Troops. I took a crash on I-275 where a 10-year-old boy was killed. He was from Jackson over on the east side visiting a friend. I sent Jackson troopers to notify his family with this boy being the youngest of four brothers; how horrible. I investigated too many fatals to talk about each one individually. We also had to do death notifications for suicides, natural deaths, and murders! Toward the end of my career it was suggested that we take a post chaplain with us to assist Troopers with this horrible task. Why didn't we think of this sooner? It was also department policy to send two troops, not knowing how the family would react. After I retired, one of my buddies was working with the Kent County Medical Examiner's Office asking me if I wanted a part-time job. He was on call and would respond to examine deaths, from vehicle crashes to murders, to determine if an autopsy would be required. "Thanks, but no thanks, I'll pass." I had dealt with death and sadness so much throughout my career I didn't want to deal with anymore. I stopped going to police officers' funerals also unless it was someone I personally knew.

A young recruit was seriously injured at the State Police Academy while boxing. He was transported to the hospital and had permanent injuries that would exclude him from becoming a trooper. I had my clock cleaned during Recruit School while boxing and also had to go to the hospital because staff thought I had a concussion. I was able to get a quick medical clearance and return to the Academy. The MSP

Command decided boxing is too dangerous, even though thousands have participated in it for years, and quit using it as a training tool. It appears that because of one unfortunate/fluke incident the feckless MSP Command gets rid of a key part of our training that helps prepare us as road troopers. Let's hope criminals realize we quit training with boxing so they won't punch us in the face during riots, arrests, bar fights, or any other incident where some shithead decides to assault a Trooper.

Every five years or so Michigan State Police T&E's (tests and evaluates) new handguns to transition to. This is usually done by the Shooting Range Staff at the Academy. They obtain firearms from manufactures to test and then give to Troops or Sergeants in the field to test. The first handguns I received in Recruit School were a SIG Sauer 9 mm semiautomatic pistol and a Smith and Wesson snub nose stainless steel 5 shot .357 magnum revolver as a backup. Both were great weapons. About five years in they decided to move from the SIG 9 mm to a SIG .40 caliber as primary still keeping the .357 for more stopping power. The new SIG .40 also had the MSP Shield engraved on the top of the slide, which was badass, being able to be seen in the holster. We then switched to a double action SIG .40 when an instructor shot himself in the leg while shooting a shotgun from the hip at the training academy. He forgot to de-cock his single action Sig in his holster so when he shot the scatter gun it hit the Sig that went off going down his leg. The Troop at first didn't realize he shot himself, duh, okay, could happen to anybody, I guess. Five years later we then switched to the Glock 17-9 mm semiautomatic gen 4 for the primary weapon and a Glock 26 smaller 9 mm semiautomatic for the backup. Wooooaaaahhh, hold on, people were pissed off at this move big-time. Why are we going from a .40 caliber bigger weapon back to a 9 mm? Better ammo with more stopping power per the Range staff. No more .357 Snubby to a smaller Glock. Changeable ammunition primary to backup made great sense. I liked both the SIG and the Glock, so I didn't give a shit either way. Our ES (Emergency Support) tactical guys bitched the most. A lot of them were actually able to keep their SIGs or go to the Glocks their choice, no choice for the rest of the department. Every time the MSP switched handguns they gave us the option to purchase our previously issued weapons. I am not a big gun guy/collector, but I decided to buy every one of the handguns I was issued and carried on patrol. Why not? I would leave them to my kids to leave to their kids. We switched long guns only once during my career. The department switch to M-4 rifles from H&K's when I had about 10 years in. They did not allow us to purchase the H&K's, what a shame because they were sweet rifles. The M-4's were okay, I had used and qualified with them in the Army, but totally preferred the H&K. Easier to shoot, shorter profile, and badass-looking for an intimidation purpose with mass shitheads at critical incidents in the 'hood. You get out of a Blue Goose with that H&K rifle at the ready, it was like the parting of the Red Sea. The Michigan State Police had rifles for years before other agencies. Many agencies had finally seen the need for rifles on patrol after the Bank of America shooting in LA, where the street cops were totally outgunned by the bank robbers. They had to go to gun stores to get rifles before the SWAT team showed up, which is ridiculous. We had Remington 870 shotguns when I came in the department, most with wood grain, which I liked. They were smoother to rack than the plastic polymer ones. We ended up switching to the plastic/polymer around the same time as the rifle transition. Again for some reason the department did not allow us to purchase the wood grain shotguns. Damn it, Jim, I'm only a Trooper.

Veterans, I'm a veteran of the US Army and appreciate veterans, especially after 9/11. If I stopped a vet, most of the time I thank them for their service and kick them loose with a warning. If I stopped a vet that had been drinking, I would call someone to pick them up and park their vehicle to be picked up at a later time. Like a New York State Police captain told me at a Trooper picnic out East when I was a young Troop, "When you work in a pencil factory, you get some free fucking pencils!" The same applied to other law enforcement or first responders.

We call it professional courtesy. I was working the downriver cruise on my MSP motor when I stopped this young kid on a crotch rocket who was popping wheelies and doing burnouts. He had marine tattoos and stickers on his motor cycle. I brought up being a vet and told him I was in the Army years back when he started laughing, saying, "If you ain't a Marine, you ain't shit." Oh, hell no, here's your careless driving ticket, Skippy. Be thankful I'm not writing you reckless and towing your motorcycle. Mess with the bull, get the horns. I remember in the Academy some instructor saying we don't write attitude tickets; boy, was he full of shit. Being a traffic guy most of my career, it was the opposite of what he implied. My first training officer told me, "If they give you sugar, treat them nice; if they're an asshole, give them spice!"

Every State Police post has a property room to put contraband such as illegal drugs, weapons, and currency, where it's stored pending a final disposition, trial, or destruction. A State Police Uniform Sergeant (Sgt.) is in charge of and runs the property room. Every once in a while, we'd have a Sgt. somewhere in the state that decides to scalp money or take some drugs/evidence from the property room because they have a gambling problem and or alcohol/drug problem. Very rarely did it happen, maybe a couple times in my 23-year career, where somebody falls from grace and fucks up! Other times you have a Sgt. that's a ball buster about hard working Troopers taking property on the road, hence more property seized, more work for them keeping track of it. One Senior Trooper got pissed at the property Sgt., having his cub put a dead squirrel they ran over in a vacuumed sealed plastic bag and then in a property locker? When the Sgt. found the dead squirrel, we thought he was going to have a heart attack! "Who's the mother fucker that did this? I'm gonna have their ass!" What else do you say but "Not me, Sarge." It didn't appear the Sgt. was going to take prints of the dead rodent or call the District Crime Lab in to look for DNA!

Michigan State University lost a basketball playoff game, so all hell broke loose on campus in Lansing. The first night the campus cops and Lansing PD thought they could handle the ruckus until the rioting turds demolished/rolled over and set a Campus Patrol car on fire. Oh shit, time to call the Big Dogs in. We were mobilized from Detroit to head to the state capital when troublemakers decided to wreak havoc on and around Michigan State University. Here comes the cavalry (MSP Troopers). We rallied behind our State Police HQ, which was on Harrison Rd., actually on MSU's campus. The university leased those buildings and property for $1 a year since the inception of the State Police, I believe. We had 200 Troopers lined up in formation behind HQ getting our briefing from the Lansing Post commander and the First District Captain. They were both badasses that didn't put up with any shit. There was a white box truck off to the side, full of leather gloves and riot shields. All the other gear was already issued to the Troops, riot helmet, gas masks, riot batons, etc. The Lansing PC was very blunt, "If any of these little bastards look at you sideways or think they are going to torch a Blue Goose, they have another thing coming!" After telling us their expectations, three of us jumped in a patrol car, one empty space for an arrest if needed. We turned our emergency lights on, the red bubble oscillating, and left HQ, half of us turning right and half turning left. We also had three or four unmarked, black Chevy Tahoes being driven by ES (Emergency Support) SWAT guys at the tail end. It was an impressive sight to see. Both groups of Troopers drove around campus to let it be known the full-grown Bears were in town and the bullshit/rioting was going to be put to an end! Along the route, a couple of college kids decided to throw debris at one of the caravans of Troops as we were driving by. Big mistake! The whole convoy stopped, some ES Troops in the Tahoes jumped out and put the habeas grabus on their ass, cuffing and stuffing them in the SUV. They went to jail for disorderly conduct and throwing missiles at a moving vehicle. Lots of arrests were made throughout the rest of the weekend, and no more patrol cars were burned, especially a Blue Goose! You're welcome, MSU! Lots of traffic stops were made that weekend!

Highland Park is a run-down city that is actually within the city of Detroit. They have many problems like any other small urban city. There were other smaller cities in Michigan that were well known as being shitholes including the Park, Royal Oak Twp., Inkster, Benton Harbor, and last but not least, Flint! The Highland Park Police Department couldn't handle all the crime, and most of their cops were corrupt. Case in point, we fired a desk Sergeant from the Detroit Post for theft, and Highland Park hired him! The powers to be decided to send Troopers and Wayne County Deputies into Highland Park to curtail the high crime levels. There was one day when a group of gangbanger shitheads had a shoot-out with another gang of shitheads across the street from house to house. We didn't want to go in there (Road Troops), risking our lives with minimum staffing to accomplish what? If you're going to take over a city to stop crime, you send in 100 Troops, stop everything that moves, take everyone to jail, and roust the shitheads out! Well, that never happened, so it got to the point where troops were assigned to work in Highland Park and strangely become sick for that shift. Now Command had to mandate low seniority Troopers to go in, which is not good because they are inexperienced and don't know what the hell they are doing, been there done that. Just like a military operation, do it right with the right numbers, don't half-ass it expecting a good outcome. The politicians want numbers, but they don't support you. When shit goes south. Upper command used to support the Road Dogs, but that has waned over the years.

Election year prior 2003, Bush running for reelection against the Green/ Tree Hugger John Kerry. I had my Pop's 1957 Ford Fairlane convertible, "Sea Foam Green" in my car garage. I can't fit my State Police Harley in the garage, so I leave if off to the side of the garage, put a sheet over the bike, and handcuff the front fairing to the front wheel. We didn't have keys to the Harley, so they could be stolen easily. Luckily, most people didn't know that we didn't have keys! We were doing motorcade after motorcade, busy as hell. I get up at the butt crack of dawn, jump on my Harley, pop it in gear, release that clutch, and hear this clanking metal to metal noise almost falling off the bike. Fuck, I forgot to take the handcuffs off. I took a pry bar trying to straighten the front fender as best possible. Thank God the bike is still drivable, I head to the rally point at Detroit Metro Airport and have to tell the Motor Sergeant I'm a dumbass and bent my front fender. "Gosh, darn it, Bomber, what were you thinking?" What else could I say? "Sorry, Sarge." My Motor Sergeant rarely swore (he was a pastor) and surprisingly didn't at me this time.

All the other Motor guys, including Detroit and Wayne County, were laughing at me calling me a dumbass! I took my lumps, did the motorcades, and took the bike into Motown Harley down from the post for the cosmetic repairs after the election was over. Bush prevailed and beat the Tree Hugger for another four years.

Party Patrol: A local police officer with Grosse Isle PD came up with a detail to work downriver (out-Wayne County) to curb underage drinking and bust up high school parties with drinking and possible drugs involved. Okay, I'll go with that, especially because it was another overtime detail wearing civilian/soft clothes and no uniform. We would wear necklace badges, carry our SIG 40s in an off-duty holster, and put a pair of handcuffs in our lower back, which were rarely needed. Most of the kids were issued appearance citations for underage drinking or MIP (minor in possession) and released to their pissed-off parents. We would also send police explorers (minors) into bars or party stores to see if they would sell booze or cigarettes to the kids and then do the same appearance citations. I signed up for "Party Patrol" every time it came around; we had a blast. We would usually get hot tips from the police explorers on who was having after Homecoming or Prom parties and where they would be. We went to a Motel 6 after getting a hot tip some kids would be there. All of us Troops, City Officers, and Deputies look like cops, short hair, no beards allowed back then. Some 17-year-old kid steps from his motel room asking what's going on, holding a beer. Oh no, you didn't, Skippy. Give me that beer and identification. Come to find out he had two hotties in a room with a hot tub that were also underage and drinking. One of the girls was pissy and argumentative when she found out we were the po-po. She changed her tune when given a ticket and her parents showed up, again pissed off to pick her up. She lied about where she was going, saying she was spending the night at her girlfriends, not staying at a dingy motel with some schmo! All I can say about the boy is, dumbass, you could have the time of your life with two hotties and a hot tub, instead of coming outside, being nosey.

On patrol in the "Silver Surfer," a semi-marked patrol car on Telegraph Rd. when I attempted to initiate a traffic stop on some dude for not wearing his seatbelt. The seatbelt law in Michigan for years used to be a secondary reason for the traffic stop, you had to have another primary reason to stop the vehicle, such as speed, stop sign, then piggyback with the seatbelt not being on. I turned my police lights on, and he looked in the mirror, hit the gas, and jumped the curb driving onto the lawn of a church to the right of us. Okay, here we go, dickhead. He guns the accelerator again spinning out in the grass with me on his ass and then goes back onto the roadway headed to an industrial area nearby. I guess he thought he could hide behind the business, not! Other troops cleared the post, which was just up the road, and headed to back me up. We found the dipshit hiding in a dumpster near the car he bailed out of. Police work 101, never leave a dumpster or trash container unturned, trash usually likes being in trash! One of the younger Troops had his .12-gauge shotgun out so he takes the end trying to butt stroke the guy like a butter churner. "Give me that shotgun, Cub." I took it away from him telling to relax and take a couple of deep breaths. We get the perp in cuffs and funny thing he says, "I thought you were a Taylor cop. That police car threw me off. If I knew you were a Trooper, I would not have taken off; sorry, sir!"

Ralph, badge number 666? What can I say, his name says it all! He was already on the State Police Motor Unit when I transferred from Jonesville to Metro. I wouldn't say he was my main motivator to getting on the bikes, but he was like Grossman from *Chips*, always getting into shit and funny as hell. His brother was also on the motor unit, which made it even more amusing because they were nothing like each other. Ralph pulls up to a crash topside in Detroit, gets off his motor when a wood utility pole comes crashing down and strikes him across the forehead almost scalping him. Holy shit, he's rushed to Detroit receiving hospital, where emergency room staff leave him bleeding out on a gurney in the hallway. His brother got a case of the pissed off and chewed doctors' and nurses' asses to treat Ralph, probably saving his life. Makes you wonder if they left him lying there knowing he was a trooper? He is treated and recovers from that incident. Thank the Lord. Back on patrol, Ralph loses his badge when it flew off his leather jacket at high speeds. This happened a lot to a lot of Motor Troopers. Very rarely are the badges ever found. We had to bend the shit out of the pins on the back of the badge to try to prevent them from flying off at high speeds/wind. Ralph just happened to lose his badge during a motorcade, so he had to write a "special" memo to the colonel advising why he lost his badge. The badge is never found, so he goes to Lansing quartermaster to get a new badge. He's looking at the badges available for replacement and comes across the BADGE #666. "Don't do it, Ralph! Look away and into the light!" He takes that badge and proceeds to have horrible luck the rest of his short career. Case in point, he's on patrol on I-96 on his Harley not paying attention when traffic slows, rear ending a semitruck. He should be dead but lived through that crash with that damn 666 badge on. He gets out of the hospital and brags how when people ask for his name and badge number he is able to throw that 666 at them. He's gassing his bike at a service station when a retired member of the MSP bust his balls for leaving his motor running. I am not quite sure why he would leave the bike running; they vibrate so much at idle I'm surprised the hog didn't fall over on its side from that alone. Anyways, retiree, who should mind his own business, gets in Ralph's grill. Ralph tells him to "go fuck yourself, and my badge number is 666 by the way." He used that like a badge of honor. Ralph ended up getting a duty disability retirement a short time later and leaving the department. They never and smartly re-issued that goddamn badge again. Rest in peace, badge #666!

Ride-Alongs: Our department had various ride-along policies throughout my career, sometime super liberal, anyone can ride, just sign the one-page waiver form in case you kill a ride-along, to extremely conservative, no one can ride except media or college interns. All ride-alongs had to wear a bulletproof vests and get the typical safety speech.

"If I make you uncomfortable, blah, blah, who gives a shit, blah, blah, here's the radio, blah, okay, let's go!" I always carried two long guns in a goose, an 870 shotgun and a H&K or M-4 rifle. I would always ask if they had any experience with the weapons in case we were in a shootout so they weren't left blindsided. They are a target for shitheads just like me. Men should wear shirt/tie and dress slacks, with women wearing a dress or dress slacks and a nice top. I had one college intern show up with nose rings, tattoos, and piercings. Oh, shit, I thought the desk Sergeant was going to stroke out! He sent her home and chewed the ass of the recruiter trying to recruit her. Today she would be welcomed with open arms! During my career I had various people ride, multiple college interns that went on to become Troops, family, and friends. I also had my future wife ride along. She worked at one of the local courts, so I sold it to the sarge as work related. This was also that time when everyone could care less who rode. We were on patrol when Dispatch advised there was an armed robbery with the suspects headed eastbound on I-94 near Metro Airport. I didn't want her to get hurt, so I dropped her off at a Shell gas station just off the freeway, then took off lights and sirens looking for shithead. Van Buren Twp. PD lost him in the airport, go figure. She had used the bathroom at the gas station taking off a butterfly ring to wash her hands. She realized it, went back to get it, and it was gone, bumming her out. Her mom had picked her up from the gas station that they lived close by. I picked her back up then went back to the post at the end of the shift and emptied the patrol car. I had her look in the glove box to make sure nothing was left in there. I had left her engagement ring in the glove box and told her it could replace that butterfly ring while asking her to marry me. She started crying, saying, "Yes." We went into the post and Sarge asked what was going on with her crying. "He just asked me to marry him in the parking lot." "Damn, Bomber, didn't know you had it in Ya."

The National Socialist Movement (Nazis) wanted to have a rally at the state capital, in Lansing. The dipshits had the right to organize and speak their bullshit just like anyone else, but it definitely caused a ruckus with other political groups. The Nazis had probably 30 people in their group with outside protestors in the hundreds. We weren't worried about the Nazi noobs but with the other group of noobs that wanted to kill them and hurt us. One such group, "BAMN" (By Any Means Necessary) would throw rocks, bottles full of piss, and other flying objects at the Nazis and us. What did I do? I'm just a lowly Road Dog trying to keep the peace, damn it, Jim I'm only a Trooper! We had special arrest teams of our ES guys that would rush in and put the "habeas grabus" on these assholes. About 10 or so went to jail for instigating a riot and assault. Whenever we were mobilized for potential riots we never fucked around, it was all about business. MSP Command was very clear, "No Blue Goose was gonna get burned, no innocent people would be hurt, and any shithead that needed to go to jail, would!

Same thing that happened to Officer Scanlon happened to a fellow Troop. Shots fired! Send the cavalry! A good friend of mine, Topher attempts a traffic stop on I-75 Service Dr. near Fort in the city of Detroit near the Lincoln Park border. Again, stopping a car in Detroit by yourself is very risky. The suspect (18 years old) keeps driving in circles in a residential area (usually means they are close to home, which was the case). The suspect bails out of stolen car with my trooper buddy in foot pursuit hopping fences with troop finally catching up to him. The fight is on in a back yard in the 'hood. The turd reaches for the Trooper's handgun and tries to disarm the troop to kill him. In the process of wrestling for the gun a shot goes off striking shithead in the shoulder. He is handcuffed and brought back toward the troop's Blue Goose and suspect vehicle when shithead's family and friends come out of the woodwork, pushing the Trooper, trying to wrestle their boy away. Luckily DPD and other Troopers make it to the scene and disperse the crowd with H&K rifles out. Animals in the hood don't respect authority of any kind. They do respect and H&K rifle at the ready! The case went to trial with myself and other Troops in attendance for support. The incompetent judge that presided over the jury trial actually ignorantly stated, "I've always questioned the State Police authority off the freeway." Are you fucking kidding me? How did this incompetent toad make it through law school and get elected judge. We are the Michigan State Police, not Highway Patrol, you fuck-tard! The jury saw through the bullshit and convicted shithead, sending him to prison for minimum of five years. But wait, that same moron judge disregarded the minimum sentencing guidelines putting him on probation after trying to disarm/kill a cop! This egregious decision by the corrupt judge was appealed immediately.

Ba-boom! Ba-boom! Bills introduced all over Metro Detroit area to quite car stereos. Technology is a great thing until you lose your hearing or shake people's windows as you're driving by in your hooptey ride with a kicker blaring bass so loud that you can't even hear the music. Most dipshits would turn the music down when they saw a cop, but some always wanted to test the waters. There is a disturbing the peace statute in Michigan, only problem is the police officer cannot be the complainant. Most of the cities adopted ordinances covering excessive noise so they would write the hell out of them. A state law was proposed in Lansing supported by 56 legislators from across the state but never passed. They wanted to use the decibel measurement, which would require police officers to carry decibel meters, which was not feasible. The city ordinance only required the officer to able to hear from so many feet away to take enforcement action. There are a multitude of citations in the Michigan Motor Vehicle Code that can be written in lieu of excessive noise and were written. More than one way to skin a cat!

News Article: "Retirements Cost Michigan State Police" Well, no shit, Sherlock? The State Police has numbered Recruit Schools or Academies. I graduated from the 114th Trooper Recruit School. The number crunchers in Lansing are aware of what schools are coming up on retirements, who turns in retirement papers, and a ballpark guesstimate of how many troopers we will have on the road on a yearly basis. The first governor that I worked under knew this and always kept our Trooper numbers up. He never wanted uniformed Troopers around him but knew a large number working the road kept Michiganders safe and the economy intact. The latter governors also knew this but didn't seem to care all that much. As I continued my career in the State Police it appeared that the hiring of civilians and promoting of command officers took priority over keeping uniformed Troopers working the road. One Governor laid off Troopers using us as a political tool and only running two or three low-number Recruit Schools during her eight-year tenure and the next threatened to lay off again using us as a tool to accept major cuts in benefits as supposed to giving state monies to be given to Sheriff's Departments to hire Deputies instead of Troopers. The number one priority of Sheriff's Departments in Michigan is to operate county jails, marine patrol, and provide security at the county court house. What a joke! Most Michigan citizens were unaware that the Michigan State Police had close to 3000 employees with only around 1000 being uniformed Troopers. A Senior Trooper once gave me advise that I gave to my cubs (junior/probationary Troopers) that kept you grounded is "You don't work for the post commander, district command, Lansing command, or even the Governor, they all come and go. You work for the citizens of Michigan that beep their horn at you as they go by after you stop some yahoo for driving recklessly or the victim of a rape where the turd goes to prison for life."

Great news, the wife finds out she's pregnant. I am working the day of our first ultrasound and tell her I can't make it to the appointment. My desk Sergeant, all knowing, tells me to comp out and go to the ultrasound. "Don't be a dipshit, Bomber!" "Okay, Sarge, you're right, I should go." At the appointment here's one heartbeat, then the nurse moves the scope, "What this? Another heartbeat. You guys are having twins, congratulations!" Good advice, Sarge. If I had missed that I would have been so pissed at myself! The Bommarito twins, Dominic and Olivia, were born during Hurricane Katrina, when Lansing sent Michigan troops to New Orleans, Louisiana, to assist with the tragic aftermath.

Senior Trooper at the post in coma after ice hockey accident. He was at his boys' practice helping the coach when he fell on the ice striking his head, going into a coma for weeks. This Trooper was a single dad, his wife dying from cancer years prior. He was raising two young boys on his own as a widower. He ended up coming out of the coma but was never the same in the head. He was always a happy-go-lucky guy, but something was off. He had to be put on a Retraining Order (usually for cubs) before he could come back to work as a Road Trooper. Myself and the "Mad Irishman" were both FTOs (field training officers) chosen to reintegrate him back to the job, rating him like we would a cub fresh out of the Academy. This was awkward, being he had at least 10 years seniority on both of us. He wasn't all there, he was driving the Goose one day, came up to a red light, looked both ways thank God, and ran the red. WTF are you thinking? There were some wires crossed. I had him pull over to a parking lot where we could talk. He was frank with me as he started crying, "I'm sorry, Bomber, I can't lose my job as a Trooper, I have to raise my boys, the love of my life died, and I need your help." I sat there dumbfounded. What to do? What to do? Ever since I had joined the State Police I saw broke dick Troopers that tried their damnedest to leave the Department on a medical or sue the department over bullshit. He was actually trying to keep his job as a public servant. I talked with my partner, the other FTO about what had happened, and we decided to get him through the retraining with a little "help." He was able to come back to the road with us relaying to the PC to get him promoted to Sergeant as soon as possible to get him off the road. He was on a crash with his police lights activated when some asshole sideswiped his patrol car and kept driving down I-94. He called it out to Dispatch and didn't pursue that schmuck. Somebody sideswipes my Goose, I'm chasing that mother fucker till my wheels fall off! Not quite all there, something's off, Troops got on radio, "Are you pursuing the car that hit you Mikey?" "Nope." "Ooooookkkkkkay?" Again just like people trying to leave on bullshit medicals, there were plenty of Troops that tried to get promoted to get off the road; why not him? He did get promoted to Dispatch down in Detroit shortly after returning to the road with no major issues arising. He made it to retirement a couple of years before I did and ending up committing suicide a month before I retired. So sad, my friend. If I had only known or reached out to you, who knows? I would tell you to get your head out of your ass and you would respond, "Okay, Bomber, you asshole."

Had to do another Retraining Order with a seasoned Trooper (again, usually for cubs on F.T.O.) with an Academy classmate of mine that was a huge fuck-up. He was constantly leaving the post area, dinking around, meeting women while on duty, etc. One discipline issue was getting a blow job from a married women (he's married too) he met on a traffic crash prior in the median in his Blue Goose! That actually made official correspondence seen throughout the Department. "Trooper receives 10-day suspension for receiving oral sex in a patrol car in freeway median." "Fuck, Lt., he's out of my Recruit School, totally awkward. Can you get another FTO to rate him?" "I've got confidence in you, Bomber, that you'll do the right thing." "Fuck, ., okay, I guess. Yes, Ma'am." This specific trooper must have thought, "Sweet, I have Bomber as my retraining officer, he'll hook me up." Wrong. He was an embarrassment to the Department, and I slammed him every chance I could. He was constantly doing shit that was way out of bounds. The mayor of Detroit had a small caravan of vehicles speeding down I-94 from Metro Airport, which is not in Detroit. This Trooper got out front of two or three Cadillac SUVs giving them a lights and siren escort to the city like he was a king when he was actually a turd! The Trooper violated Department policy and Michigan law for who knows what favor from the mayor? I get thrown into a Goose with dumbass and right out of the shoot he drives to a titty bar in Detroit. "Hey, Bomber, you wanna come in?" "No thanks, I'll pass." Again we are on a Retraining Order. "Are you fucking kidding me?" I call my PC at home and tell her we're at a titty bar and I'm sitting in the parking lot in a Blue Goose. "He's gonna know I called you." "No, he won't, I'll tell him a citizen inside the club bitching and complaining about a uniformed Trooper sitting inside the titty bar fucking up business." She calls the desk Sergeant at the post and tells him to have us Signal 3 to the post. My classmate won't answer the prep radio, so I have to go in and get his ass from the club. I've got topless girls coming up to me flirting; back off, broads! I snag his ass and tell him we have a call and gotta go. That was the final straw. IA (Internal Affairs) dropped, and he's given the option to resign or be charged criminally for other incidents he took part in. They had a discipline folder on him as thick as a calculus book! Bam, short time later he was gone, took his badge and gun and all his other shit. Back to the civilian world for his stupid ass, good riddance!

My buddy, the "Mad Irishman," was on a traffic stop on a residential street just off I-96 in Detroit. Single officer straying into Detroit by himself, hmm, trouble about to pop? He stops a white shithead/Hood Rat, goes to get him out of car for drugs and fights on. He's screaming on radio for help (Ofc. Scanlon, DPD, ring a bell). I'm on a crash about two miles away in Redford Twp. with citizen in back seat of my Goose. "Excuse me, sir, can you exit my car and return to yours please?" Actually it was more like, "Hey, get the fuck out, my partner needs help, I'll be back." I boogey ass over to his stop as he's chasing shithead on foot through back yards by himself in Detroit. I get there with neither one in sight, sinking feeling not being able to help right away. Out of nowhere this lanky Black dude runs by my partner and clotheslines that prick. I catch up to them on foot behind some yards a block away from the stop. That upstanding citizen wasn't even out of breath. Damn how appreciative were we? We gave him a "Get out of jail free card" (business card) and thanked him for knocking dickhead on his ass for us. "My pleasure, Officers."

College football games, I worked many U of M games at the "Big House" and other college games in Michigan. As I watched games on television growing up as a young kid and throughout my career as a trooper

I realized that most universities, especially down south, Alabama, Georgia, Florida, etc., always had State Troopers around the coach at the end of the game. We never did, of course we would work the games with the Deps and campus cops but U of M and state always had the campus cops around the coach at the end of the game; why is that? Is it this is my turf issue? Our MSP Command doesn't want to pull weight and piss off the campus cop chief? Anyways just something I noticed that raised an eyebrow! I worked Central and Western Michigan games also, never Michigan State (which I can't stand by the way). Go Blue!

An off-duty Dearborn Heights police officer pulls up to a video store on Telegraph Rd. a couple miles up from our post. He gets out of his truck to drop a couple VHS tapes in the drop box when a crackhead W/F jumps into the driver's seat and steal his pickup truck in front of his eyes. She locks the doors, flips him off, and hits the gas. He chased her on foot through the parking lot and then called 911 reporting the fresh steal. Big problem, he left his duty weapon tucked between the driver's seat and center console. My buddy Topher and I hear the call and go out over Dispatch that a Westland officer is pursuing her. We head north and pick up the pursuit on I-96 in Livonia. She now has a Westland Cop on her ass and us two Troops in separate cars behind him. He drops back and lets us take over primary pursuit because he is out of his city, and I call out the pursuit being the second MSP car. Okay, now we're in the city of Detroit with DPD and MSP Detroit jumping in the pursuit. She rams one of our two-man MSP Detroit cars putting them out of commission. The pursuit ends up going down Michigan Ave leaving Detroit into the city of Dearborn almost full circle. I get cut off by a DPD scout car and have to take the right turn lane to get around the DPD cars out of their jurisdiction. Get out of the way, dummies! We finally box her in crashing onto the lawn in front of the Dearborn Police Department. She locked the doors and wouldn't exit the pickup, so we had to smash the windows out to drag that twit out of the driver's seat. The handgun was still sitting there, thank God, she didn't grab it and try to smoke one of us when we ran up on the truck. She was high on crack and cuckoo for cocoa puffs! We ended up taking the case because it went through multiple jurisdictions. Topher and I had to transport that crazy broad to a psychiatric hospital for evaluation after being lodged. Really not our job; the Sheriff's Department should have done that. The off-duty Heights cop was happy to get his pickup back even though it was demolished. "I'm just glad you guys caught that crazy bitch."

Hazel Park Police Officer Jessica Nagel-Wilson, 26 years old, killed by a shithead responding to a dog off a leash call. She had gone up on the front porch when he shot her in the neck twice, killing her. I attended and assisted on motors with her funeral service days later with a heavy heart. What a senseless killing of a great cop by some monster that has no heart over a dog-at-large call. Officer Nagel-Wilson's funeral service was held at a church half a mile from where I grew up on Sterling Heights. Rest in peace, Officer Nagel-Wilson!

Less than two weeks later Detroit Police Officer Scott Stewart, age 31, was shot and killed while making an arrest at an after-hours gambling party. He had placed one subject in custody putting him in a scout car when the subject's shithead brother-in-law walked up and shot Officer Stewart, execution style, like a coward. Another monster takes a Michigan Police officer's life within two weeks, WTF? Officer Stewart's funeral was also at the same church that was half a mile from my childhood home. I attended and assisted with motor escort and found it interesting that Officer Stewart's family did not want any Detroit Police command at the funeral. Officer Stewart was a Cop's Cop, and his family had no respect or sympathy requested from the upper brass. I guess I couldn't blame them; that's their prerogative. Rest in peace, Officer Stewart!

"25-19 copy a single-car crash on I-94 near the Big Tire. The female driver appears to be intoxicated." "25-19 will be en route." I get on scene and just as Dispatch advised, there is a fubar'd (fucked up beyond all recognition) female in the driver's seat. I was working by myself in a Goose during the winter months and not on a motor. She fails field sobriety tests and refuses to take a PBT. She was also being a flaming bitch! Okay, here we go. "Dispatch, I have a refusal and will be taking her to the clinic in Dearborn for a blood draw." Sometimes we went to local hospitals or other times specific clinics that did blood draws for Police Departments. At this point in my career we **did not** have in-car cameras. We had a policy to call out starting mileage from the scene and ending mileage upon arrival at the destination with females or kids. The old CYA (cover your ass) policy, which actually worked. I get to the clinic with this chick, and she tells a couple of nurses that I raped her on the way to the clinic! "Really?" I tune Drunkie up, "Stop lying to those nurses." I tell them to take the blood and then lodge her ass at Dearborn PD. I call a desk Sergeant at the post and tell him what she said. His response was, "Fuck that bitch, she's just drunk and trying to get out of being arrested! She'll forget about being a dumbass when she sobers up. I heard you call out your start and end mileage, you're good. Don't worry about it, Bomber." "Okay, Sarge." Never heard anything about that arrest again, she actually pled straight up to drunk driving! It appears the old salty Sergeant was right!

Arrested another drunk where blood was drawn on a refusal to take a breath test. This case involved a traffic crash near the county line where the intoxicated subject went to St. Joseph's Hospital in Ypsilanti, the next county over. About a week later I took an investigative subpoena signed by an assistant Wayne County Prosecutor over to the records department at St. Joseph's Hospital to obtain a copy of the blood test/ results. I was in full uniform when asking for the record when a clerk advised that they would not give me the results per the office manager. I ask to speak to her supervisor, the office manager, who comes over to the counter with a snide attitude. "We have no obligation to give you those records." I explain to the lady she is obstructing my investiga- tion, can face arrest, and then advise her I'll get back with her. Hmm, I go out to the parking lot in my Goose and call the prosecutor. I give him the rundown, and he advises me to again advise her that she is obstructing my investigation and if she doesn't release the record, she will be arrested for felony obstruction! I tell Dispatch this over the radio when a Detective Sergeant from the Ypsilanti Post pipes up, "Whoa, whoa, hold up on that, Trooper Bommarito, I'm on my way up there." Okay, the Ypsilanti Post is just down the road, I can wait a bit. He comes to the hospital wearing his sweater vest and khakis and persuades her to give up the blood record. WTF? I'm in full uniform and that stupid bitch listens to him and not me. Well, I guess it was her lucky day, she had no idea how close she was to sitting in a cesspool Wayne County Jail overnight with no bond allowed on a felony.

I had a buddy that was a Drug Abuse Resistance Education "DARE" Officer with Livonia PD. They put on various functions at the local schools mainly educating young children on the danger of using illegal drugs. I was lodging a prisoner at Livonia PD when he showed me a note that a little girl had given him during a luncheon at one of the elementary schools. "Hey, Bomber, look at this note." I looked at it and laughed my ass off. I told him to make a copy so I could stick it in my scrap book. The note read as follows:

Dear Officers,

My dad says he pays your Salary. He says you guys have nothing better to do but pick on innocent people. He also says you're over paid and over weight. Hope you had fun at our lounchen [mispelled], you ate for free.

Signed: Jenny Smith

I had two not so good contacts with DPD (Detroit) cops when I worked at Metro. Myself and a cub (probationary Trooper) were shutting down a freeway ramp on I-96 in Redford at the request of another Trooper on a fatal crash. A Jeep Cherokee comes driving the wrong way up the ramp head on toward our patrol car directly at us! The driver hangs a badge out the window yelling, "I'm DPD." I advised him that you can get badges out of bubble gum machines and that I needed to see his Michigan Ops and Department ID. He refused to produce either, getting real shitty, real fast. "I told you I'm DPD." Here we go, step out of the vehicle. Ask them, tell them, take them. Again he refuses, so I proceeded to remove him from the Jeep and place him into custody for failing to produce a driver's license, reckless driving, and disregarding a police officer. Through a further investigation it was determined that was an off-duty DPD officer. He did have a semiautomatic pistol in his waist band that was also secured on my dashboard. The Detroit Police Department always had two roving Inspectors that were available in the city for any incidents that arose. One came to our scene and asked what we were charging his officer with. I told the inspector he could remove his guy from our rear seat and remove him from the handcuffs and he could deal with him internally, that I would not be charging him with anything. The Inspector was very thankful, and when his guy started to chirp up, he was told to shut his mouth and be thankful he wasn't going to jail. That same off-duty DPD officer later filed a complaint saying we violated his rights, which was a joke. The incident didn't go anywhere; the upper command handled it among themselves. My PC realized he was a dink and relayed that appropriately. I had another incident with another off-duty DPD officer when I was working on my Harley on the Southfield Fwy. in Dearborn. I stopped this female for speeding, expired plates, which at the time was a misdemeanor, and failure to wear a seatbelt. She had a male passenger in the vehicle who was wearing his belt, no reason to contact him or ask for ID. She had an attitude right from the beginning. "What are you doing walking up on my passenger side, I'm over here, so I don't get run over you, idiot! She wouldn't know or appreciate that because she doesn't do what I do. "I'm DPD." Here we go. She was extremely contemptuous and given two tickets, one for speed (18 mph over) and one for expired proof of insurance. I gave her a warning for expired plates and failure to wear a seatbelt. Boy, was she pissed, no professional courtesy for her, discretion is usually the better part of valor, but not in this case.

On patrol on I-75 on my State Police Harley when a fast, fearless flying hornet hits me in the right eye near the top where the lid is. We still had open-face helmets at the time. Damn, that hurt, I'm amazed I didn't crash that hog. I immediately pulled over to the right shoulder and turned my police lights on. I knew of an urgent care a mile or so away, so I carefully drove to the outpatient clinic amazingly not crashing. By the time I got there my eye was swollen like I was in a boxing match. The docs put some ice on it, pulled out the stinger, and put some save on the lid. Good thing I had my sunglasses on might have hit me in the eyeball? I told dispatch to send a troop in a car to pick me up and bring a Motor Man to pick my Harley up. I took the rest of the day off at the suggestion of the PC. She called to check on me trying not to laugh at the same time. "Bomber, you're the only one I know to get stung by a bee on your police motor, you're a shit magnet in more than one way or another." "It was a hornet, not a bee, Ma'am." We both laughed.

Benton Harbor, Michigan, and St. Joseph, Michigan, the tale of two cities. A bridge for the most part separates the cities. Local Township cop who is white pursues Black male on crotch rocket motorcycle who crashes and dies. Weird concept, "Stop for a Cop" riots erupt in Benton Harbor, which is a mostly Black community where residents say they are tired of being harassed by police. Does this sound familiar? Michigan State Police Troopers are mobilized from around the state to restore law and order in area and assist the locals.

Shortly after, patrolling the area on a regular basis near the initial flash point where riots started prior. One week later at 4:15 a.m. at least a dozen shitheads are lying in the middle of the road, not one or two, a dozen! A two-man Troop car rolls up to investigate why they are lying in the middle of the roadway like a roadblock. Danger, danger. Bad news, as the Troopers exit the patrol car, they are shot at by nearby car. They return fire striking one suspect with one Trooper being struck in the arm with non-life-threatening injuries. A State Police Lt. gives a statement that he doesn't think it was an ambush? Are you fucking kidding me? I was confused at the time, thinking this is political correctness at its worst. Black Shooter, White Trooper? Hmm, I guess if we had two dead Troopers, then it would have been an ambush? Benton Harbor eventually calmed down when the shitheads realized they weren't going to get away with mayhem now that Troopers were patrolling the city and surrounding area.

Working at the Metro was fun when we were at full staffing. Senior Troops always said you know it's time to leave when you're not having fun anymore. The post was putting out three to four two-man cars on midnights covering out Wayne County with Detroit and Metro North putting out about the same. We were tearing it up getting into pursuits all the time, arresting bad guys and sending them to prison. Dispatch advised the Feds (DEA) had a hot tip a some schmo leaving Detroit/Metro Airport with a kilo of cocaine in the vehicle. They were looking for a roller to stop the suspect vehicle. Shit, we couldn't answer up fast enough. Before you knew we had all four Blue Gooses chasing that cocksucker up and down I-94 in front of the airport. He finally crashed out into a snow- covered ditch and was taken into custody without incident. That kilo of cocaine was in the vehicle as the DEA said, so they arrived on scene shortly after to take possession of it. One of the Troops was talking to Dispatch with us hearing pecker-head chirping in the background on our prep radios. I opened up the back door of the Goose and chirped back at him, "You're in contempt," him replying, "Contempt of what?" "Contempt of Trooper, mother fucker" just as my buddy ET was transmitting on the radio. Oh shit, that went out across the whole district frequency. I get back to the post, desk Sergeant catches me in the hallway. "Contempt of Trooper, mother fucker, eh" with a smirk on his face. "Don't swear on the radio again, Bomber." "Okay. Sorry, Sarge." Case closed.

Michigan Football, working the football games at the Big House was one of the highlights of my career. We had a large contingency of troopers from the Metro Posts, Detroit and Ypsilanti Post whose post area covered Ann Arbor. In the ten years I was at Metro I worked at least 20 home football games. They would beef up law enforcement during the big games, Ohio State, Michigan State, etc. They also beefed up security after the 9/11 attacks. I really enjoyed working the games and established a reputation of taking care of the Ohio State Marching Band escorting them to and from the practice field and the Big House before and after the games. Command put me in charge of a squad of troopers to protect the band from hecklers and drunk morons that try to get in the way of the band. We would march them over by the tail gating slushies (drunks) sometimes having to push them back as they were poking at band members. One slushy yelled out, "Why are Michigan Troopers sticking up for Ohio State?" I told him, "That's what we do, dummy!" I actually received a thank-you letter sent to U of M from the Ohio State Band Director, thanking me personally and my squad for protecting his band members. The main priority after the game was always keep the students and fans from tearing down the goal posts on the field. If I wasn't on marching band detail, we were at the gates coming in before games, on the sidelines during and after the game to prevent to goal posts from being torn down. U of M command, not MSP basically said do what you gotta do to keep those goal posts up. Okay, sounds good to me. The stadium would make a public address announcement before the end of the game not to rush or attempt to pull the goal posts down! We would set up a circular perimeter around each post with Troopers, Deputies and campus cops. Some young kid came rushing at me so I cloths-lined him knocking him on his ass backwards. "Sir, why did you throw me to the ground?" "Get up, turn around, and get your ass out of here." He responded in a rapid manner vacating the area!

The Michigan State Police Motor Unit usually had around 20 or so bikes during the escorts, which came from Detroit, the Metro Posts, and some of the instructors from the drive track at the Academy in Lansing. Being an election year, 2004 was a huge year concerning presidential motorcades. We escorted then President Bush, VP Cheney, Senator John Kerry, and his sidekick Senator John Edwards. The two "Johns" is what we called them. We always had Secret Service motorcade training before an election year. All the big players would go to the General Motors proving grounds for the training. The Michigan State Police, Detroit Police, and Oakland, Macomb, and Wayne County Sheriff's Departments were the only agencies allowed to have Police Motors perform the escorts. This allowed for joint training having everybody on the same page for security and safety reasons. You don't want to be doing 100 mph on a motorcycle during a motorcade and have some Podunk PD officer that thinks they know how to ride a motorcycle pulling out of you and killing somebody very important! The Secret Service would advise on security protocol concerning motor down procedure. The ambulance in the motorcade at the rear was for the dignitaries, not crashed motors. Didn't give us a warm fuzzy feeling but at least we knew going in where we stood in the pecking order, toward the very bottom. Lord knows we had plenty of motors go down during motorcades in the fifteen years I was on the Unit. I participated in four election year motorcade campaigns. The first two were on Harley Davidson Electra Glides in blue and the other two on BMW RTP 1200s in a sharper blue! Only thing worse like taking a gut punch than hearing Motor down over the radio is officer down, which I had heard too many times over the years.

The Woodward Dream Cruise is held every August and runs on Woodward Ave. from 8 Mile all the way up to the City of Pontiac. The busiest area is Royal Oak, where the MSP Command Post is. The MSP Motor Unit worked this detail every year, so I worked it for eight years straight while I was still assigned to Metro. We tried to let people have fun unless they were stupid drunk or driving like an idiot. I was talking to my brother one year with some other Motor Men when Dispatch advised there was a stolen Ford Mustang convertible right near our location per the owner of the stolen vehicle they were on the phone with. We found the stolen car with four young men inside. The car was boxed in and had nowhere to go. They were extricated like puppets when they failed to exit the vehicle in a prompt manner. The dumbasses should have known better to stay away from the cruise where there are a shit ton of cops! That was our first felony arrest at the Woodward Dream Cruise. Thanks, boys!

News Article: "State Trooper Charged with Drug Possession." Really? It should have read Drug Courier! WTF? And what a dumbass! I vaguely knew the guy but come to find out he was running drugs from Detroit to the Brighton/Lansing/Flint area for years. What a piece of shit. Instead of facing the judicial system, he decided to commit suicide by driving his personal car into a tree at over 100 mph. Whatever, I guess he saved the taxpayers some money!

Michigan State Police Trooper Kevin Marshall, 33 years old, shot and killed in the line of duty. Trooper Marshall was posted at the Newaygo Post in West Michigan. The Newaygo area is one of a few areas in Michigan where anti-government shitheads/Michigan Militia live. They believe that they don't have to follow the rules like the rest of us? They don't have to pay taxes, don't have to have license plates on the vehicles, don't have to obtain a driver's license, etc. A lot of "Don't Tread On Me" flags and bumper stickers. We were advised of these shitheads in the Academy and to look out for them if posted in rural areas of the state. You don't see these Wood Ticks in the urban areas because they would get eaten alive by Hood Rats. Most of these groups don't recognize City Officers or State Troopers as having any authority to enforce Michigan laws and only recognize Sheriff's Deputies because the Sheriff is elected. Well, the last I knew Governors and Mayors are also elected, you fucking ignorant morons. A couple Sheriff's Deputies went to this turd's house to execute a search warrant when he opened fire on them, threatening to kill them for being on his property. Weird, I thought these assholes recognized Deputies' authority? I guess it comes down to a shithead is a shithead is a shithead. The Michigan State Police Emergency Support (SWAT) Team was requested to assist the Sheriff's Department with arresting this turd. The upper command decided to have a team of ES guys use forced entry to apprehend their guy. He set up a sunken sub floor near the main entrance and opened fire on the Troopers with an assault rifle striking and killing Trooper Marshall instantly. They retreated back out with one of my Recruit School instructors pulling Kevin out of the house. Same Trooper later committed suicide, not sure if this incident affected that decision or not? The murderer was able to put on dark clothing and low crawl out the back of the residence under the cover of darkness later that night. "How the fuck did that happen?" Somebody on the perimeter fucked up hugely! A few days later they received a phone call from a citizen putting him in a vehicle not far from the area of his house. Multiple ES Troopers responded to the scene, advised him to exit his vehicle and give up. He chose to get out of the vehicle with a gun; big mistake! They made Swiss cheese out of his ass. Trooper Marshall grew up over in Sterling Heights, where I was from. I had the honor of escorting his body with the MSP Motor Unit and also stood guard over his casket during the pre-funeral visitation. Rest in peace, Trooper Marshall.

Besides being on the motor unit for years I also was an MSPTA (Michigan State Police Troopers Association) rep for years. Anytime there was a trooper involved in critical incident, including shootings, I would respond to the scene looking out for the best interest of that Trooper.

I also handled disciplinary issues and hearings for the Troopers. One of my good buds JB was in a pursuit/shooting with a crackhead that was actually lighting and smoking a crack pipe during the pursuit. The shithead had left the road driving onto a lawn near a double wide trailer crashing into a pole barn. A Trooper, Deputy, and Township Officer all in the pursuit exited their patrol cars when the shithead backed up, striking the Troop car and then driving at the Township Officer, trying to run him down. All three shot at the turd, stopping the threat to their lives with him expiring at the scene. When I got there I talked with the command officer, got the Trooper another firearm, and took him back to the post. It was a good shoot and closed out as such shortly in the near future. (Chapter 8 will discuss the MSPTA more in depth.)

Sterling Heights Police Officer Mark Sawyers, 30 years old, was ambushed/shot and killed while completing a crash report sitting in his patrol car in the parking lot of a Target store. Piecemeal information was coming out that the suspect was a white male/cop hater who executed Officer Sawyers with a shotgun, stealing his duty weapon. Word from Dispatch was that the suspect was driving a Geo Tracker, green in color. Come to find out he was in a red Camaro and had probably driven right by us on I-75 headed out of state. Fuck, the cocksucker probably drove right by us ready for a gunfight because there would have been a gunfight! The turd made it down to Florida and when cornered by police committed suicide, fucking coward! We were fat with staffing at the Metro South Post that day. I had a cub in the patrol car with two other two-man cars waiting in the median of I-75 for the shithead suspect to drive by us on his way out of state toward Ohio. I should have called Sterling Heights Police direct instead of relying on our Dispatch. "Shit in, shit out!" I attended the funeral and assisted with motor escort for Officer Sawyers. Rest in peace, Officer Sawyer!

Unwritten rule, stay out of Detroit unless you have a partner. Let's take a shortcut and drive through Detroit to get back to the post. Detroit troops are two-man cars, Metro Troops are not, usually being single officer patrol! Fuck, what was I thinking, here we go, I'll cut across Warren to the Southfield freeway back to Metro. I'm driving down the road. I look over to the right and see this large white biker dude, wearing his colors (motorcycle gang vest), sitting on top of a female pinning her to the ground with his legs locking her arms. Kind of like my older brother would do to me when he was kicking my ass or teasing me as kids. I pull to the right curb, turn my police lights on, and chirp my siren to get his attention, no time to call anything out on the police radio. He looks over at me with contempt, then keeps pouring beer out of his red Solo cup onto her face. They both appear to be highly intoxicated. I exit my patrol car and with a loud, stern voice say to him, "Hey, fucker. Get your ass off her." Hmm, no response? So a quick soccer strike / boot to the head knocks him off her and then a boot on the throat keeps him on the ground. As I call out for backup to Dispatch, she gets up and starts to come toward me. "What are you doing to my boyfriend?" Are you fucking kidding me? I push her back as DPD is rolling up. They grab shithead under my boot and take her into custody also. The classic female at a domestic; she is getting her ass kicked and humiliated by the male but then goes after the cop trying to help her. Two shitheads turned over to DPD. "Dispatch, show me clear." Back en route to post.

Detroit Day Care Shooting: Another one of my Trooper buds Johnny that decided to take a shortcut through Detroit when he was flagged down being advised of a shooting that just occurred at local day care. He responded with the complainant to the business immediately requesting DPD and MSP backup. Upon entering the building, two adult women had been shot and were unconscious lying on the ground. Two children were shot in the head, one dead, one in critical condition. We live among monsters! What monster shoots children execution style. The incident was turned over to Detroit Homicide with multiple agencies looking for and finding that monster that did the shooting. Turned out it was a domestic involved incident.

Detroit Police Officers Jennifer Fettig, 26 years old, and Matthew Bowens, 21 years old, killed in the line of duty on a traffic stop on Michigan Ave. near the Detroit/Dearborn border. "No such thing as a routine traffic stop, right?" You hear that over and over, time and time again; it doesn't change anything, just reiterates the monsters that are out there mingling among us in society. Monster on traffic stop came back to their patrol car executing her; when he tried to administer first aid to her, shithead came back and executed him. Again we live among monsters! I attended the funeral and assisted with motor escort for these officers. It's bad enough to go to the funeral of one police officer, but to attend and escort the bodies of two that were killed together is a really hard endeavor. I was honored to assist with the escorts of these two heroes! Rest in peace, Officers Fettig and Bowens.

Care packages sent to Cavalry Troopers in my old US Army Unit stationed in Iraq. I got with some of the other Troops at the post and local Police Departments including Dearborn, Taylor, and sent a large supply of care packages to my old Unit the 3/17th Air Cavalry station in Iraq. The packages included baby wipes, candy/chewing gum, and other non-perishables that the Cavalry Troopers could use and help raise their morale. I loaded up the boxes roof-high in one of our State Police Tahoes and took them to Selfridge Air National Guard Base in Mt. Clemens, Michigan, for shipment over to Iraq. The Cav Unit sent us an American flag that they took flying with them on missions in Iraq and a thank-you letter for the care packages. Pretty sweet, hung up in the conference room of the post. One can never do enough for Veterans and War Fighters!

News Article: "Michigan State Police Investigators Claim the State Attorney General Impeded the Probe of the City of Detroit Mayor."

Strange that the state attorney general would not issue subpoenas to the State Police? Supposed celebration party thrown at Manoogian Mansion with strippers that ended up missing and dead? Not so weird when the Attorney General came from the Wayne County Prosecutor's Office, which covers the city of Detroit with the sitting Governor all being Metro Detroit cronies and the good ole boy club! As a young Trooper, I scratched my head saying to myself, WTF? The Feds eventually got that Mayor on other corruption charges, and he ended up going to federal prison. To show how arrogant he was, he actually took a Harley Davidson from the DPD Motor Unit for personal use. I took my motor to Motown Harley Service, and tech said Detroit Mayor's bike was there for service over mine. "Oh, hell no." A call made to local television station broke that story about that schmuck! He ended up caving in to news media pressure and gave that motorcycle back to the DPD Motor Unit! The same Attorney General that had obstructed the State Police investigation had tried a DPD officer for murder a few years prior when he was an assistant Wayne County prosecutor. The officer and his partner were responding to a domestic dispute when a deaf man with a heavy metal rake charged them, almost taking his partner's head off. The DPD officer used deadly force to stop his partner from getting murdered. I watched that trial in awe on *Court TV* and actually interviewed that DPD officer after the trial concerning a background investigation for a family member. The officer was acquitted by a jury of his peers but was put through hell by that prosecutor, again later to become the state AG. He would fit in well today with the many progressive woke prosecutors in many large cities throughout the country!

CHAPTER 7: RIDING OUT THE METRO

WORKING AT a Metro Post as a State Trooper is dangerous, exciting, and a little fun at times! Add a motorcycle working on two wheels instead of in four is even more exhilarating. Many people throughout my career thought I was fucking nuts for patrolling on a police motorcycle. I always said working eight hours on a bike was like working 12 in a car. Your head has to be on a swivel. I've been hit three times in a patrol car and luckily never on my motor. Our Department had a no-pursuit policy on the motors, which was very smart and I had no problem with. A spike of the brakes or swerve into my motor by some shithead, and I am toast. There were plenty of occasions when I would be on patrol on my motor when Dispatch or a Sergeant at the post would advise of a pursuit. I would boogie ass back to the post on my motor to jump into a Blue Goose so I could assist with deadly force pursuits. I would go into the gun room, grab a long gun and the keys to a high mileage patrol car, and bust ass to assist with the pursuits. Metro Detroit is a very high-crime and violent area to work. For many years the FBI listed Detroit, Michigan, as the most violent city in the nation. Lots of armed robberies, carjackings, drive-by shootings, etc. Our use of deadly force involved murder or its attempt, armed robbery or its attempt, CSC (criminal sexual conduct) with a weapon or its attempt, kidnapping or its attempt, and arson or its attempt. We were in pursuits with carjackers on a regular basis. Sometimes I thought this shit is like the Wild West; does this happen elsewhere like this, or only in Detroit?

"Post 25 cars BOL [Be on the lookout for] a Jeep Cherokee, silver in color, wanted in a carjacking, handgun used, suspect is a Black female.

The vehicle is traveling W/B on I-94 from the city of Detroit." "Dispatch, 25-11, I am on I-94 set up in the median, looking for the suspect vehicle." Lo and behold she drives right by me and gives me that "fuck you" stare as driving by. "Fuck me?" No, fuck you. The pursuit is on. Here we go in and out of traffic at a 100 mph plus. And there we go by Telegraph Rd. where two more Troopers jump in the pursuit behind me, which is good because they can call out the pursuit while I focus on the turd in front of me. Woooh, right by Detroit Metro Airport we go, she hits a median, turn around headed back eastbound and then crashes in the right ditch and bails on foot. Foot chase in on. She loses and goes to prison on multiple felonies. Armed robbery, felony flee and elude, and obstruction for attempting to fight when being placed into custody. A little pissant .32 semiauto handgun was found in the Jeep. Dispatch later advised that moron carjacked another carjacker. WTF! First and last time had that scenario. She ended up having a huge rap sheet of prior felony convictions and went to the Big House for 20-plus years. She can get out when I retire from the State Police I guess!

Working in Metro Detroit as a Road Dog on Sundays can be tedious at times, slow days just like any other profession. The post had beefed up staffing during the week to cover rush hour. Sundays were usually short-staffed so we might have three cars covering our patrol area, which was fairly large, with not enough troopers. As young troopers, we were told by senior troops that crazy, weird shit always seems to happen on Sundays. One Sunday afternoon we were advised by Dispatch there was a naked woman, described as a young Black female walking down the right shoulder of I-94 in the city of Dearborn. Holy shit. The three of us working jumped on the radio, advising we were en route. I was the second closest, driving fairly fast to get there, no lights and sirens though. This was one of the worst calls I responded to in my career. I was a five-year trooper, and the first on scene was a 15-year troop. He got on the radio, "Bomber, pick it up, we have a problem." Oh shit, I wasn't too far out, turning my lights and siren on. When I pulled up behind the 15-year trooper the naked woman, who appeared delusional, was wrapped in a yellow emergency blanket that we carried in our Gooses next to his patrol car. The 15-year troop, who was Black, was awestruck and pale. I've never seen him like this. He was one of my mentors. There was another yellow blanket on the ground, covering something on the shoulder. "Bomber, this is fucked." "What's fucked?" "Look under the blanket." I lifted up the blanket, seeing a dead infant with its eyes gouged out! There was a rigid six-inch-long piece of pipe on the trunk of his patrol car. The piece of pipe looked like it could have a been a deep socket used on a wrench.

An ambulance responded to the scene and took her to the closest hospital, which was Oakwood Dearborn. My partner asked me to follow the ambulance and stay with her until they decided what we were gonna do. The third Troop stayed at the scene to help him. The medical examiner had to respond to the scene. A Post Detective /Sergeant also had to be called in to assist the troop with the investigation. Turned out the woman had the baby with her boyfriend that didn't want a kid, so she decided to kill the baby so he would stay with her. Are you fucking kidding me? Thinking about the incident after, I was amazed she didn't wander into traffic to get run over, killing herself and the baby. Not sure when she killed her baby though. The baby did have rigor mortis by the time we arrived on scene. I sat with her at the hospital until released. She was very pleasant and friendly toward me, never asking about her baby. I was friendly and pleasant back with her, she asked if I could hold her hand, which I did. I didn't quite know how to feel, anger toward her for killing her own baby, compassion for some sickness she might have, … wow, many emotions for many reasons! Our shift partner who was first on scene was fucked up mentally by this incident; he had kids, the other two of us were single with no kids at the time. That Senior Troop who was first on scene, my friend, would go on to have many problems, the most serious, alcohol abuse, which led to a divorce and, eventually, his death. He was a great troop that for years tried to get promoted to Sergeant to get off the road with the upper command overlooking him time and time again. They contributed to his problems but would never admit it! They should have helped him and they never did? There were plenty of other incompetent morons in the State Police that got their stripes instead of him. He left Metro and transferred to the Flint Post, where he was from originally. I lost touch with him after he left but heard years later two Troopers were sent to his apartment, where they found him dead; he had drunk himself to death, so sad! Rest in peace, Mikey!

The 2005 Major League Baseball All-Star Game was held at Comerica Park in downtown Detroit. We couldn't have asked for a better day to ride a motor during a sweet detail. What a beautiful day for baseball and to be an MSP Motor Man! Alex Rodriguez and David Ortiz "Big Poppy" were in the parade of players down Woodward Ave. in front of the Fox Theater. Great detail for my MSP detail bucket list. The Yankees and Red Sox had a majority of the players for the American League. The MSP Motor Unit along with DPD and Wayne County Sheriff's Department were assigned to the detail. The same units that did the Presidential motorcades every election cycle. We always trained together in the spring prior to motor season starting. Two bikes were in front of every convertible with the ball players sitting up on the back seat/trunk area. Too cool! We were able to watch some of the game and then had to stand by our motors toward the end of the game to escort the players back to their hotels or Detroit Metro Airport. The game was won by the American League, which was fitting because Detroit was an American League team. Too bad there weren't any Detroit Tigers in the starting lineup for this game on their home field though; go figure.

We had over 20 different district courts in the Metro Detroit area that we could work in writing tickets and arresting perps in. I was at the 34th District Court, in Romulus, for some traffic hearings. I would always run the driving records for the magistrates and judges who might ask to see them. I also wanted to see if suspended drivers would be stupid enough or have the balls to drive to court on a suspended license. I had a joker that did this one day and wanted to test the waters and my authority. He lost the test. I saw him drive into the parking lot of the court, called him out in the lobby, and arrested him for a misdemeanor committed in my presence, taking him in front of one of the three judges for direct arraignment. I also called for a hook (tow truck) to remove his car from the court parking lot at the request of the judge. Sounds a little hardcore, but a message had to be sent to some morons: there is a rule of law, and it will be enforced!

Grosse Isle, Michigan, is a unique community, lots of money and expensive homes on the Detroit River looking toward Canada. It's an island with two bridges, one required to get on, and one required to get off. Crime is super low on Grosse Isle because they know the police will just shut the bridge down to keep them from fleeing, so they would have to swim their way off, like escaping from Alcatraz. Working as a Motor Man, I was able to work many a cool detail. One was an old-time naval air show at the Grosse Ilse Airport, which was a naval air station during World War II. Myself and my motor partner patrolled around the airport between the parked planes looking pretty and basically being there for visibility and public relations. There was an Air Force A-10 Warthog there with the tech who maintains it, having my same last name, Bommarito. Now how badass is that! Didn't think we were related, but sweet anyways. The air show had many World War II vintage aircraft doing flybys also. They included P-51 Mustangs, Japanese Zeros, B-17 Bombers, and many others. Hard to believe I was getting paid overtime to ride around on a Harley with my partner around aircraft that I loved, being an aviation buff from college and the US Army. Somebody pinch me—this shit's awesome! The Grosse Isle Police Department loved us troopers and treated us well. They would lodge prisoners for us if needed, have us work other overtime details with them, etc.

I worked a "Click it or ticket" detail with Grosse Isle PD watching peeps as they crossed the bridge. We actually had large signs posted stating, "Seatbelt Enforcement Zone," so the morons had the chance to put their belts on before entering the zone, duh? One joker wasn't wearing his belt and was issued a ticket by a Grosse Isle cop, which set him off, instantly becoming a dick! He refused to take the ticket from the Grosse Isle officer and refused to move his vehicle. I abruptly interceded, asking the man to take the ticket and contact the court. He again refused to take the ticket and/or move his vehicle from blocking the roadway/bridge. We then told him to do as told, again him disregarding a police officer, which is a misdemeanor in Michigan. I went back to what I was taught in Recruit School, "Ask 'em, tell 'em, take 'em." Ask them politely to do something, tell them to do something when they refuse, and then the take their ass to jail when they continue to refuse—pretty easy concept. He was removed from his vehicle and placed into custody and lodged on the misdemeanor. His pickup truck was moved over to the shoulder, to be later lodged and towed off the bridge. What a dumbass. He turned a zero-point, $65 seatbelt ticket into a day in jail. A few days later I had a Trooper that had been fired from our department and who worked with this dumbass call me and bust my balls for arresting his friend/joker. He received an earful, with me basically telling him to fuck off and don't worry how I do my job as a Trooper, with all the shit he pulled before he got fired.

Now, let's talk about that fired Trooper. He was senior to me when I first transferred to Metro, having about seven or eight years on me. Okay, being a military guy I respect seniority up to a certain point. He was from an MSP family, brother and father both in the department. Didn't know them, but from what I heard they were stand-up guys. It appears he was the black sheep of the family. First sign this troop was a moron was when our PC and APC(Assistant Post Commander) had to go to a topless bar over by Metro Airport after receiving complaints that he was sitting in there, drinking coffee in uniform, watching naked girls dance. The owner said a state police car in the parking lot and a uniformed Trooper inside were scaring off their business. He was probably banging one the dancers, but that never came out of the wash. Are you fucking kidding me? Supposedly not the first time either! Then come to find out the moron was checking in for service on day shift, going home, parking his patrol car in his garage, and then doing construction work on days while being paid as a Trooper. I'm sure the taxpayers would be happy to hear that! We had a lot of Troopers at the time, so Dispatch would just stop calling the dumbass for calls when he didn't answer the radio, knowing they could call somebody else. He did this for months before one of his neighbors ratted him out. Still he was not fired. The final straw was him stealing items from a gas station while in uniform, telling command when confronted that the gas station's owner told him he could have food and candy on the house. This was the final straw when they fired his ass and threatened to charge him criminally, which should have happened. What a piece of shit and embarrassment to the MSP. A bunch of us young Troops were in the squad room at shift change when he took a call from his wife. Not, "Hi, Honey, how are you and kids doing?" It was, "You fucking bitch, I told you not to call me at work, I don't give a shit what the kids are doing!" Wow, maybe explains his hanging out at topless bars? Again he actually had the balls or he was just stupid enough to call me and bust my chops for arresting his dipshit civilian work buddy after he got fired by the department.

The Michigan State Police was always testing new equipment being offered by various companies for various reasons. Be it patrol cars (Michigan is home of the Big 3, Ford, General Motors, Chrysler), side arms, etc. Visteon was a high-tech company based in Van Buren Twp., Michigan, which was located in our post area. They dealt with state-of-the-art automotive and aviation technology. Visteon took one of our MSP Crown Vics and put some fancy electronic shit including a heads-up display monitor near the windshield and some other voice-activated controls. Three of us Troopers (Road Dogs) at the post were chosen to evaluate this patrol car and advise how well it worked for road trooper application. We had the car for about a year using it on different shifts and putting it through different tests. When I said, "Alley light left," it would turn on the left spot light. It was easier for me to flip the toggle switch on the spot light. When I was behind a car and said the license plate aloud, it was supposed to recognize my voice and run the plate in LEIN (Law Enforcement Information Network). This was all done before we had in-car computers allowing us to just put in the plate or name and get an instant return instead of having to go through Dispatch and wait for returns. The voice recognition would never work properly. It constantly repeated a wrong plate number, which was very frustrating. There was a hand controller mounted to the right of the radio tree in the center console, which was too awkward to use without being a distraction. We were constantly calling the Visteon techs to come look at the car and update the programming on the voice-operated system. Time and time again, it would not work as they stated it should. The one cool thing it did have was a siren built into the horn on the steering wheel. I could get behind someone push that horn on the wheel, and the siren would squeal loud as hell. For some reason I was sent to a static display/demo put on by Visteon for a Senator from Tennessee who was in town for who knows what. There were MSP command from district there and suits from Visteon. When asked by the Senator how the car performed with the Visteon equipment added, "Horrible" was my response. Holy shit to see the look on their faces (command and Visteon). The Senator was actually pretty funny and seemed to appreciate my forthright answers about the poor performance of the system and advising it was really not needed for what we did on patrol.

"Stick Man", one of my buds, fellow Paisano transferred to the Metro Post around the same time I did. He ended up becoming a district crash reconstructionist. Each district in the Michigan State Police has a recon Sergeant. They are usually selected as Troops and then reallocated as

Sergeant after two years in the position. When I first started in the unit they had full-size black Ford Econoline vans with no police marking. I think his might have had a siren and some flashing lights in taillights and wigwags up-front. Are you kidding me? If I had some black van come up behind me with a siren on, I would throw up the bullshit flag and probably call 911 on their ass! We called his van the "Scooby-Doo" van to fuck with him. He parked it in front of the garage bay doors where we parked our patrol cars. One day I took a shit load of orange "abandoned vehicle" stickers and plastered them all over his van; boy, was he pissed. He bitched to the Desk Sergeant, who called in our shift asking who had sticked the vehicle. Of course we all looked up at the ceiling and said we didn't know. He threw a VHS tape on the table saying, "Okay, you pricks, I got you on surveillance tape; better fess up!" "Okay, Sarge, I did it." "Ha, you dumbass. I knew it was you, Bomber. There ain't shit on that tape." We all laughed and bolted out of the conference room.

U-Haul trucks are pretty popular and are seen all over the place. I'm sitting in the median on I-94 in my Blue Goose when a midsize U-Haul drives by me with the truck tilted hard right almost looking like the thing is going to tip or roll over. I follow the vehicle and initiate a safety traffic stop to conduct a vehicle inspection. Upon contacting the driver, I find out he is suspended with a couple traffic warrants for his arrest. I tow the truck and open the back to conduct a search subsequent to arrest and inventory search for the impound. When myself and the tow truck driver up the back door, there are around 200 cases of beer. The driver was transporting beer from one party store to another. I contact an agent from the Michigan Liquor Control Commission, and he tells me that this transport is a felony and has to be done by licensed alcohol transporters (distributor beer trucks). Okay, I get a felony warrant for the driver, so I sent a notice of warrant to his home address for him to turn himself into the court. The illegal transport was not the crime of the century. He never responds to the letter, so I go to his house to arrest him at a later date in Detroit by myself, again big mistake—don't do anything in Detroit by yourself! I knock on the door, and his nutty wife answers with a baseball bat. They obviously got the notice of warrant I had sent. I step off the porch, and the bitch comes out threatening me. I tell her to step back, and thankfully she complies so I don't have to knock her on her ass or shoot her. (We didn't have tasers at the time.) I call for backup with DPD and troops responding fairly quick. Her husband shows up and is placed into custody on the felony warrant. Come to find out this schmo is an informant with the ATF (Alcohol/Tobacco/Firearms) unit in Detroit. "Hello, Trooper, this is Agent Dick Head with the Detroit ATF. You arrested Mr. Schmo, who is an informant of ours, and we were wondering if you could help us out on his charges. My response, "Fuck no!" Especially after his shitbat crazy wife came out of the house threatening to bash my face in with a baseball bat. We go to trial, and he loses. He appeals the circuit court decision, and years later the Michigan Appellate Court dismissed the case because they said the LCC (Liquor Control Commission) law was too vague. Learning experience for me. Never seize hundreds of cases of beer anytime in the future. My shift Sergeant made me empty all those cases of beer, pouring out one at a time. I then had to take the bottles in for the 10-cent returnable refund to sign over to the State of Michigan for all my hard work! What a pain in my ass! Never again.

Super Bowl XL, held in February 2006 at Ford Field in downtown Detroit. Pittsburgh Steelers vs. Seattle Seahawks. East Coast vs. West Coast, damn what a great matchup! The motor unit Troopers, minus motors, too damn cold and out of season, were assigned to escort each team for a week or so leading up to the Super Bowl game. The Detroit Police Department, Wayne County and Oakland County motor officers also assisted with the detail. We were running mini motorcades all over Metro Detroit for 10 days prior to the big game. We each had our own fully marked Crown Vic w/bubble. They wouldn't let me use my "Silver Surfer" slick top semi-marked patrol car for the detail. The higher-ups wanted full visibility even though my traffic car had better LED lighting than the Blue Gooses. They split the unit in half, and I was assigned to the Steeler detail, which was "bad aspirin" because I was a Steeler fan. This detail was definitely on my bucket list of details. We got to meet the players, coaches, and other big wigs. No pics per the NFL though, but that's okay. The teams stayed at the Ritz Carlton and Hyatt Regency Hotels in Dearborn which was a couple of miles from the Detroit Lions practice facility in Allen Park. We would escort them wherever they needed to go. The Motor Men had no other responsibilities except for the Super Bowl. Another Desk Sergeant at post, "Hey, Bomber, I need you to follow up on this hit and run crash." Fuck that, I'm on the Super Bowl detail, talk to my motor Lieutenant, Sarge!" He'd got pissed, "God damn Motor Men think your shit don't stink." At the time the Motors were split between different traffic posts, but that would change later on after I left the district, go figure, where the whole unit became a district unit, not post to post. A couple of days before the big game, Detroit PD decided to call off sick with the "Blue Flu." They were pissed off over pay and contract talks, and what better time to call in sick across the board than Super Bowl week, when there are thousands of people downtown? Okay, now what? Our department decides to mobilize Troopers from across the state to fill in the gaps. Righteous idea, but stupid implementation. The motor unit was pulled to work downtown while not doing escorts until other Troopers could arrive from around the state. The upper command wanted to put single Troopers on street corners in downtown Detroit for visibility and traffic control. Being a union guy, we cried foul, "Oh, hell no! Officer safety, officer safety, officer safety!" Case in point, one of my buddies who was the district union rep had contact with an intoxicated homeless shithead who was strong-arming citizens with a stolen Detroit Police flashlight actually swinging it at them if they wouldn't give him money. He was doing this right in front of a uniform Trooper. My partner and I look down to the next street corner and see him tussling with this asshole. Wham, Bham body slam to the ground, one in custody for disorderly person and assault and battery on a police officer. A Detroit City councilwoman happened to be walking near the incident. "What are you Troopers doing to that man?" Really? We're placing him under arrest, too bad he didn't assault your stupid ass with the stolen police flashlight! This information was immediately relayed to MSP Command explaining why we needed two Troopers to every street corner! We didn't even mention the city councilwoman, no need to. Game day finally arrived with all the entertainers coming into town. The Rolling Stones were performing at the half-time show. Aretha Franklin was singing the National Anthem. The Motor Lieutenant was able to escort the Stones, and they used the rest of us to escort other notable stars. We were able to watch the game from the inside until we had to get to our cars for the escort to the hotels near the end. The Steelers ended up beating the Seahawks, yeah! Great game, great detail!

Motorcycle pursuits were constant in the second district/Metro Detroit. Shitheads would tuck their plates up under the rear wheel well or cover them so they were illegible. Throughout my career I had been in around

20 pursuits with crotch rockets. Most of the riders were shitty and didn't know how to ride a bike, but everyone once in a while you would have some slick dick dude that could really ride, which made it a challenge for us. I never had a pursuit with a chick on a bike, weird? I light this dude up on I-94 by Metro Airport, he looks back at me and blips that throttle—chase is on. In and out of traffic over 100 mph. He takes off toward Belleville on the west end of the county, which is fairly rural with dirt roads and corn fields. I maintain sight with him till he goes off road, ditches the bike, and flees on foot. No biggie, I have the bike and the plate (tucked away hidden), run it, and it comes back to a 75-year old grandma that lives close by. I contact the old lady, who is super nice and cooperative, and she rats out her grandson who asked her to put the bike in her name for insurance purposes and apparently so he can drive around Metro Detroit like an asshole! I get a statement from her, finally catch up to him, and he lies about it being him on the motor-cycle that I had pursued. I get a warrant for his arrest and later find out that he is a state security guard at a boys camp near Brighton. What a turd! I contact his boss to let him know what happened, and his boss confirms he's a turd and he's been trying to find a reason to fire his ass. I attended a termination hearing for the dude, and an arbitrator decided to let him keep his job because the original felony flee and elude charge was reduced to a plea of misdemeanor reckless driving. Damn, that little prick got away with a felony and was able to keep his job. Oh well, you win some and lose some.

I was an FTO for 15 years of my 23-year career. Took a lot of patience but was well worth it and rewarding. It was also nice having a partner even though they were newbies; figure if they can make through the Academy like I did they must be somewhat reliable. I wasn't the greatest recruit, kind of tried to keep a low profile and fly under the radar. I learned that in the military, you don't draw attention on yourself unless you're a dumbass! We investigated a lot of drunk driving incidents and arrested a shit load of drunks in the Metro Detroit area. Our afternoon

Sergeant would actually have contests: whoever popped three drunks first could go home, and he would carry you on the daily log for the rest of the shift. There were many occasions where we could pop back-to-back drunks and get three for a hat trick. We would also have to go to local hospitals for blood draws on slushies that refused to take a breath test. Get a quick search warrant for the on-call/after-hours magistrate or judge and take their ass over for a blood draw. We had official state police blood kits with paperwork and test tubes in the kits. They were used by all agencies in the state. Sometimes we would run out of them at the post and would have borrow a blood kit from a deputy or local cop. One summer night my cub and I took a drunk into the local hospital across the street from the post. During the blood draw, the phlebotomist dropped one of the tubes full of the suspect's blood. Fuck. We have hospital security watch Slushie, while we go out to the car to get another kit. As we're walking out to the Goose, some dude walks by us with a stab wound holding his gut and bleeding as he's walking, giving us a dirty look. I ask him, "What happened to you?" His response, "Leave me the fuck alone." My response, "Ok fuckhead, don't bleed out in the emergency room." We've got blood from the draw on the floor, this dude bleeding walking in, most have been a sign. We got our second tube of blood and took the drunk to jail for testing and lodging. I told the cub to call Taylor PD and let them know they had a uncooperative stabbing victim at Heritage Hospital ER if they were interested in talking to the moron. With all that blood we've seen, it's time for lunch; lets hit the Coney Island!

"Arts, Beats, and Eats" was some festival put on in downtown Pontiac in Oakland County. "Let's try and have a fun time in one of the most violent cities in Oakland County like we do in Birmingham." It ain't the same environment, dumbasses. Turns out the Oakland County Sheriff's Department and Pontiac PD overestimated the crowds and hooligans that would show up. They mobilize the full-grown Bears, a shit ton of Troopers from the district, and send us in four-man cars to the party.

We renamed the festival the "Arts, Tarts, and Farts" festival—enough said! Our sergeant at the time was as salty as you can get; his first name was Harry, and we called him Happy Harry Hard-On! "Come on, you fuckers, we have to go up to Pontiac, seems the brown clowns and city kitties can't handle the crowds up there! "Load some Gooses four Troops to a car. Don't forget long guns rifles and shotguns, you idiots." "Okay, Sarge." We get up there, after stopping at a gas station for snacks and check in with City Command. Damn, felt like I was back at the state fair, two-man foot patrol looking pretty until fights break out. It was only going on for one weekend, thank God. We went the next two nights making a pretty penny in overtime. Thanks for overtime, City of Pontiac!

People named after other people: We had a Trooper at the post named Dave (Davey) Crockett, who was a full-blooded American Indian and a badass trooper. He had a trial with a Wayne County prosecutor that was a huge Star Wars fan, changing his name to Luke Skywalker, no shit. There was a magistrate/defense attorney in Wayne County named Ricky Nelson. Holy shit, what are the chances they would have a trial together the three of them at the same time. "We have Luke Skywalker representing the people, Trooper Davey Crockett as the lead investigator, and the defense being represented by Ricky Nelson." Now that's some funny shit, somebody call TMZ!

News Article: "Quick Action by off-Duty Officer Helps Save Toddler" One of my city officer buds (Woodhaven PD) was at his residence when a young mother crying frantically pounded on his door asking him to help her daughter. The young girl lost consciousness in a swimming pool when the mother turned away momentarily. He jumped into action grabbing the toddler from Mom and bringing her back to life after she had turned blue and stopped breathing. He was sitting at home with the family when the mother knocked at his front door. Great job, buddy! He lived outside his jurisdiction and was going to be recognized and given a Life Saving Award for saving that little girl. Police officers do more that arrest criminals and write tickets, just saying!

What are motor carrier/commercial vehicle officers? I briefly discussed motor carrier officers early on. They are **not** certified police officers in the State of Michigan, but they should be. They do carry handguns and long guns same as Troopers but have no authority off duty. They attend a shortened Academy that emphasizes commercial vehicle enforcement. Troopers have arrest powers off duty 24/7 throughout the entire State of Michigan. Troopers receive ERC (emergency response compensation) to carry their weapons off duty at all times. Troopers pay rate is significantly more than a motor carrier officer. Motor carriers, jokingly called "Diesel dicks," enforce commercial vehicle laws and used to be part of the Department of Transportation before being moved over to the State Police. They have limited police powers, only able to initiate traffic stops on commercial vehicles or suspected intoxicated drivers. They cannot stop a passenger car or other motorized vehicles for speed or other moving violations. They can get involved in felony incidents, i.e., pursuits, if available, which is nice having an extra gun around if you're chasing some shithead for armed robbery or other serious felony! I had no idea what a motor carrier officer did until I joined the State Police. I knew they had light blue "robins egg" patrol cars and SUVs instead of the dark blue that Troopers had. Each post usually had one motor carrier assigned to it unless they had a weigh station in their post area or were by the border of other states (Indiana, Ohio, Wisconsin) or the Canadian border. Those posts had three or four motor carriers. Didn't see our motor Carrier at Jonesville much because it was a rural area with little commercial traffic or just the fact that she always got lost, was at lunch, or doing other things.

When I transferred to Metro we had usually two or three Diesel dicks at the post that had a ton of work to do in the Metro Detroit area. When the State Police introduced Chevy Tahoes into the fleet they left the motor carrier SUVs the same dark blue as the troops vehicles. They also changed the door shield and not the motor carrier shield on the door. There was a huge bitch from the troopers including me that Joe Citizen has no idea of the difference between a Trooper and motor carrier except for the color vehicle and uniform they wear. The motor carrier uniform had a light blue shirt instead of dark blue, and all of a sudden, they have dark blue fatigues to wear and are looking more and more like Troopers. This was done during financial cutbacks and mileage restrictions under the same Governor(Jenny on the block) that only ran two or three Trooper Recruit Schools during her eight-year tenure as governor. Smoke and mirrors. "Let's make motor carriers look like Troopers so people think there are more Troopers on the road?" We actually proposed bringing the motor carriers into our union with a grandfather clause having them take a criminal law update at the Academy. This proposal was turned down by the department and Governor them not wanting to pay more money to them and have more members in our union. As a union rep, I had to go toe to toe with post command trying to give Trooper overtime details to motor carriers, which should have been a nonissue. They have their own overtime budgets and their own union. I was in court once, and a magistrate kept referring to a female motor carrier officer as Trooper. I corrected the magistrate saying she was an officer, not a Trooper. She went back to the post and complained to the PC crying that I embarrassed her at court. I had two female Lieutenants on either side of me pestering me because they knew there was nothing they could do to me for correcting her title. I literally felt I was being harassed for being a male getting hit with an artillery barrage. Whatever, I stuck to my convictions. I advised them she should have corrected the magistrate and not let him keep calling her Trooper. I busted my ass in Recruit School to obtain the title of Trooper, and I would defend that title with great vigor! I've been in court throughout the years and been called officer or deputy, and I always corrected the judge or magistrate.

News Article: "Troopers Jobs May Be Cut." Here we go again. The Governor using us as political pawns to get what she wants. Really? The Michigan State Police budget is insignificant when you look at the entire state budget. The biggest sucking vacuum is Social Services/State Welfare. They don't lay off social workers or the over 1000 paper-pushing command and civilians our department has, but let's lay off the Road Troopers that actually work for a living, responding to criminal complaints and traffic crashes to help the citizens. Many cities have in their police contracts that before any uniform police officers are laid off, the civilian secretaries, dispatchers, and noncritical staff have to be laid off first, Janitors, etc. Wow, that seems like common sense, doesn't it? I brought that up at an MSPTA Union meeting, and most of the members on the executive board looked at me like I was an idiot! At least five times during my career we had snow/ice storms that shut down everything for days. Per executive orders by the Governors, didn't matter Republican or Democrat, all nonessential state employees were to stay home. The only state employees to go to work were Michigan State Police Troopers/Sergeants and Michigan Department of Corrections officers for the prisons. Everyone else was to be furloughed until advised to return to work. They admitted that all the others were nonessential. The department would never go for that, Bomber. Well, no shit; you put the proposal in front of an arbitrator and let them apply common sense to impose the department to do it. Sometimes I thought I was living in "Bizzaro" world with everything upside down. The longer I was in law enforcement, the worse it got! Around the same time she was using us as political pawns again to get her budget from the opposing political party. One day I was sitting on a freeway ramp on my Harley Hog waiting for a motor school that had been run in Lansing to drive by so I could jump in for an outstate ride with them. I was sitting on the ramp for about 45 minutes watching cars drive by and noticed something strange. At that time Lansing/state government had Chevy Cavaliers, little pissant cars that worked fine for social workers and other state employees. They had a little round "State of Michigan" sticker on the front doors of the cars. In 45 minutes I was bored, so I counted over 30 of the Cavaliers with State of Michigan stickers drive by and no Trooper, Deputy, or city Officer cars. Hmm, why don't we lay those state employees off instead of Troopers. Seems like the smart and right thing to do, just saying!

News Article: "Trooper Held in Homeless Man's Death." One of my buds was working a two-man Troop car with a female Troop that had just left CID (Criminal Investigation Division) for three years and went back to uniform for her first night back on the road. She was a good Troop; I had worked with her in past years. They are in downtown Detroit by the Detroiter sports bar, which was packed because there was a home Detroit Tiger game in town. The homeless guy was pissed off, highly intoxicated and irrational, and started throwing rocks through the windows of the bar. The Troops happen to be driving by and turn on their police lights when they see the commotion and exit their patrol car. The male Troop gave multiple orders for the man to stop and show his hands; instead the suspect reached into the front of his pants which could be construed as reaching for a weapon, refusing to show his hands and charged the Troopers in an aggressive manner. The male Trooper again gave him multiple verbal commands with the suspect not complying. He had no choice in fear for his and his partner's life, so he used deadly force to stop the threat. He double tapped the man, dropping him instantly. We initially handled the shooting with a Lieutenant from MSP, getting into an argument with an Inspector from DPD. It was said things got heated at the scene and that the DPD Inspector was trying to take over the investigation, saying he would have Detroit officers arrest any Trooper that gets in their way with the MSP Lt. telling him, "I'll mobilize Troopers from around the state and arrest your whole night shift." Things calmed down; our department backed the shooting as following department policy for use of deadly force. Three days later with calls being made from the Detroit mayor (later gone to federal prison himself) to our illustrious Governor then to our Colonel (who disagreed), advising our guys to turn the investigation over to DPD, which was bullshit. Typical Detroit/Wayne County politics: let's not do the right thing, let's do the "try to stick it to the Trooper thing" (thanks, Governor). This was the first time in the department's history that a Michigan State Trooper was charged with murder in an on-duty incident in the performance of their duties when our department backed him!. Here we go, this case is gonna cause a political problem! The Michigan State Police conducted their own investigation concluding the shooting, while unfortunate, was justified by our Trooper. The Wayne County prosecutor thought otherwise. The first Black Director/Colonel of the State Police actually gave that trooper $50,000 out of the department budget for his defense. If you are charged criminally as a Trooper, our department has no obligation or legal basis to defend you or give any department funds for your defense. The Trooper charged with second-degree murder was acquitted by a jury of his peers. That same Trooper later ended up suing the Detroit Police Department for monetary damages for tampering with evidence and various other atrocities. He ended up getting a very large settlement.

Here we go again with another first? Same prosecutor charges another one of my friends with assault and battery while working the state fair detail. I worked three state fairs early in my career as a young Trooper. It was held every year at the end of summer leading up to Labor Day weekend. The Michigan State Police (MSP) handled everything on fairgrounds, which is state property, and the Detroit Police Department (DPD) handled everything outside of the fairgrounds. I wasn't at the fair this year but had one of my Trooper/friends charged criminally again for doing his job in the performance of his duties. He was working the band shell/concert detail when a highly intoxicated, off duty, female Detroit officer was causing a disturbance. She refused to leave the concert and actually pushed him away, forcing him to put her on the ground and take her into custody, placing handcuffs on her. Instead of taking her to jail for disorderly conduct and assault on a police officer, she was released by a feckless Lt. running the fair detail at the time. What the fuck? The next day after she sobers up she goes to her DPD precinct, where she works, has one of her buddies take an assault and battery report against our Trooper, and lies about the entire incident. One of my favorite quotes that I will keep referring to is "**The worst form of police corruption is incompetence.**" There was a shitty/incompetent MSP Lieutenant in charge of the fair detail that had a hands-off policy that year. She was trying to get promoted and stuck to her hands-off policy on most low-level arrests, which is ridiculous, basically to remove and or eject unruly patrons off the fair-grounds instead of arresting them and lodging them, which was past policy. Our moronic Lt. basically gave the off-duty turd DPD officer a basis for charges to the prosecutor. Well, why didn't you lodge her or arrest her if she did what you're claiming? A funny twist, our Trooper that they arrested, was married to a DPD officer. She was told by other officers they had a warrant for her husbands arrest. He turned himself in to the local DPD precinct and was denied bond. They made him sit in jail for a couple day just to say, "Fuck you, Trooper." A misde-meanor charge under Michigan law shall be allowed bond. Being the post union representative, I threw a fit with command. "God damn it, someone needs to get their ass down there yesterday and get him out of jail." They wouldn't let me go down because they thought I would probably get arrested by DPD for cocking off, which I didn't give a shit. "I'll sue their ass." They ended up sending a Sergeant, who was able to get bond for our Trooper. We go to trial again, listened to her bullshit lies, and my friend is acquitted by a jury of his peers. Loss number two for you, Wayne County prosecutor. We spoke to some of the jurors after the verdict, and they told us, "That DPD officer was lying. We love having the State Police in Detroit. Keep up the good work, Troopers!" Holy shit, that was nice to hear. He ended up suing DPD for falsifying information and other atrocities, again receiving a large payout. I saw the writing on the wall; if I got a chance to get the fuck out of Metro Detroit and Wayne County, I was going to jump on it!

I was working a different week of the same state fair with the Mad Irishman when Osama above got jammed up by shitty Fair Command. We were working for the same shitty command when an admin Troop was screaming on the radio for help on I-75 off fairground property. He went to get Burger King for lunch and came across some shithead teenagers stripping a Lincoln on the shoulder of the freeway. We ran across the fairgrounds, jumping into our Blue Goose, and took off, hitting wooptie dooooos along the way with lights and sirens activated. Watch out, people, we're coming through. "Trooper calling for help," in other words, "Get the fuck out of the way!" I took the wheel and almost lost it on a service drive at over a 100 mph in one of the shitty Crown Vics with the black bumpers. "Hold on, sir" to my partner as the tires are screeching almost rolling the car over. "Damn, great recovery," says the Mad Irishman! We arrive on scene with a two-man Detroit car rolling up with three in custody. Great job, Troopers! Three dumbasses thought they would strip a car in broad daylight, don't think so!

News Article: "Trooper Reads Lips." I signed up to work most holidays and overtime details at the Metro Post. I was working on St. Pattys Day around 3 p.m. when a lady pointed to the car in front of her looking directly at me and mouthing, "Almost hit me." I clearly saw what she said, so I turned on the suspect vehicle, following through a nearby bar parking lot, initiating a traffic stop on his vehicle. He was subsequently arrested and lodged for drunk driving. He later took the case to trial with his attorneys saying I had no basis for the traffic stop, since the witness/lady never stopped at the scene of the traffic stop, hence fruit of the poisonous tree/bad stop. Whoa, whoa, whoa, defendant and defense attorney. He lost the district court trial and appealed it to the Michigan Appeals Court, where he lost also. Bam! I should start a Trooper lip reading class at the Academy in Lansing, Haha!

The Woodward Dream Cruise: We had multiple cruises in Metro Detroit. What else would you expect from the Motor City, birthplace of automobiles and the transportation revolution? You had the Downriver Cruise, the Gratiot Cruise, and the Big Daddy of them all, the Woodward Dream Cruise! Being Motor Men, we always worked all the details every summer, every year. The motors had the unique ability to work these events to cut the lanes in between cars, get to crashes expeditiously, fights with drunk morons (the fights always involved too much booze), or other incidents faster than patrol cars. It was also harder for careless and reckless drivers that felt they had to impress the crowds by squeezing their tires, doing burnouts and drag racing. The cruise command wanted participants and spectators to have fun while avoiding catastrophic incidents. One year an idiot in a Ford Mustang thought he was cool doing a burnout until he lost control, crashing into a crowd of people on the curb and sidewalks. Luckily there were only minor injuries and the dumbass didn't kill anyone, which could have easily happened. We usually had at least 100 motors for the Dream Cruise, 20 of which were MSP bikes. Oakland County Sheriff's

Department had a larger unit than us; they had around 30, with other smaller city departments filling the gaps with their motors.

What a blast getting paid to patrol on a State Police Harley on a 10-mile stretch of Woodward with over 100,000 people in attendance. All the classic cars and events were too cool. We would ride two Motor Men in pairs for officer safety, never alone. Sometimes they would pair a Troop with a city Cop, Deputy, or mainly two Troops together. I didn't mind either way. Belonging to a unique fraternity of Motor Men for 15 years of my career was the bomb. All Motor Men go through the same "Northwestern" motorcycle course. Okay, okay, Oakland County did have a female motor officer; she was cool, talk about feeling isolated being the one female out of 100 dudes, just saying. We had one of our Criminal Investigation Division (CID). Lieutenants that lived in Royal Oak, where a large portion of the cruise was held. He had a pig roast every year and invited the Motor Men to stop by for food on break. You'd go by his house, and there would be 5–10 MSP Harleys sitting out front, in the drive and on the grass. The neighbors never bitched; they thought it was sweet. At the end of every cruise, the police motors would line up on the main drag with all our emergency lights activated. They split us into three different platoons of about 30 bikes each. We would roll down the roadway and sidewalks clearing and corralling people like cattle, getting them to leave the cruise area. We would get on our motor PA systems, which were very loud, and say, "You don't have to go home, but you can't stay here." The sirens on the police bikes were also very loud because they were mounted directly on the front of the bikes. Sirens and air horns are muffled on cars and SUVs because they are mounted inside the grill under the hood. There were plenty of times that I would blip my siren or air horn on my police motor and scare the shit out of people. Sorry to scare you—not really—get the hell out of the way! I worked many Dream Cruises and other cruises while on the bikes. Woodward was the most fun.

I had worked a drunk driving detail from 7 p.m. till 3 a.m. one night before having to work the Dream Cruise. My partner and I got in a pursuit with a very distinctive crotch rocket (café-style motorcycle) with no plate in the city of Detroit around 1 a.m. in the morning. We chased that dipshit all over the freeway system being at a disadvantage, driving in a Ford Crown Vic, which were slow as hell. I did fairly well, keeping up with the turd, finally us terminating the pursuit when we lost sight of him. I worked the cruise the next day on noons, so I didn't have to be there till later in the day. We're sitting around on our bikes, and out of nowhere, four or five crotch rockets in a group pull up to talk with my motor sergeant. Holy shit, one of the bikes was the turd we pursued the night before. I told my motor Sergeant, who didn't know they guy but said, "Bomber, do what you gotta do." I couldn't prove it was him but knew it was him. I approached that asshole and told him, "You either have big balls or are really stupid for showing up here after running from Troopers last night." "What? What?" was his response. My response after copying his plate down, "You have two seconds to get the fuck out of here before I find a reason to arrest you." He couldn't get his motorcycle started fast enough to get the fuck out of there! Dumbass!

Southgate and Northville Psychiatric Hospitals were both open when I transferred to Metro but then closed due to budget cuts. Big mistake! In fact Governors around the country were closing mental hospitals to save money, putting extremely dangerous monsters and innocent people that needed help on the streets, telling them and their families to have them self-medicate. Really? My buddy called it, saying the future would tell a story of all these mental patients being left to be dealt with by law enforcement and families that didn't have the ability to control them. The moronic politicians, didn't matter which party they belonged to, decided it was better to save money then keep these dangerous people away from the public. As State Troopers, we would get dispatched to the mental hospitals to take various reports, from simple larcenies including assault and battery up to more serious cases such as CSC (rape). Most of the reports were bullshit, but every once in a while, there would be a legit complaint/incident. I received a letter of commendation from the Southgate Psyche hospital where the administration had fired a staff member that had made some threats. I contacted that subject and advised him in not so nice terms to cool his shit and stay away from the hospital. I would perform property inspections at the hospital with other Troopers for a period of time until things settled down. They ended up closing both those hospitals before I transferred out of the Metro area. Every once in a while, we would get trespassing complaints of young teenagers breaking into the Northville Hospital and drinking around in the underground catacombs. Some organization bought the Southgate Psyche Hospital, but the Northville Hospital stayed vacant for years.

Politicians fighting over budgets and our Governor decided to lay off 100 Troopers to prove a point. Really? Give her the money she wants, or she will jeopardize public safety and blame the other party. How the fuck did she get elected? Same Governor that put our Road Troopers on mileage restrictions three times during her tenure. Lansing figured out some stupid formula by how many calls you responded to the miles you could drive per shift. The first time it was like 50 miles, the second time less down to 40, and then the third restrictions was the worst, around 20. What a fucking joke! I bitched to a Sergeant who threw their hands up in the air. "I'm on a bike which gets better gas mileage than a patrol car, give me 20 extra miles." They just laughed. Being a union guy, I was interviewed by the *Detroit News* concerning the mileage restrictions and layoffs. I got a phone call from my motor Sergeant after the story went to print. I guess the District Captain wasn't too happy with my comments. He was actually a Troopers Captain and a great guy. He probably caught shit from the higher-ups and Lansing. Nothing ever came from it. Are they going to discipline me for telling the truth to a reporter? I think not. There are actually whistleblower laws that do protect employees, and sometimes the higher-ups have to be reminded of that! A couple of my favorite quotes on the front page of the *Detroit News* article, which was titled "Troopers Told to Park It!" Well, now we are like firefighters, totally reactive instead of proactive. Let's sit at the post and respond to calls like firefighters. I said it was like getting ready to run a marathon and then right before the race starts, they (the Governor and Lansing) blasts you in the leg with a baseball bat, telling you, "Good luck with the race!" Our Troopers Association actually gave the Governor and State of Michigan $300,000 to avoid laying off 100 Troopers, reducing the number laid off to 29? Those $300K were supposed to be reimbursed sometime in the future. This was put to a vote of the association's executive board, about 12 and not the rest of the membership! I was vehemently opposed to this offer and voted against it. This might be a surprise. She still laid off those 29 Troopers, and our association never got that $300K back—shocking! The State Police budget is insignificant compared to other state agencies including Social Services/Welfare, which is the biggest sucking vacuum of the taxpayers' money!

Two of my cubs from the last Recruit School received their letters to their home address from Lansing. "As a result of the budgetary shortfall, the Michigan State Police is forced to abolish your position which will result in an indefinite layoff." Wow, what Governor would do that to the citizens of Michigan and her Troopers for political points? Sickening, with no shame! This same Governor put us on "banked leave time" (BLT),which meant we would work 80 hours in a biweekly pay period yet only get paid for 76. The state would bank four hours of our pay every pay period to save money. She did this for a short period, which was the max that federal law would allow. This vote to accept or not accept was put to the whole association membership, Troopers and Sergeants, not just the executive board. I did vote for the BLT because there was a stipulation that when we retired, we get paid out in the hours at the retirement hourly pay rate, not the rate at which it was taken out, which for me would be significantly higher.

Newspaper Article: "Michigan Needs Troopers, Not New Buildings." Another hot topic around the time of the layoff of those 100 Troopers was the governor building a new MSP Headquarters in Lansing on a flood plain by politically connected developers. We were leased our original headquarters on Michigan State University property on Harrison Rd. for a dollar, yes $1 a year, and our lease was still good for many more years to come.

Dearborn Heights Police Officer/Corporal Jason Makowski, 31 years old, killed in the line of duty. The City of Dearborn Heights was three miles up Telegraph Rd. from our post. Too close to home! Jason was responding to a call of a man arguing with garbage men. Really? Who argues with garbage men? When the Dearborn Heights officers arrived on scene at the residence, the shithead homeowner opened fire on the police, striking Officer Makowski in the face as he tried to take cover near a neighbor's house. The shooter continued firing toward Jason, not allowing his partners to extricate him from danger to render first aid. What a monster! The shooter was finally shot and killed by a Heights officer with a rifle from a distance away. I was off that day but did have the honor of assisting the Dearborn Heights Police Department on the motor unit with the funeral of their hero. Rest in peace, Corporal Makowski.

Tennessee State Trooper Calvin Jenks, 24 years old, shot and killed while conducting a traffic stop. I was asked by the association to attend the funeral of Trooper Jenks like I had previously for Oklahoma Trooper Evans. This time I would be driving an MSP patrol SUV to Tennessee for the funeral. A Sergeant from the post went with me so there would be two of us. We took a Chevrolet Tahoe down to the funeral, which is fitting. Our department had a policy that another outstate Trooper's funeral had to be within so much of a distance or else we had to fly. The Troopers Association always paid for the outstate funerals, including airfare, lodging, and meals. The department would allow us to use fleet gas cards for fuel if we took an MSP patrol Car or SUV. On the way down to the funeral there was a Kentucky State Trooper on the right shoulder with his lights on We stopped to check on him, seeing him running around in a ditch near a wired fence. He was trying to corral some cattle back into the pasture, away from the freeway. He looked at us with are red bubble on, walking up in uniform, with that "WTF look" on his face. Then he realized we were headed to Trooper Jenks' funeral. Weird thing most Troopers know when another Trooper gets killed in the line of duty around the country; it's a Trooper thing! In a classic southern drawl, he said "I'm all set, fellows; thanks for checking on me." The funeral service had Troopers in attendance from all over the country. During the traffic stop Tpr. Jenks noticed there were illegal drugs in the vehicle at which point the male passenger shot Tpr. Jenks in the head and torso. They then stole his service weapon and ran his body over when fleeing the scene. Another needless murder of a Trooper by monsters that have no respect for police. They were arrested in

Nashville, approximately 13 hours after executing Trooper Jenks. Rest in peace, Trooper Jenks.

Retirement is supposed to be the next step in life. Walk away from law enforcement, etc. We had a retired Detective Sergeant, who was buddies with the Colonel at the time, come back in the State Police as a Trooper, quit then back again as a bus inspector! WTF? Word is that his buddy the Colonel had a conversation with him and after a year he would be reinstated as a Dick Sergeant with full pay and seniority? Throughout my career I had seen a few leave the department and go elsewhere, Feds, other law enforcement agencies, private sector. Their MLEOTC certification expires one year after they separate or leave the department. Back to the bus inspector. Bus inspectors go around the state and inspect school buses for operational safety, righteous job, I guess, not my cup of tea. Well, the year was getting ready to expire. The MSPTA and civil service got involved when they got word of the deal between the Colonel and the retired Dick Sgt. We would have shift pick and vacation pick with all us young guys letting him pick first even though he was at the bottom of the list. The guy had 30 years in the State Police. I would never do what he did. Fuck that! He did have a weird personality like didn't give a shit about much like being the lowest Trooper in seniority in the Michigan State Police with 30 plus years.

One of the local towing companies came up with a great idea for Metro Detroit. It was called the "Courtesy Patrol." They partnered with MDOT (Michigan Department of Transportation) to have standard white full-size vans travel the Metro Detroit freeway system and assist motorists if they run out of gas, need a jump start, or have a flat tire. At first, we liked the idea because it would free up Troopers from constantly getting sent to car assists on the freeways and M (Michigan Trunkline) roads. Some of the local cops would call us "AAA with a badge." Ha, at times they were correct with their slam! They put our red bubble on the vans, which at night would make it look like they were a Trooper in a Blue Goose. Being a union guy, myself and other Troopers had a problem with this choice of light for their vehicles. The department's stance was that other agencies could use the same rotating bubble we use, so Courtesy Patrol could do the same. The fact that the light was red also came into play because if the light was blue, they would not be able to use it. Per federal regulations, only law enforcement agencies can have blue lights. We had only red for the longest time like the New York State Police when the Feds came out with a regulation that all law enforcement across the US had to put a blue light somewhere on their patrol cars, motorcycles, boats, etc. It could be a mirror light, deck light, or overhead bar with some form of blue lighting. The Courtesy Patrol drivers were allowed to park their vans in our post parking lot. Some of them were good peeps, others were downright criminals. One guy was stealing property from people's cars, and another one was making peeps pay money for assistance. They were fired and charged criminally. Maybe our department and the MDOT people proving this service should have done background checks on these people? It also became a problem where morons would purposely run out of gas and then call 911 for free gas!

Belle Tire: There is a huge tire in our post area on the side of Interstate 94. It was used during a World Fair, back in the day, as a Ferris Wheel and somehow ended up on a freeway in Metro Detroit. I don't know, Detroit the Motor City, maybe a consideration. It has "Uniroyal" written on the tire, sometimes changing. One year they put a nail on the top and a new slogan on the hubcap, "Uniroyal takes on nails." There's another tire, Belle Tire, whose headquarters are located in close proximity to the Big Tire. We would use the Big Tire as a reference during pursuits, car crashes, and other incidents. "I'm chasing a red Ford pickup E/B on I-94 just west of the Big Tire." I'm at the post one day, and a desk sergeant hands me a copy of an arrest warrant for the CEO of Belle Tire. "Is this a joke, Sarge?" We actually had generic "Notice of Warrant" letters we would send out to defendants to contact or turn themselves into the court. We didn't have the manpower to look for every Tom, Dick, and Harry that had a warrant out for their arrest. They also have fundraisers where fake warrants are issued for higher-ups in the community where they are taken to a fake jail and have to post a donation/fake bond to get released; this was *not* the case with this warrant. I take my happy ass over to Belle Tire and speak with three different people, the final being the CEO's secretary. I had no intention of arresting this guy, it was a misdemeanor warrant with a $500 bond. I can't even remember what the warrant was for, something chickenshit. When I first talked to the secretary she thought it was a joke. I advised her it wasn't and told her to give the copy of the warrant to her boss and contact the court. I advised her I would check with the court in a few days to make sure it was taken care off. I did contact the court, and they said he took care of the warrant that same day within an hour of receiving it. This is an example of officer discretion. Could I have taken him into custody if he didn't have the $500 in cash? Sure. I also have the authority to notify the defendant to contact the court and/or turn themselves in within a reasonable time frame. Arrest the CEO? Ain't happening! I would look like a flaming asshole, and the department wouldn't fare too well either.

"Metro Dispatch, I am in pursuit of a Volkswagen Beetle, yellow in color, on I-94 E/B near the Big Tire." There was a huge, sweeping ramp from the Southfield Freeway that I and other Troopers would sit up and observe E/B traffic with a handheld laser. "Bing, 83 mph", "Bing 87", "Bing 95." I can't remember what I had this joker at, but my cutoff for the most part on speeders was 15 mph over the limit or faster on the freeways and secondary roads. If it's 86 or faster on a freeway, I'm coming out; 71 or faster on 55, I'm coming out, etc. This turd took off to about a 100 mph for a couple miles when I lit him up. I ran the plate with Dispatch, with the vehicle coming back stolen. He pulled over in the center median and bailed on foot, running across four lanes of traffic, with me hot on his heels, luckily neither of us getting run over by W/B traffic in the process. Out of instinct I grabbed and put my garrison hat on with it falling off my noggin after about three strides. Now keep in mind, I am wearing a 30-plus lbs. gun belt, a clip-on tie with wool pants on a hot summer day. State Troopers have to look pretty, which is fine, but damn, sometimes it was a pain in the ass! One of my Trooper buds, Topher, gets to my patrol car lights and sirens still on. VW driver's door open, my driver's door open, my hat lying in the median. He stated he had a knot in his stomach. Shit, where's Bomber? I'm chasing this asshole, yelling at him to stop, probably calling him an asshole while chasing for at least a mile and a half. He finally petered out and stopped running, with me cloths-lining his ass to the ground. We tussled a smidgeon, so I deployed my pepper spray to take him into custody. I had no idea where we were, only behind some industrial complex. Topher finds us and has a nice cold bottle of water for me to drink. Dumbass has his eyes rinsed out and then has the balls to ask for water to drink. He was given a minimal amount of water to get his ass to jail, so he didn't pass out. "Why are you guys being mean to me?" My response, "Why is your dumbass speeding in a bright yellow stolen bug?" You would think you would drive like a grandpa knowing you're in a stolen car and also having a suspended license!

We used to always say we will never go out of business due to the number of stupid criminals in society.

My buddy Topher and I worked an OWI enforcement two-man car for a couple of quarters together. This was when we were fat staffed with plenty of Troopers for every shift. We worked 8 p.m. until 4 a.m. looking for drunk drivers, which was pretty easy in Metro Detroit. A lot of times we would go for a hat trick, getting three drunks in a shift like three goals in a hockey game. We would get involved in other shit while working this gig. Oftentimes we helped locals with bar fights usually around bar closing time at 2 a.m. One night, Dispatch advised Detroit Troopers were pursuing a stolen Cadillac Escalade, white in color, close to our location. Topher and I would swap out every other night, one driving as the wheel man and one in charge of the radio, riding shotgun. I drove the night before, and for some reason didn't gas up the patrol car at the end of the shift. Big fuck up! You always gas the Goose at the end of the shift. We get involved in this pursuit in the winter, chasing this fucker all over the city of Detroit. The residential streets were like an ice rink, slipping and sliding all over the place. Detroit Public Works sucked, they never plowed or salted the side streets. Dispatch had On Star on the telephone with constant updates where this asshole was. So if we temporarily lost him, they would tell us where he was within a block or so. Oh, shit. The low fuel light popped on in the patrol car. "Dispatch, we will be out of the pursuit for now." We stop at some gas station, and my partner jumps out and tries to use our fleet gas card. It doesn't work! Fuck, just give the guy $5 so we can catch the prick in the Escalade. Nope, we had to go to another gas station where the gas card worked. I don't know how, but we were able to get back in that pursuit and caught that shithead after he crashed and bailed on foot. "Dispatch, one in custody; send a hook [tow truck] for that stolen Escalade."

The city of Inkster, located in our post area, was known for having lots of shitheads, dopers, and a district court judge that didn't really like the state police. The Wayne County Sheriff's Department had a sub-station there to assist with all the crime that happened there. Years prior, in 1987, three Inkster officers were executed at the Bungalow Motel, which was on Michigan Ave., a main trunkline that runs between a lot of cities in Wayne County. A mother in her late 60s and her three adult sons had taken the two Officers and Sergeant hostage in the motel room all over a bad check complaint. They lured them in the room, tortured them, and then summarily executed all three of them. Every time I drove by that motel it gave me the heebie jeebies. There was a subsidized apartment complex/HUD housing (federal slums) in Inkster called "Little Saigon" by the cops. Word was never to go in their alone, and if you do go in there, go hard and heavy. They would shoot at the city cops and deputies from various apartments. If we went in, they never fucked with us. Guess they knew the phrase "Mess with the bull, get the horns." Being a Trooper was different in the urban areas because the majority of the citizens had little contact with us and when they did, they seemed to show us a little more respect than the city Officers or county Deputies. We would roll up on a scene, and people would come talk to us and ignore the local cops. I think part of the problem was they deal with and see the locals all the time, so they build contempt for them when they won't do their bidding. Little did they realize we weren't going to put up with their bullshit either. We had worked various details in Inkster while I was at Metro. "Weed and seed" drug detail, fugitive sweeps, etc. We would send three or four two-man cars in the city, shaking and baking, making lots of traffic stops looking for drugs and guns. It's always about drugs and guns. Little accomplished because you would arrest shitheads only to be way undercharged by the Wayne County Prosecutor's Office. You arrest somebody for possession with intent to deliver (PWIT) dope, and they would reduce it to no ops on person. WTF? As junior Troopers, we would get pissed off, and the Senior Troopers would remind us just to do our job and have fun, don't worry about shithead judges and prosecutors that don't do their job; easier said than done at times! My partner and I were backing up Inkster PD at a local party store when some turd came up on us highly intoxicated. "I have a felony warrant for my arrest and I have AIDS." "Turn your ass around and get the fuck out of here." He complied, stumbling down the sidewalk. We were on a traffic stop on Michigan Ave., latest fad, little LED lights in the washer sprayer inlets that are illegal. We stop a Mercedes Benz with these lights, and my partner tells and asks this Arabic man, "Hey those lights are illegal dude. You don't have those on your camel, do you?" We write him a ticket and send him on his way. We go back to the patrol car, he's laughing. I'm like, "Holy shit, dude, that was ballsy!" He laugh it off, "What? What, Bomber?" Same Trooper, currently a command officer at headquarters in Lansing? Just saying.

One of my my buds, Topher again, goes to traffic court on some young teenager he wrote a speeding ticket to. No biggie until a Dearborn Heights "DARE" cop shows up to testify against my buddy about speeding factors and the character of the kid the Trooper wrote! I would never contemplate doing what this cop did. Are you fucking kidding me? Turns out my younger cousins went to school where this turd cop was the DARE officer. They told me stories of him having parties at his house with young kids and smoking dope with them. Weird that short time later he gets arrested for the same after someone tipped off the higher-ups at Dearborn Heights. They fire his ass, and he sues the department a couple years later, saying he was harassed because he was Hispanic. What a loser, his ass should be in prison, not just fired. These are the kind of bad apples that should never be in law enforcement and scolded for what they do.

State Police K-9s: We have a great K-9 program that has a long and outstanding history performance in the Michigan State Police. The department received most of the dogs from a breeder in Germany and had all the police dogs receive their veterinary care at Michigan State University near our HQ in Lansing. Most posts in the urban areas had at least one K-9, some having two dogs with the same handler. There would be less dogs in the UP due to less population and less crime. I'm not sure if the UP police dogs had a Canadian accent or not, eh? All were tracking dogs and some could be cross-trained for bomb detection and drugs sniffing. I had put in for one K-9 school, ran the run in Lansing at the Academy, and got water logged, falling into a swamp soaked from the neck down. First time tried and last time, not my cup of tea. I ended up getting on the motors shortly after the K-9 run instead with no regrets. Police dogs are just like cops or Troopers, some are great and some suck. Our dogs did seem better trained than the locals, so if possible and we needed a dog for a track or sniff, we would try and use our dogs. If one of our dogs weren't available due to training or other reasons, we would have a local dog come out. There was a badass

K-9 at the Richmond Post that would react to his handlers opening of his hand cuff case. That dog would go after the first person he saw to chomp on their ass until called off by command by the Troop. He would fuck with Troops and Sergeants walking down the hallway of the post on that slick tile floor making them shit their pants with "Dino" scrambling, slipping, and sliding down the floor coming at them, ha! Nobody ever got bit, but pretty funny though. We had lost a K-9 at the Metro Post to cancer, so we buried him behind the post and had a small ceremony for him. The local paper did a short news story on it and some dickhead wrote the editor saying, "It's only a dog that's not worthy of that attention." Fuck off, you insensitive prick! We had a senior K-9 handler at our post that was a slight rebel. He got into it with the PC pissing Lansing off, with them telling him they were going to take away his dog. Weird, just before they were going to come get his dog, a gate was left open, and the dog took off. Turns out he had a buddy in Ohio that needed a good police dog, and he just happened to catch that dog down in Ohio somewhere! A horrible tragedy that did occur while I was in the department was swept under the rug with one of my former Recruit School instructors, great guy, but screwed up big time. He had a long day at work having two K-9's with the State Police and was in a rush to get home for his kids sporting event. Parked his Blue Goose leaving the two dogs in the K-9 wagon turned off with no air conditioning on a hot day. Both dogs died from heat exhaustion, which is horrible. I mentioned it to the K-9 handler at my post, and he got all defensive. "Where did you hear that from, Bomber?" Uhh, two of our police dogs are dead, WTF, nobody's saying he did anything on purpose but still majorly "FUBAR!" Me being a union guy, I was always looking for consistency with incidents that happened in the department, which usually was not the case. If they like you, they usually take care of you! Our department also does not recognize our police dogs to be killed in the line of duty when left to die in vehicle from heat exhaustion. I totally have a problem with this seeing how they die due to no other reason than handler neglect. Does it suck for the handler? Absolutely!

Recognize those police dogs, damn it! Other agencies do on ODMP (Officer Down Memorial Page).

Things happen to people who work as a law enforcement officer just like any other career field or business out there—it's called life. One of the Troops at the post, who was married, was having an affair with a motor carrier officer. Everyone knew it, except for command or people with their heads in the shell. It turned out that his midnight partner was a fellow Italian like myself. The Troop breaks off the affair, wife finds out, female officer threatens to kill herself, all hell breaks loose. I get called into the old man's office, the PC. "Hey, Bomber, what's going on with you two?" "You have the wrong Italian, Lt., I have no idea what you're talking about." I knew a little hearsay but wasn't gonna say shit to him, not my business. The only thing I did tell him was who the right Italian Trooper was, which he should have figured out on his own; duh, they were midnight partners for a while. That Troop ended up leaving the department a few years later to become the chief of police in another department in Michigan. I ended up working with that motor carrier officer in another district years later also. Same Trooper was involved in a shooting in Detroit; prior to leaving goes up to the UP to get away for a while. He gets stopped for speeding 10 mph over by another Michigan trooper. She writes him a ticket for 5 mph over and scolds him telling him he should know better. I wonder if that bitch knew his officer girl-friend. He just paid the ticket being that kind of guy but her name got around the department fast as the douche in the UP that writes fellow Troopers, unheard of at the time! She obviously never heard the quote "When you work in a pencil factory, you get some free fuckin pencils" that came from a Captain in the New York State Police at a Trooper picnic out east.

Four of my Recruit School classmates were assigned to the Richmond Post out of Recruit School. The Richmond Post covered my home of application in Sterling Heights. There were four of them sent there because the Richmond Post was a fairly busy complaint post located in the northwest part of Metro Detroit. It was a newly built post with all the bells and whistles like the Metro Posts. They had holding cells, a data master for drunk driving arrests, and plenty of space for other operations. One weird thing was they shared the building, a small portion, with the City of Richmond PD. There were 30 Blue Gooses and two Richmond PD cars in the parking lot. Shortly after those after Recruit School there was a pursuit on Gratiot where three Troops were pursuing a shithead for a traffic violation. Two of the Troops were brand-new cubs out of my school. The fleeing shithead leaves the roadway and runs over a 10-year-old boy on his bike, killing him instantly. How fucking horrible, the Troops were traumatized at what this shithead did. Nobody's fault but his, obviously. The department was scrambling to justify our pursuit policy advising changes would be made. What changes? Shitheads make the decision to run and not stop for a cop. They could be suspended, stoned or drunk, mental, or have a dead body in the trunk. Problem is nobody knows what their problem is and why they hit the gas when those lights turn on except for them. Proverbs 28:1 says, "The Wicked flee when no one pursueth." The Richmond Post also had a weird policy with the US Coast Guard station on Lake St. Clair in their post area. If the Coast Guard (Coasties) arrested a drunk on the water, they would call the Troops to take their prisoner and transport them to Macomb County Jail for testing and lodging. Hmmm, I never knew this until one of my buds got jammed up for an incident involving one such "Coast Guard" arrest. He was in a two-man car sent to pick some schmo arrested by the Coasties, swap cuffs, no problem. Wait, that was the problem. His partner did not put the cuffs on tight enough while en route to Macomb County Jail, slushie is able to slip his handcuffs, whip out his hog, and piss between the seats on the two Troops. Brakes slam, slushie comes forward, and my buddy socks him in his snot locker, instantly breaking his nose! Oh shit, now he's bleeding all over the place. They have to stop the patrol car, resecure slushie in handcuffs, stop the bleeding, and take him to the jail all fucked up. Not sure what I would have done, probably the same. The Troop was suspended and charged with assault and battery and took a plea to keep his job. After this incident, it was determined by the MSP and Coast Guard that they should transport and lodge their own prisoners. Duh, that's the way it should have always been or let the Sheriff's Department do it since they have Marine Patrol that work with the Coasties!

When I was a young Trooper at the Metro Post we were fully staffed, tearing it up, and having a great time trooping! We had a code on the radio to return to the post. It was a "Signal 3." Usually used when the old man or boss wants to talk to you or bust your balls about something. Could be a Desk Sergeant wanting a lunch break, etc. "Signal 25" for Post 25, or your car number, Signal 25-17, was bad, meaning you needed help or might have been taken hostage but can't put it out over the radio. If a "Signal 25" or "Signal 25-22" went out, send the cavalry because some shit's about to go down! "Cars 25-11, 25-16, 25-19, and 25-30 Signal 3 to the Post" goes out over the radio one summer day. All four of us single young hard-charging troopers working afternoons. "Shit, now what have we done?" We all get back to the post from different patrol areas assigned. The APC calls us into his office as we roll in. Throw your civi's (civilian clothes) on, grab a shotgun from the gun room, and meet in the squad room. "Ooooooookkkkkkay, what's up, sir?" The State Senator called and needs and MSP trap shooting team to go to the downriver shooting club for a fundraising benefit/steak dinner. Damn, I get to get off the road and go shoot a shotgun at skeet while getting paid and then get a free steak dinner, thanks Lt.! Off we go, jump in a Blue Goose wearing T-shirts/shorts and departmental shotguns in hand. Out of 10 teams or so, we came in ninth place, probably because we were unable to hit shit with the choke on the Police Remington 870s we brought. They are made for shooting criminals, not skeet!

Michigan budget hit hard, governor laying off Troopers, time to look elsewhere for employment. I had enough seniority that I was pretty much protected from getting laid off but still pissed off at the whole issue of using Troops as political pawns. One of my Recruit School classmates' father who was also a retired Troop had moved to Arizona and somehow gotten into a high-ranking law enforcement position out there. Same Troop that was on the cover of the *Detroit News* when I had gotten out of the Army in that article that my mother showed me, how ironic. He sent some Arizona DPS recruiters to Michigan to try and entice some of us to go out there. I was on the motors riding a slow rollin' Harley. The recruiters in Arizona DPD uniforms offered us BMW take-home motors with them also counting our time in service with Michigan toward Arizona's seniority; damn, pretty sweet offer. Arizona also had a 20-year and out retirement, not 25 years like Michigan. I thought about it hard, weighed all the options, and decided it was best to stay. One of my good friends actually swayed me a little, "We don't need to lose a bunch of great Troops to be stuck with moron ladder climbers." I can't remember how many Michigan Troops ended up leaving and going out to Arizona. I thought there would be a lot more. Things are cyclical, the current unappreciative Governor would be gone soon enough, we could ride it out. I learned throughout the rest of my career that getting a new Governor didn't really change anything significantly—they are all self-serving.

Off Duty Incidents: Hmm, yes they do occur, especially for State Troopers that have authority 24/7 anywhere in the State of Michigan. Our department paid us emergency response compensation, which was not much, approximately one hour of pay a day to carry our weapons off duty and take action off duty if needed, be it a car crash, robbery, etc. I would estimate throughout my career I had probably been involved in call back off-duty incidents around 10 times, one every couple of years. If we put ourselves in service per our contract, we would get three hours of call back overtime unless we were tied up on something longer, i.e., a critical incident. We had Troopers that were terminated for not taking action. One troop was at a wedding where some schmuck pulled a knife and cut somebody; he did nothing, didn't even call 911, and his excuse was he had been drinking and didn't want to get involved. There was a Troop out of my Recruit School that was at a party where he pulled a knife on someone, not his duty weapon, and was fired for that. Not surprised he had issues during the Academy and was on suspension when he pulled the knife. We had Troops, Sergeants, command officers, and civilian employees get popped for drunk driving. If it was a first offense, no problem, they could say they have a drinking problem, take a plea, and move on. Off-duty Troops call on "Nextel": "Blip Blip Blip, are you working, Bomber?" "Yes, sir. What cha got?" "I'm following some asshole, could be drunk or just driving like a schmuck." Then I would head to cut off and make a stop and the perp. When "Nextel" phones first came out, we wouldn't even tell Dispatch what was going on till we were making a stop. Sometimes Dispatch would call us, "25 cars we have an off-duty Troop/Police Officer/Deputy following a possible intoxicated driver." We would get these calls into Dispatch all the time in the Detroit Metro area, no shortage of shitty drivers! I would follow someone driving like a yahoo, get a good look at the driver, write their plate down, and pay them a visit at a later time while on duty. They always had that dumbfounded look on their face when I wrote them a careless or reckless driving ticket at their house. I would act like a third party had called in their driving and then I would tell them, "Ya, I'm the one that witnessed your driving, Skippy. Contact the court within 10 days." Very rarely would they go to court, they would just pay the ticket and take their lumps.

One of my buddies who was off duty was following some dude that "road raged" him. He calls me on Nextel to pull him over for careless. I stop the guy, and my buddy jumps out of his pickup truck pointing his snubby revolver at him. Hokey pokey, put that gun back in your pants, partner, settle down, and take a deep breath. I write out a dooker (ticket) stating what he did and have the off-duty Trooper sign the ticket and give to him. No need to point guns at careless drivers. After the stop he said the guy pointed his hand/fingers at him like a gun? Okay, hand still not a weapon/gun. Another buddy of mine on his way to the post to work midnights when a drunk sideswiped his brand-new pickup and kept going. Oh, hell no, not his brand-new pickup truck. He rams the side of this dude's car, forcing him off road into the median. By the time we get there he's got him out of his car on the ground with his knee in his throat. Okay, we'll take it from here. Drunky failed all the sobriety tests we gave him and went to jail for operating while intoxicated and hit & run.

Promotions in the State Police: You would think that civil service would be all over this to make sure there was a fair process, but NOT! There were five Troopers, all white males, that sued the department over reverse discrimination when I first joined the State Police. They were known as the "Fab Five." The testing process at the time was strictly written and strictly by points on that test. The department established a list for promotion, and highest scoring would be promoted; sounds like common sense, right? For some unknown reason white males were getting passed over for promotion even though they had done extremely well for the testing process at the time. The department lost the lawsuit, had to promote all five to Sergeant, give them back pay as Sergeants, and changed the testing process so it was fairer across the board for everyone. I ended up working with three out of the five Sergeants and knew the other two during my career, all great guys and Sergeants! When I took the Sergeants test it was broken down into two sections, one for uniform and one for detective. I passed the uniform part and failed the detective part. Oh well, never wanted to be a Dick anyways. I was only interested in two Sergeant positions with all the specialties in the department. One as a motor Sergeant and the other as a Sergeant/pilot in the Aviation Unit. Both were considered uniform positions. Promotions in the command ranks, Lt. to Lt./Colonel were different since they were in a different civil service tier than that of Troopers and Sergeants. The Director/Colonel was appointed by the Governor. I knew I would probably be a Trooper my whole career, so I really didn't care how command moved up the ladder other that a lot of ass kissing and jockeying for position that went on. There was another saying we had among the Troops, "Screw up and move up." We had a female Troop at Metro that kept crashing patrol cars. She became a Sergeant rather fast after the third crash, get her off the road to get rid of her. She's a liability on the road. Sergeants don't work the road; send her to Dispatch to monitor civilians or put her on desk. The latter part of my career the department came up with a promotion system where you had to take a written test still and have an interview with command for the position. This was called "Targeted Selection." Basically, if you were their target, they would select you for promotion. They set up the interview process so they could manipulate points in a subjective way instead of objective way. What a bunch of bullshit. I saw so many morons get promoted to different positions in the MSP that left me scratching my head over and over! WTF, how did they get promoted?

Six to eight of us afternoon Troops and the shift Sergeant were sitting in the squad room at end of shift around 10 p.m. when a young woman beats on the back windows of the post, yelling, "We need help up front, one of your troopers is fighting a man." Holy shit, it was like a herd of cattle running down the hallway to the front of the post. We scramble out the front door and see one of our boys fighting some asshole on the front sidewalk with another guy standing near him. Game on, boots flying, fists flying, and pepper spray flying. One in custody fairly quick and dragged into the post to one of the holding cells. The woman and her daughter were traveling down Telegraph Road when some drunk pulled up alongside them, making sexual mannerisms with degrading comments yelling at them to pull over. The woman see the State Police Post and pull into the parking lot for help. A troop just happens to be at the front door after interviewing a suspect on a different incident when the ladies yell to him for help. He contacted slushy at the driver's window smelling alcohol and observing he was clearly intoxicated. Dipshit throws the car in reverse and tries to flee with the Troop hanging in the window fighting him to get the car back into park. The hit and run suspect was trying to help the Troop. He took a couple licks before yelling out I'm helping you guys. "Sorry! Dispatch, send us a wrecker to the front of the post for one in custody. Also send a Taylor Fire Rig for a wash down for blood on the front sidewalk." Can't have blood stains (not sure whose) on the concrete leading into the post the next day, wouldn't look good, just saying! During a search subsequent to arrest, we found cocaine in his car also. What a dumbass, being so drunk and on cocaine, that he followed those women into a State Police Post now facing OWI, resist, obstruct the police, assault on a police officer, and felony possession of cocaine. Great job, boys; one more shithead off the road for a while. That same dumbass actually took his case to a jury trial instead of taking a plea. The jury found him guilty, and he looked like an idiot when the mother/daughter took the stand testifying about the sexual comments and motions he had done. His wife started crying and stormed out of the court room.

All enlisted members had to shoot three times a year and qualify once a year. The civilians didn't have to because, hmm, they weren't Troopers. The fall shoot was the fun one where instructors would come up with some cool targets usually involving balloons, bowling pins, and even shooting out the windshield of a shitbox car sometimes. I only shot DE (Distinguished Expert) once in Recruit School, never again throughout my career. I was always happy shooting "Expert." I thought the badge looked better and was easier to see, at least that's what I told myself. We practice shooting with our police motors also until one of the sergeants shot the front police light off. "Damn it, Jim, I'm only a Sergeant!" Most of the time I enjoyed shooting unless we had some instructor that acted like a military drill sergeant having us run and do push-ups before shooting to get our heart rate up! Hmm, I don't remember doing push-ups before my active shooter shooting I was involved in later in my career, just saying!

Hot Chicks on Harleys! We would constantly be asked during motor season to participate in static displays all over the Detroit Metro area and even rural parts of the state. A static display is where you clean your motor, make it shiny and pretty, go park it at a fair or other event, and let little kids and hot chicks sit on it and get it all dirty again with finger prints all over the place. No dudes allowed to sit on my Harley at events! Two of our Motor Men, not me, damn it, were on a detail in downtown Detroit at Hart Plaza with their Harleys. There was a NASCAR display set up with some hot chicks in bikinis. Two of the bikini-clad women wanted to sit on the Harley, which was a request that obviously the troops could not deny. Cameras are flashing, troops are smiling just when the district command pulls up in their unmarked Chevy. A female Inspector who was a horrible leader and the District Captain who was a good shit get out of the car. The Troops try and scurry the girls off the bikes. "Fuck, now we're in trouble." She gets out of the car rushes over to the motor Troops with a stupid look on her face, probably thinking, "I've got you fuckers now." The Captain steps in front of her, shakes the Troops hands, and says, "I'm glad Troops are still being Troops." She goes back to the car in a tizzy all pissed off. When we were on rideouts with the entire motor unit we had hand signals to let other Motor Men what the formation would be. Single finger up, single file, two fingers up, side by side, surfer thumb and pinky movement staggered riding for safety. If we slapped our helmets it was a signal to the guys behind to look right because we were passing a hot chick! The sirens on the Harley had a cool wail that sounds like a cat call when you passed a hottie. "Whirp Whirl." What a great gig being a Motor Man! Sometimes I had to pinch myself, holy shit, I get paid to ride around on a State Police motorcycle, write tickets, arrest people, and look pretty! Highlight of my career as a trooper riding a Harley for eight and BMW for seven for a total of 15 years!

News Article: "Illinois State Police Unveils Bew Motorcycle Enforcement Bureau." Wow, Michigan brought back motorcycles for patrol and special events in 1994. Illinois starts a brand-new unit in 2007, 13 years later with more bikes than we have? What a bunch of bullshit, Lansing; put more bikes out there. It's all about politics because motorcycles are way cheaper than patrol cars as far as the monthly mileage and lease payments and cheaper to operate concerning gas prices. A Sergeant that works at the Drive Track/Academy in Lansing actually put a study together showing how much money Michigan is wasting in leasing vehicles instead of purchasing outright, which had been done for years. A former Governor had transferred all State of Michigan vehicles to a lease program with a company named "Wheels", which was based out of Illinois. We were paying a high monthly lease/mileage fees for the vehicles all the way from small Department of Social Services passenger cars, MSP patrol cars and motorcycles, and DPW snow plows and other equipment. The department also got rid of the gas pumps that each State Police post had. They issued Wheels fleet/gas cards that were put in each patrol car/motor for use at most gas stations. Problem is you have an emergency such as a power outage and all of a sudden, our gas cards don't work, hmm? When I was at Metro we had a four-day power outage in Detroit where they thought a fuel plant in southwest Detroit was going to explode, so evacuations had to be made. We had to find a local PD that still had gas pumps and borrow gas from them. Okay, that's embarrassing! Another key issue he stated that we pay for mileage from mile one until they are turned in. We didn't get the three-year/36 free miles, which is the norm! Holy shit, we were paying a shit ton of money that didn't have to be paid to a company in another state. WTF, we're the State of Michigan with the Big 3, Ford, General Motors, and Chrysler Headquarters in our state. You would think they could strike a sweet deal with the Big 3! Again, this is one of those dirty little secrets most people are unaware of until someone brings it to light. That Sergeant was basically told to squash his study, shut his mouth, and let it go, or he would be finding another job away from the Drive Track. Typical political/department bullshit when a bunch of feckless people are in charge and beholden to politicians and not the citizens of Michigan. When I first joined the State Police we would keep patrol cars in service until 60,000 miles and then turn them in for new cars. Then about half through Lansing decided, okay, let's bump that up to 70,000, then 75,000, then 85,000 for patrol cars and 100,000 for SUVs by the time I retired. Why would we keep cars for more and more miles when paying higher prices? I asked this question for officer safety purposes. The longer you keep vehicles, the more shit breaks; easy concept, right? I was in a pursuit in a high-mileage Dodge Charger slick top when a huge plume of smoke blasted out the tail pipes. Oh shit, just blew an engine, I'm out of the pursuit! Lansing's response: "Well, cars are made with a better quality today, so they can be kept in the fleet longer." What a bullshit response! The Drive Track guys always tried to get us the best vehicles available but were constantly cock-blocked by certain upper command and department civilians in Lansing. When we switched over to Dodge Chargers from Ford Crown Vics in the early

2000s the Drive Track ordered 100. Some MSP civilian dumbass canceled the order saying they were too fast. First of all, dipshit, Ford had discontinued producing the Crown Vic; what do you want Troopers to drive? A Toyota Prius if you had your way! A Lt./Colonel with some balls who later became director for a short time called that civilian and advised them to reinstitute that order for the 100 Chargers or find another career field. Bam, take that, you pogue!

CHAPTER 8: MICHIGAN STATE POLICE TROOPERS ASSOCIATION (MSPTA)

WHAT TO DO? What to do? Troopers and Sergeants went door to door back in the day getting enough signatures from Michigan citizens to give Us binding arbitration and other rights in the MSPTA. The citizens of Michigan thought this was important enough to support those men and women for years to come. Should I stay in the Troopers Association or be an ass kiss and try to rise through the ranks as a command officer. I have a Bachelor's degree from WMU, I am a military Veteran, and have a great deal to offer as a leader. I decided to stay with the Union and the Road Dogs. Most command officers I dealt with throughout my career were administrators and not leaders. Most of them were self-serving and always looking for the next promotion or who to align themselves with for the next leg up! We did have a few great command officers, but they were few and far between. It seemed like the longer I was in the department, the less I saw of these leadership traits I first witnessed when I was a young Trooper. Probably a combination of getting salty as I progressed toward the end of a great career or a reality of the times were a changin'. The MSPTA has an executive board, and the department has an executive council. I like the sound of "board" better, just saying. We have a President, Vice president, Treasurer/Secretary. There are seven districts in the State Police so each district has an MSPTA district representative on the uniform side. Then there are Sergeants reps within region 1 and region 2 that cover uniform and detective Sergeants throughout the state. Each post had at least one post rep, maybe more for larger posts in the urban areas of the state. Most post reps were

Troopers, but Sergeants were allowed to be post reps also, which very rarely occurred due to a conflict of interest with them being in the chain of command between Troopers and the Lieutenants. I was involved with the MSPTA my entire career until I retired and held rep positions for 16 years. I was a district rep in Metro Detroit for a little over a year and a post rep for 15 years on the East and West side of the state.

There has to be some perks to being a union rep. Post reps would receive $50 per meeting and mileage paid for post, district, and quarterly meetings. We attended quarterly meetings in different parts of the state. The best would be the fall meeting on Mackinaw Island near the Upper Peninsula, which was a great location to take the family. The Association would pay for the hotel rooms for Troops, and you make up the difference for family members. The actual meetings are attended by members only, and family can hang out at the pool, go site seeing, etc. Department issues are discussed, any changes to policy, contract talks, grievances, etc. They put on a nice buffet/meal for troopers/sergeants and their families. We had meetings in Detroit where we stayed at the Greektown Casino, meetings in Traverse City at the Great Wolf Lodge water park, Boyne Mountain where they would put on a golf outing to raise money for MSTAF (Michigan State Police Troopers Assistance Fund), and a lot of other great resorts and areas in Michigan. It was like having a mini vacation every three months for years. District reps would get a stipend of around $475 per month because they handled more issues and represented more troopers. The Troopers Association President and Vice president were paid at their rate by the department, either Troop or Sergeants pay. We voted as a union to give an additional stipend to both, equivalent of a Captain and Inspector pay. Both the President and VP work out of the Association office in Lansing, dealing with Lansing HQ on a multitude of issues from labor contracts, discipline issues, legislative lobbying, etc.

Troopers and Sergeants get in trouble purposely and unknowingly. We are human too! Shit, even command officers get in their share of trouble, but they don't have the protections we do in the MSPTA. If you are a Troop or Sergeant and getting disciplined, you have way more rights than a command officer. All serious discipline is handled through Internal Affairs (IA) and Human Resources within the MSP. Minor offenses could be handled at the post level by the PC. This changed later on toward the end of my career where one of the directors was in charge of everything. She wanted IA in Lansing to handle almost everything at the Vatican, which is bullshit. The department can bounce command officers via transfers or demotions on a whim if they decide to. One Lieutenant screws up, and then they bounce him or her to a different district. I've seen this happen multiple times throughout my career. There are disciplinary transfers for Troopers and Sergeants, but it is way more difficult for the department to do. If you fuck up in the UP (Upper Peninsula), they might send you down to Detroit and vice versa. There aren't too many troopers that want to go work in the UP from Detroit, myself included. Compared to the fast-paced work in Detroit, it would be boring as shit. I once had a nightmare that I was sent to work in the UP as a Troop where I was dispatched to an IGA (grocery store) for a bad check complaint and some fat cashier was flirting with and hitting on me!

They told us in Recruit School that the three B's would get you in trouble be it working or off duty: beer, booze, and broads! Hmm, I guess that makes sense. We were told that women wanted nothing more than to hook up and get our Blue Cross/Blue Shield insurance. I first became an MSPTA rep when I had about five years as a Troop, the "John Wayne" time frame. Being a union rep is comparable to being a defense attorney. I would have to walk a fine line defending the Troops and being reasonable trying to understand the department's position. If a Troop or Sergeant dicked the dog, I would let them know and try to get their discipline rendered as light as possible. Discipline could involve the lowest level of verbal counseling all the way to the highest, which would be termination. If department members were charged criminally and the department agreed with those charges (very important), they were basically on their own. Minimal assistance from the MSPTA (lawyer contact advise and nothing required from the department). The State Police believes in progressive discipline, which makes sense. The more you fuck up, the bigger the consequences should be. I would sit on discipline panels as a post rep and termination hearings as a district rep.

We also responded to critical incidents where troopers were involved, including fatal pursuits, and shootings, including fatalities.

Retro (retroactive) Pay? The MSPTA fought hard with the office of the State Employer and command through the Governor for at least three years when I first joined the State Police trying to get a decent pay raise in our next contract. They kept demanding concessions for giving us cost-of-living or better pay increases. We held out and took the state to arbitration, where the state lost big time! The arbitrator decided the state had the ability to pay the Troopers and Sergeants, so he made them pay big! We were awarded one of the biggest pay raises we had ever seen as an association without having to give anything up, such as health care or other benefits. I received around eight grand in retro pay; damn, as a single Trooper that was a huge bonus at the time. I always wanted a Porsche, so I bought a used 1986 Porsche 928S that I still have to this day. It was sitting in a doctor's driveway in Riverview with five other high-end cars. The Porsche had a cracked windshield, a flat tire, and was a work in progress that I was glad to take off his hands. This made his wife extremely happy to have some extra space for her vehicle. I also took a five-day trip to Las Vegas with some other troops. "What happens in Vegas, stays in Vegas!" Thanks for the retro pay, Governor!

We gave Troops cards that told them what to say if involved in a shooting, which in Metro Detroit occurred on a regular basis. "How many shots were fired? In what direction? And was anybody hit?" That's it. Until a rep shows up, don't say or offer anything else. That was with our command also. Don't say shit to other agencies, a big no-no!

Early on in my career most of the IA (Internal Affairs) complaints that I dealt with representing troops were serious complaints concerning conduct where Troops were fucking off while on the clock, not working taking complaints, crashes, or writing tickets, etc. Toward the end of my career the department was going after Troops for actually doing their jobs, too many cars in a pursuit, using profanity on camera, and other chickenshit incidents that would have been laughed at when I first joined the State Police. We were taught in Recruit School during patrol when dealing with shitheads, "**Ask** 'em, **tell** 'em, **take** 'em!" Case in point, you make a traffic stop on a suspended driver. You ask them for their driver's license. They don't produce it as required by Michigan law. You **ask** them to step out of the vehicle. They refuse to exit the vehicle. You **tell** them to exit the vehicle, but they again refuse. Finally you **take** their stupid ass through the vent window, call for a tow truck, and take them to jail. Easy concept that can be applied to multiple scenarios. A great quote told by a senior FTO when I was a young Troop: "If they give you sugar, treat them nice; if they're an asshole, give them spice!"

You might remember when I talked about the dumbass Troop that was hanging drywall when he was on the clock. Same one hanging out at titty bars while working in uniform. He finally got fired with the threat of being charged criminally for stealing swag from a gas station while on duty. He would actually walk into gas stations and take a pop and candy bar walking right by the cashier. That turd got coming what he had coming. What an embarrassment to the uniform and the citizens we serve. Then there was my classmate that was offered the same deal, accept termination without fighting it or get charged criminally. Wow, these guys were like criminal defendant shitheads we arrested on a recurring basis?

I represented a Troop that was at the Detroit Post when he was injured while on the job and off for over a year. He then kept calling in sick for long periods when cleared by his doctor and a department doctor to come back to work. As an enlisted member of the department you accumulate four hours sick time per pay period. He was reimbursed his injury time under Workmans' Comp but had little sick time when he came back to work. I actually agreed with the department on this one. If you can't work, then apply for a duty disability retirement and stop calling in sick all the time. It was his right to use his sick time, but when you run out, there is a problem; you are put on lost time and can be bounced back in seniority to a later Recruit School. We finally came to a compromise with command allowing him to have an administration position where he wouldn't have to work the road anymore. There were lots of admin spots, vehicle maintenance officer, court officer, detective trooper, etc. He bounced around in different positions until getting promoted off the road. Many people think, "Use it or lose it" so they take some sick time off at the end of their career. I did, figured I earned it, wouldn't get reimbursed for any lost sick time and busted my ass for my whole career as a Road Dog.

I had a really good rapport with my first PC as a Post Rep. She was the one who sent me to Motor School and appreciated my work ethic. She didn't jam Troops up over chickenshit, only righteous violations of official orders (written policy covering everything and anything in the MSP) or department policy. Troops were working hard for her and people would come into the post with bullshit complaints, most saying, "The Trooper was rude and unprofessional." Can't tell you how many times people come up with that bullshit line. She would address those people accordingly and advise her assistant PC and Sergeants to do the same. They came out with the in-car-cameras in the early 2000s with VHS tapes. Those things were archaic, but they did the job. A defendant and his father came into the post one day to complain about a Trooper writing his son a window tint ticket. Ironically the troop was my classmate that was eventually fired, yet she defended his actions were correct for the traffic stop. The son was in his early 20s, so his father had no basis to be at the post other than trying to take of a momma's boy. She had them sit down in her office and had a desk Sergeant pull the VHS video to play for the two. They might not have been aware that he turned his camera on as the car drove by catching the tint in clear view. They kept saying the car did not have illegal window tint on it. She located the traffic stop as the car drove by with the tint showing it to the father/son combo. She then rewound it multiple times asking them if they saw it and needed it shown again. Both dad and son got shitty with her using profanity when she picked up her phone on the public address system and requested Troops come to her office. When the Troops went in, they were advised to throw their asses out of the post and if they refused to leave, then arrest them for disorderly conduct and trespassing. Wow, she's a Badass. I loved working for her!

Lots of Shootings: Troops in pursuit headed E/B on I-94 into Wayne County. Two suspects in the fleeing vehicle crash into the center median near the airport with shots fired. I respond to the scene with multiple Troops from my post. I am driving a semi-marked Crown Vic with a cub in the car. We get to the scene, I talk to the Troop that fired shots before command gets there. I go to put the Troop in my patrol car when my cub taps me on the shoulder from behind and advises our car is driving E/B on I-94. WTF? I call on the radio multiple times for whoever was driving that car to respond, advising other Troops that someone just stole our patrol car and is heading E/B. Two Troops set up ready to ram the car when they see a Senior Troop from the post was driving. He finally answered the radio and stated he jumped in the wrong car to go back to the post. What a dipshit. He was one of the problem children at the post that was constantly getting into trouble for doing stupid shit. The car he took to the scene was the regular MSP blue patrol car with the bubble on top. I had a silver slick top, semi-marked with a door shield and state police marking on the passenger side. The moron took the car on purpose to be a smartass! I tried to get his stupid ass jammed up even as a post rep, but the current PC had a soft spot in her heart for the dumbass. Anyways, back to the shooting. "How many shots were fired, what direction, and was anybody hit?" I ask and then swap out his handgun and send him back to his post, easy-peasy. There was another Ypsilanti Troop that had left the post to get into the pursuit. He and another Troop were put on indefinite desk duty because of a hazing incident. They hazed a cub when he first got out of the Academy being assigned to the Ypsilanti Post. One Troop who this cub had never met acted like he was a criminal and was put in the holding cell. Anther Troop, both FTOs (field training officers), gets him out of the cell to fingerprint him with the cub present. Troop acting like the criminal scuffles with uniform Troop. They had put blank ammunition in an H&K rifle that the cub had going to load a patrol car. Undercover Troop runs out back door with uniform Troop grabbing the rifle and shooting at him in the back as he ran away. They used fake blood and had the cub shitting his pants. Lansing command didn't find this incident, which they kept calling hazing too funny. Both Troops were proposed to be terminated but were able to keep their jobs through arbitration while having to sit desk for almost a year. The arbitrator must have agreed more of a joke than hazing when the cub yelled at the undercover bad guy, "That's what you get for running, mother fucker." Again the cub not knowing bad guy was a real Trooper.

The Senior Trooper above that took off in my semi-marked patrol car was always doing stupid shit. He worked the state fair one year when I also worked it. There was a group of Hawaiian Tropic high divers that put on a show climbing a high ladder and diving off at various heights in a fairly small pool below. I was on foot patrol with my partner when someone called over the radio that a female Trooper was about to jump off the high dive. We looked at each other and then busted ass at a fast run across the fairgrounds toward the high dive. Shit, we got there after she had already jumped and was getting out of the pool. She was a civilian with an MSP shirt with tie and pants on. She did look pretty hot getting out of the pool soaking wet. Problem is command didn't find it all that amusing! Command opens up a UD-93 (Internal Affairs investigation). They interview hotty high diver, and she implicates dumbass Trooper that gave her the uniform and coaxed her and her buddies to do the dive. They interview dipshit, and he says someone broke into his hotel room and stole the uniform. Classic case of the cover up is worse than the incident. All he had to do is admit that "ya, it was a stupid idea. Sorry." He lies making it way worse and gets jammed way more that needed including unpaid time off. The Michigan State Police has annual inspections of the posts and district HQ where command officers look over reports, check patrol cars and equipment, etc. This same Troop pissed off about discipline he had gotten allegedly decides to go into the gun room just before inspection, making a rifle here, a shotgun there "hot" by racking a round in the chamber. Big no-go, the post fails the inspection, huge officer safety issue also. The PC and assistant PC gets their asses chewed by district HQ. They never proved he did it, but everyone knew he did! Same Troop has a teenager that likes to drink underage. He decides to take a PBT (preliminary breath test) home to test his kid to see if he's been drinking. During inspection it comes up that a PBT is missing. Strange, we wonder who has it? The PC finds out he took it home, which starts another IA with more discipline! As a union rep you handle enough IA's from Troops like him and you start to wonder, "Are you really that stupid or just have huge balls?" I'm going with the really that stupid!

"State Police Sergeant gets arrested for shoplifting" on the local Detroit TV News station. Fuck, how embarrassing. Really sucked that his usual rep was on vacation and I had to represent his stupid ass. Again, I'm a Trooper representing a Sergeant. He goes into a drugstore and steals razor blades. Only a misdemeanor, and he claims he has a problem. Hmm, same Sergeant used to be a Motor Man supposedly stole another Troops leather jacket from his open locker. Couldn't prove it, just speculation. Okay, kind of solidified that theory, leather jacket, razor blades, no other suspects? There wasn't really much to do for his defense, he did it. He was just trying to get less days off on suspension. Same Sergeant has another discipline hearing couple years later, and again I somehow get picked to sit on discipline panel. Fuck, what are the odds? I have the worst luck. He kept coming late into work saying he had childcare issues. The PC had given him plenty of slack and finally had enough. We were sitting at district for the discipline hearing when the secretary advises the sergeant is running late because of a flat tire. Uggghhh, okay. I have time to talk with the command officers prior to the hearing with all of us just sitting there shaking our heads in disbelief. He's being disciplined for being late and is late for his hearing. It might come as a surprise, but he was found responsible and given more time off.

Shots Fired: Two Troopers are sitting in their Blue Goose in a gas station parking lot finishing up a crash report in the city of Detroit when they are startled by gunfire in the next parking lot over separated by some high arborvitae bushes. A couple is parked parallel with them when another car pulls up, two mopes exit the car, and try to execute the couple for a previous drug deal. The two Troops exit the Goose, one grabs a rifle and the other his handgun. They engage the two shooters in a face-to-face gunfight. They kill the closest and shoot the other until he drops and the threat is stopped. I went to the Detroit post to help the Troops with the report and help them with any issues they might have. Job well done, Troopers. Assassination attempt stopped by the two heroes. The department psychiatrists showed up and talked with the Troops. The one suspect that survived takes his case to a jury trial where he told the jury he was just walking down the street when the two Troopers jumped out of their car and shot him for no reason. Hmm, only in Detroit, that's some funny shit! He was found guilty and full of shit by a jury of his peers and sent to prison for a nice stint.

More Shots Fired: Undercover Trooper on Drug Team shoots two suspects killing one. I get the call and off to the hospital I go to make contact with the Trooper. He was on a task force working with the ATF in Detroit when an ATF agent was taken hostage in a drug deal gone bad. Our guys never go deep undercover like seen on TV or the movies. They use CIs (confidential informants) to arrange their drug deals. The ATF on the other hand act like the CIs or drug dealers. Two shithead dealers made the undercover agent inside an abandoned house in Detroit. They had him kneel down and were getting ready to execute him from behind the head when the troop rammed his M4 rifle through an outside window killing one turd with the other running out of the room out the front door. The Troop ran around the side of the house and shot turd #2 in the ass dropping him in the street. Damn, son, he saved the ATF agent's life and took down the two shitheads by himself, impressive. As far as going to the hospital, when he jammed the M4 through the window he had cuts on his hands from the glass. "Great job, trooper!"

News Article: "Troopers told: Park It!" Being a union rep in the largest district in the Michigan State Police I was approached by the union president to be contacted by a reporter from the *Detroit News* along with another trooper from the Brighton Post to give our perspective about being placed on mileage restrictions by the Colonel at the direction of the Governor. Hell ya, I'll be more than happy to talk to that reporter. One stipulation was he had to reference that we were from the MSPTA and not the MSP. "Troopers told to Park It" was the title of the article, and it was a huge article on the front page of the *Detroit News*! I had some really great analogies for the article. I told him we were like fire fighters totally reactive and not proactive because the Governor was using us as a bargaining tool to get what she wanted in her budget. We were put on mileage restrictions to save gas three times during her tenure. It was one of the most asinine proposals enacted at the detriment of the citizens of Michigan. We could only drive a certain number of miles per shift, which meant we had to go out on the freeway, sit in the median, and not make any traffic stops or sit at the post and respond to emergencies only! What Governor would do that to her State Police Troopers? Definitely an inept one! I said it was like getting ready to run a marathon and then right before the race someone blasting you in the leg with a baseball bat while saying good luck with the race! That was one of my Italian heritage/mob references! The day the article ran again on the front cover of the *Detroit News* I received a phone call from my Motor Sergeant advising the District Captain wasn't too happy about the article. Same Captain that was a Troopers Captain.

He probably took shit from the higher-ups in Lansing, and you know shit rolls downhill. He calls my motor sergeant who calls me. My motor Sergeant was a religious man and a pastor. "Jesus, Bomber, what are you thinking?" "Jesus, Sarge, I was told to do the interview by the Union President, the same union you belong to." "Okay." What else is he going to say? Everything in the article was truthful; the only problem was the improper referencing of MSP instead of MSPTA by the reporter. Hey, that's on the reporter, not me! Jenny on the block got us three times with mileage restrictions during her tenure. Now she is the Secretary of Energy, dealing again with gas issues. Lord help us!

The President of the MSPTA was a good friend of mine. A Road Dog for years and a little off. He kissed the Governor's ass for what reason, I could never figure out. I would call him up and bust his balls or do it in person when I stopped by the union office in Lansing. We have a chance to do a meet and greet with the Governor after about her sixth year in office. Really? Myself and four other board members passed. She and her underlings did everything they could to degrade our department. She can kiss my ass, I've got nothing to say to her! There was a constant fight with our union and the higher command because of the stupid shit she was constantly doing, laying off Troopers, mileage restrictions, getting rid of semi-marked traffic cars because one of her peeps was stopped by a Trooper for speeding on the way to Lansing, etc. We knew many of the higher command were discouraged, you could see it in their eyes, and how they tried to justify her bullshit decisions. One upper command officer, a Major ,who I respected immensely and always fought the good fight for the Road Troops decided to abruptly retire saying. "Bomber, I just can't deal with the bullshit anymore, I've gotta pull the pins for my own sanity." Sir, if we lose command like you, who cares for and takes care of the Troops? We're fucked." I remember prior to becoming Governor she was the Attorney General and actually did a great job as AG. The Detroit Troops said she would bake cookies and bring them into the Detroit Post at times. She would send criminals away to prison where they belonged and make them pay restitution for damaging patrol cars in pursuits. When she became Governor, everything changed. It seemed that she had surrounded herself with the wrong people giving her the wrong advice including what to do with her own State Police Department. She became Governor around the same time the corrupt mayor of Detroit was elected, that's weird!

When I was a district rep down at Metro it was period leading up to 2007–2008 that the economy started to take a shit, and she was proposing laying off Troopers. There were many police departments in Metro Detroit that had it in their contracts that layoffs had to be civilians in a police department before any enlisted members (cops). We had an executive board meeting at a quarterly where I proposed to the rest of the board members that we fight to have a stipulation put in our contract that before any Trooper is laid off, all civilians have to be laid off first. At the time there were just a little under the road Trooper numbers that were civilian employees. The Department of Michigan State Police had approximately 3000 employees, around 1200 Road Dogs, 500 Sergeants, and 300 command with the rest being civilians. Damn, can you imagine when the State Police was first formed during World War I having 1000 civilians in the department? Fuck no! Most of them worked at headquarters in and around Lansing. What a scam, why does it take 1000 civilian employees to work supporting what we did as Road Dogs? It doesn't! The number of civilian positions gradually kept increasing higher and higher during my career. All you had to do was go to Lansing for training to see what was going on. When we had severe weather or a huge power outage like the four days in Southwest Detroit where they thought the oil yards were going to explode, only critical staff were to report to work for the State of Michigan, which always meant Troopers, Sergeants, and Corrections Officers. The state readily admitted it. Only essential employees are to report to work, all others including civilians and command officers are furloughed. Damn, present that to an arbitrator, and they are sure to side with the union. I saw an article from the Colonel of the New Jersey State

Police where he said they were getting ready to go under critical staffing for Troopers. Their department had around the same as ours, 3,000 members including Troopers, command, and civilians. His critical number for staffing shortage was going under 2000 Troopers in a state one-third the size of Michigan. Holy shit, I can't even imagine Michigan having 2000 Road Dogs. We would rule the roost. The board members looked at me like I was a moron and said, "Bomber, the state will never go for that. Done, end of story." Sometimes I thought I was living in Bizzaro world but came to realize many people even union leaders all drink the Kool-Aid at some time and forget where they come from and who they represent.

Transfers were unique when I first joined the State Police. You had to be off probation/FTO to put in for a transfer to another post. The transfer list was based strictly on department seniority with, I believe, them allowing you to pick 10 posts. This caused problems because there were Troops throughout the state that were very senior and a huge pain in the ass for the department. Those individuals would put in for a transfer, and the department would not transfer any people to those posts at the top of their list. One person could lock up 10 or more posts from getting bodies except out of Recruit School for years. The department also paid for moving expenses and lodging when offering transfers, which could come to a pretty penny of high costs for the state. They would give you a list of movers or you could choose your own depending on the rate the state was willing to pay to move an employee, which most of the moving companies were aware of. The state would also pay for lodging and meals, usually around $25 per day for up to three months. This was a nice little perk to have when transferring to another post. The MSPTA eventually gave this up for the department to guarantee a certain percentage of transfers per Recruit School because Troops were bitching at union meetings about the stagnant transfer policy. No more moving costs, lodging, or paying for meals. This was all done at the troops' expense now. Wow, what a huge concession just to have more movement!

CHAPTER 9: WHO WANTS TO GO TO ROCKFORD?

NEWS ARTICLE: "Motorcycle Troopers Return to Rockford." I was on the motor unit for six years when the Motor Sergeant asked those on the unit, "Who wants to transfer to Grand Rapids on the west side of the state?" Rockford was a pleasant community just northeast of Grand Rapids. The post was like Jonesville, built in the 1930s during the "Works" project that FDR instituted. The old brick buildings with the "Michigan State Police" in limestone on the facade. Uhhhh, I couldn't raise my hand fast enough! I had gone to quarterlies over there, had a great time, and the wife also liked it. An hour from Lake Michigan, Michigan's Adventure amusement park, the silver sand dunes, etc. We had two-year-old twins, one of each boy and a girl, still in diapers. It would be a fairly big move but nowhere near going to Arizona would have been. I can't remember if they picked two of us to transfer by department seniority or motor seniority. It didn't matter either way because I was pretty high with both, 12 years as a Troop and 6 years on the motors. It was a big move, but at the time the department still paid for transfers including moving expenses and putting you up in a hotel for up to three months with per diem for meals until you found housing. We lost that little perk in contract talks, go figure. My motor partner and I transferred to Rockford in early May of 2008 with no motors because they were still at the Drive Track for the current motor school they were running.

Motorcycle troopers return to Rockford

Motor officers the first here in 67 years

BETH ALTENA

Officers from the Michigan State Police first hoisted the public a thousand patrol on horseback are appending to motorcycles for cycles were used in daily use until 1941 when they were beings of the horses in favor of mobiles. For the first time 3 years, Kent County drivers once again will be under the response and sharp eyes of cycle patrol troopers.

side this

Two Rockford motorcycle troopers were formally introduced to the public on Tuesday, August 26, at the Michigan State Police Sixth District Headquarters on Three Mile Road, Grand Rapids. Troopers Chris Bommarito and Dave Cope have joined the Rockford Post as permanent motorcycle road patrol troopers. They are two of only 21 MSP motorcycle troopers.

According to Captain Gary Gorski, MSP Sixth District commander, the MSP motorcycle unit was reintroduced in 1993. A study by the University of Michigan

See TROOPERS page 16

READY TO ROLL—Michigan State Police has 21 motorcycle officers, including two out of the Rockford Post. Troopers Chris Bommarito, front and Dave Cope, next, have been in town since June.

While I was waiting to transfer to the Rockford Post Lansing, the Drive Track in particular took my Harley to use in a motor school. This was the same time the Detroit Red Wings had won the Stanley Cup, and they were having the usual ticker tape parade down Woodward Ave. in Detroit near the Fox Theater. The Michigan State Police and Detroit Police Motor Units escorted the players in convertibles down the parade route. Can you say bad aspirin? I had missed the last Stanley Cup win by one year from being on the motors. I was so fucking pissed at the Drive Track Lt. I could spit! He was adamant he needed my motor for training. Wait a second, I'm one of the Senior Motor Men, I bust my ass all the time on patrol and with details, and you can't spare one bike for one day? You prick! To add insult to injury my post commander at the time assigned me to some bullshit fugitive warrant detail in Detroit where Wayne County decided to do some amnesty sweep allowing people to pay partial payments on nonviolent misdemeanor and civil infractions. They were basically trying to take any cash they could get to clean up their dockets. We had to go sit at some church in the 'hood and run shit-heads standing in line that would come up to our patrol car windows where we would run them in LEIN (Law Enforcement Information Network) to see if they had a warrant for their arrest and how much they owed. We then sent them to another line to rectify it with a court employee. Let's make a deal. It's all about the money with these fucking assholes, not doing the right thing. Some dumbasses actually had felony warrants for their arrest not knowing they'd be going to jail. My partner and I had a dipshit come up to the patrol car window and after running his name in LEIN, he came back with no warrants. "What chu mean, I have no warrant, run me again, this is bullshit." "No, what's bullshit is you wasting our fucking time; take a hike, jerkoff! Then come to find out, the powers to be had pallets of water delivered for these turds, and they were actually stealing cases of water from the pallets, so Troopers, Deputies, and DPD Officers had to be put on a water security detail; only in Detroit, what a shithole! It was a three-day detail, so I just happened to come down with the two-day flu, probably from some turd hacking on me through my car window, and called in sick the next two days. I had one pay period, two weeks to go before I transferred to Rockford and couldn't get out of Metro Detroit fast enough!

Another problem the Rockford post had was too many Troops for the space, which is a good thing. They used the old garage for a squad room. No garage, where do we put out motors when we're staying at a hotel for months? The Rockford Fire Department was nice enough to let us keep our bikes in one of their garage bays. I stayed at a Choice Hotel for two months before finding a house, and my partner stayed there for three months while he had a house built. We had take- home bikes, so once we had houses, we were golden. That number of Troopers would slowly dwindle to bare bones staffing before I retired!

The first day my motor partner transferred over to Rockford, we had no motors because they were getting radio updates in Lansing for the 6th District. Neither of us were from the westside, so we had to learn the area. The Trooper we were supposed to ride with for area familiarization had called off sick, and nobody knew it. Day Sergeant says, "You Guys worked in Detroit for years, you can handle going out on your own, here take this Tahoe out on patrol to learn the area." Ooooookkkkkkay. We jumped in a Tahoe and headed out on patrol on day shift. Oh shit, what kind of trouble can we get into? We went down to the city of Grand Rapids, which is the 2nd largest city in Michigan. There is an S-curve that snakes through the City on US-131. "Be careful working in the S-curve," we kept hearing. We worked on the Metro Detroit Freeway system, which is some of the worst in the country! I was driving the Goose when I decided to get off the freeway and turn around on one of the service drives. We come across a Grand Rapids cop in uniform blocking the roadway in a Ford Crown Vic with no markings, only police lights on. He had three mopes at gunpoint that had crashed their Cadillac into a fire hydrant. I flipped on the overhead and sped up to the scene to see what was going on. My partner opened his door to jump out when I jammed on the brakes causing his door to fly open and damage the front fender. I cuff one turd up, my partner grabs the other two and cuffs them. Working in Metro Detroit for years we both carried more than one set of handcuffs on us. Turns out the GR cop that had these dudes at gunpoint was a Captain! We had heard stories from troops before we transferred to Rockford that there was a huge Dutch population in West Michigan. In fact the GR Captain was of Dutch descent. One perp kept saying, "I want your name and badge number." I'm Trooper Van Bommarito and my partner's name is Trooper Van *Y&^, shut the fuck up! The GR Captain asks "what were you guys chasing them for?" "Really, Cap?" talk about deflecting, I threw it back in his face, "Hey, Cap, I'm sure you were happy when you saw two Troopers roll up to back you up, right?" "Ya." First day at a new post, we damage a Goose and have some Captain say we were chasing someone that he was? That Cadillac they crashed turned out to be stolen. Sign of what was to come working at the Rockford Post I guess!

Still no bikes after two weeks. There was a silver semi-marked Crown Vic at the Rockford Post same as the one I had used in the Metro. Sweet, I'm back in the Silver Surfer! They were great traffic cars having no markings on it except for a door shield on the front passenger door and

State Police on the front passenger fender. You could get in the right lane and let people fly by you to the left, and most had no idea you were the police. I loved the semi-marked cars and not too many troops at Rockford used that car, so being a Motor Man I told them I'll take that car. I'm on patrol in the city of GR when another troop calls out a pursuit with a crotch rocket. I wait for them to come northbound on US 131 and jump into the pursuit. Our pursuit policy required fully marked cars to take primary and slick tops or semi-marked cars to jump in secondary. I kept waiting for him to pass me in the fully marked, and he never did. I even told him over the radio, take primary, son! Crotch rocket man gets off the freeway headed toward the hospital downtown on cobblestone street. Not a good idea, he finally pulls over and gives up, knowing we're on his ass and not giving up. I jump out of my car and clothesline his ass onto the ground as he tried to take off on foot. One in custody, Dispatch send us a hook (tow truck)!

My motor partner and I were finally able to go Lansing to pick up our Harleys. We were on the way back to the Rockford Post when some retired Lt. called the post and complained about our driving on the way back. WTF? A desk Sergeant told us he called, okay, whatever, thanks, Sarge! We had no idea where that came from, Trooper lane, Trooper speed. If two Troopers are coming up behind you in the left lane on State Police Harleys, get the hell out of the way, dumbass! Hanging in the left lane without moving over in Michigan is actually illegal and a two-point violation, and that retired Lt. knows that! I would never call in if I was off duty on a trooper, deputy, or city officer about their driving. I always looked at it like, hey, they have a job to do, I'm not going to "Monday morning quarterback" them on how they do their job, period!

I find a house to move my family into close to the Rockford Post. Sweet, now I can keep my police motor at home instead of the Rockford Fire Department. I get on my blue Hog, check in with Dispatch for patrol, and bust out of my driveway, leaving the subdivision. As I'm pulling out, I look to the right, then left, and see a shitbox turning into the sub. Wooosh, a bottle rocket flies past my face from left to right and explodes to the right of my face. Holy shit, I look left and see this joker hanging out the passenger window of a vehicle who apparently shot the bottle rocket at my head. I do a quick 180 on my Harley and turn the lights and siren on, pulling these two teenagers over. Both the driver and passenger are immediately extricated from the vehicle with the passenger saying, "Sorry, sir, we didn't know you were a police officer." "I'm a Trooper, dipshit, and you're both under arrest for assault on a Trooper!" They are put in bracelets (handcuffs) and sat on the curb while I wait for a Trooper in a Goose to transport their asses to Kent County Jail. I left their vehicle parked at the scene to save them a tow bill. The Kent County prosecutor bumped the charges up to felonies including shooting missiles from a moving vehicle and terroristic threats. Never thought of that second charge before or even after 9/11. We had a sweet court officer that encouraged the prosecutor to load them up. I did tell the boys they were lucky I wasn't some burley bearded Harley dude because they probably would have gotten their ass kicked!

Transferring to a new post in a totally different part of the state is an exciting opportunity that brings a new sense of almost working for another department. When I left Jonesville to go work in Metro Detroit even being from there was an eye-opening experience. The senior troops there knew I wouldn't stay there being from Metro Detroit and would catch the next transfer out of there. The Rockford Post's main responsibility is patrolling and taking crashes on the freeway system in Grand Rapids, the 2nd largest city in Michigan. The Rockford Post also had responsibility for all the M-Roads in Kent County. M-57, M-46, M-37, etc. Our main purpose in Kent County was traffic, traffic, and traffic! My partner and I got the cold shoulder from many senior troopers at the Rockford Post as being "those guys from Detroit." Hey, dickweeds, we went to the same Academy in Lansing, wore the same uniform, and had the same title as Trooper but were still treated like outsiders. Some were pissed off that they couldn't get on the motors before sending two troops from Detroit over them. I had 12 years in the State Police when I went to Rockford, and I was not gonna put up with any bullshit from Rockford Troops that have been at the same post their whole career. Do they really know what the State Police is all about never working at any other work site their whole career? I don't think so. There were troops at Jonesville that were the same, working there their whole career at the same post thinking they knew all about the State Police. I joined the State Police to do different things and work in different parts of the state, not be in the same post area for my entire career. People that do that might as well become city officers or county deputies. I didn't want to have to stop at the city limits or turn around at the county line. There was always something cool about being a trooper and having full authority in the state 24/7. The Rockford Post area besides the urban side of Grand Rapids also had a rural area/out-county with apple orchards to the north and many lakes and recreational areas.

News Article: "Exchange of Words Sparked Grand Rapids Nightclub Shooting, Police Later Killed Alleged Gunman." Been at the Rockford

Post for six months when I signed up to work New Year's Eve and New Year's Day overtime. My partner that night was a 20-year troop who like me had worked in Detroit years prior. He had a wealth of knowledge and experience, and I couldn't think of a better partner to have for what was about to happen. We had two two-man cars working on New Year's Eve with a desk Sergeant at the post. We ran into that Sergeant at a crash scene and we both had our "Bunny-Trooper" hats on. He didn't have his hat badge on which I pointed out. He told me that was just a target for someone to shoot you in the noggin! How ironic what would transpire later in the shift! I had the wheel of the Goose driving around downtown GR when I see some neon light off Market near US 131. I jump off the ditch (troops call the freeway the ditch because most of the freeways in Detroit are lower level with embankments that go up to the service drives). We do a drive-through property inspection of a strip club with those fancy neon lights. We come across a dude hanging out the driver's door losing his cookies (vomiting). I pull over, and my partner and I contact him. He's visibly intoxicated and has no license or identification on him. We tried to run a file and status check on him with Dispatch, but they are short staffed and not answering the radio, go figure. He was only identified as "Billy from Benton Harbor." After sobriety tests and a preliminary breath test he is arrested for OWI/drunk driving. Behind the wheel of a running car is all we need for the OWI arrest. My partner searches the car and finds a small baggie of marijuana in the car. Bang, bang, bang, shots fired in the strip club. I call out priority on the radio, shots fired, give Dispatch the location at which time I had no idea what the name of the club was. Just said strip club on Market, west of 131, send backup. We pull to the front of the club with the red bubble still spinning like a beacon to a moth! I jumped out, popped the trunk grabbing the .12-gauge shotgun asking my partner if he wants the rifle. He didn't want it because there were too many people screaming and running out of the club. A door man is at the front door yelling for us to come in, saying the shooter was down the hallway. We go in, look to the left and this giant of a man is standing there with a .357 revolver that looks like a cannon. We gave him multiple commands to drop the gun, with him raising it and shooting at us. That round hit the ground to left of me, so we opened up on his ass. Wow, he just shot at us? The man had shark eyes with no emotion. He never said a word, just fired at us. My feet were telling me to turn and run the other way, but my brain said, "You need to stop this monster." He ran up some stairs out a back door then onto a side street before stopping in the middle of the street, appearing to reload his weapon. He was given multiple commands to drop the gun with no response. I fired at him with my shotgun until the threat was stopped. He ran a short distance and collapsed on the roadway. My partner ran up and kicked the .357 away, and I waited with him for EMS to arrive, which was shortly after he collapsed. Some highly intoxicated dude came over to us saying that his car had been broken into. "My car was broken into. I need a report." He was clearly drunk and loud. We told him, "Hey, asshole, we were just in a shooting as you can see. We don't really give a shit about your car at this time. Fuck off." Two more Troops (no Grand Rapids cops), showed up so they went into the club to clear it, making it safe, with my partner. Grand Rapids officers waited across the street at the public works for backup while we were in a shooting with an active shooter thanks for the backup ladies!

My partner went to secure the Goose that was in front of the main entrance to find "Billy from Benton Harbor" handcuffed and sleeping in the back seat. Holy shit, what do we do with "Billy from Benton Harbor?" My partner woke him up, got him out of the patrol car, and kicked him loose. "Your lucky day, buddy. Call someone to pick you up." We never heard from him again, not surprised. Finally, after all settled down, with the gunshot victims tended to, the scene secure, a Grand Rapids officer came to the back street behind the club asking if we needed anything, to which I replied, "Yes sir, two large coffees with extra cream and extra sugar; we're gonna be here for a while".

It was a really bitter cold night when the shooting occurred. Our District Captain and PC both showed up to the scene, with us being able to smell booze on both of them, go figure, on New Year's Eve/Day. They sat in the backseat of our patrol car with the Captain smoking a big stogie. I remember smelling the odor of marijuana, forgetting that my partner had taken a baggie of dope off "Billy from Benton Harbor" and stuck it in his waistband. The Captain told us we did an outstanding job, the PC/Lieutenant repeated everything the Captain said, and I kept thinking to myself, "WTF, where's that smell of marijuana coming from?" We cleared the scene of the shooting around 6 a.m., five hours after the shooting had occurred. My wife had taken the kids to the eastside to stay with friends, knowing I was working overtime for the holidays. I went home and tried to sleep but couldn't, still shook up about the shooting. I couldn't reach my wife and talked to her later that day. I told her my partner and I were in a shooting, and she started crying. My three-year-old daughter saw my wife crying and asked, "Is Daddy dead?" Holy shit! This is what we deal with in law enforcement! We all started crying, and she handed her the phone so I could talk to her and she could hear my voice. They rushed home so we could be together during a critical incident. My partner and I had to go in the next day and see the department psychiatrist and finish the paperwork on the shooting. We were only on paid administrative for three days, which was way too short before going back to work. We were both still keyed up and had a multitude of emotions after the incident. There were two shooting victims at the club that night that the suspect had shot and left for dead before we confronted him, when he shot at us. He stood over one already shot and lying on the ground, stating, "I'm a gangster, mother fucker" per a witness as he put two more rounds of his .357 Magnum into the victim's body. He was also wearing a knit cap that said "Thug Life." He shot the club manager in the neck as he tried to intercede in the shooting. Both of the shooting victims survived; the shooting suspect did not!

Sex Offender and Fugitive Sweeps: They put these together yearly with multi-jurisdictional teams with City Officers, Deputies, Troopers, and various federal agents. I was looking for a sex offender in Grand Rapids when I exited my patrol car somehow losing my uniform badge off my shirt, not knowing it was missing till later in the shift. I think it snagged on my seatbelt when I got out of the Charger. Oh shit. I call the desk Sergeant to let him know I'm getting ready to write a memo to the Colonel on how my dumb ass lost my badge. The badge has to be put in LEIN as lost or stolen, and it's embarrassing as hell and just a big pain in the ass! At this point I had been on the motors for eight years and never lost my badge, with many a Motor Men losing their badges that would go flying off at high speeds. Not me, I lose mine going to look for sex offenders, go figure. I backtracked and went to one of the houses with an offender's girlfriend answering the door. (Her boyfriend was probably in the house hiding, at this point who gives a shit!) She was disheveled and appeared to be intoxicated/stoned. She walks into the front yard, looks through some leaves, and somehow sees the shiny pin of the badge sticking up, reflecting off the sunlight. "Is this what you're looking for, officer?" "Shazaam, I love you!" She found my badge that was unique to me from Recruit School and had never been worn by anyone else. "1741." I gave her a huge hug and a business card ("get out of jail free" card) to call me if she needed anything. About a month later I got a call from a Grand Rapids officer stating she had arrested her for narcotics possession and the suspect flashed my card. I told him the story about losing my badge, and he laughed. "All right, Bomber. I'll try and help her out." I didn't realize she was going to get jammed up with the law that fast; damn, girl!

Working in law enforcement you come across various people that you wonder, "How in the hell did they pass a psyche test?" We had a Sergeant that was constantly getting into trouble and should have been fired many years earlier. I was on a blocking crash on US-131 when he came up on scene asking what we had, with me telling him we had a blocker. He took his Chevy Tahoe and rammed the vehicle pushing it off on the right shoulder, causing more damage! "What the fuck, Sarge?" "It's not blocking anymore." He then took off down the freeway. Of course we used our push bumpers to move vehicles that run out of gas or are blocking after a crash, but we don't ram the vehicles from the side. He was "cuckoo for cocoa puffs". Later at the end of the shift some of us Troopers were sitting in the squad room when I asked that same sergeant why he took a Troops' newly assigned Tahoe, implying they should be for the Road Dogs first. He took the keys and threw them across the room toward my face. I had to duck to avoid getting hit in the noggin. Here we go again, "What the fuck, Sarge?" I could have ratted him on both instances to higher command, but that's what we do, I just dealt with his stupid ass in the best way I knew. He knew I had worked in Detroit for 10 years and was the post union rep and wasn't going to put up with his shit. He then got in some hot water for falsifying his daily log. We kept daily logs with our activity during each shift so the department could track what we did and tally statistics. He was putting shit on his that didn't jive. He couldn't get in touch with a Sergeant rep to be in the IA hearing with him, so I had to sit in with his ass. I knew he was mental and knew this one could lead to termination if he couldn't justify what he was doing. I made sure to sit sideways to him so I could keep an eye on him and his firearm. I had heard lots of stories about him with Troops saying if anyone had the possibility of going postal, it was him. The hearing went okay with the IA Lieutenant, and boy, was I glad to be done with that one. I had a simple rear end traffic crash in the city of GR with a female looker who got a ticket for rear-ending someone else, pretty simple. She goes to the post to complain about being found at fault and the same dumbass sergeant shreds my ticket and changes my crash report, which is ILLEGAL! I threw a fit, threatening to drop an IA on his ass and force the post commander to deal with him, and I reissued the ticket. There are many other incidents with this dude that he should have been fired for!

Took a family trip to Mackinaw Island in upper Michigan, where we stay at a locally owned Holiday Inn. The kids have little Nintendo hand-held games that we brought to keep them occupied on the long drive up from Rockford. We check into the hotel later at night, planning on hitting the island first thing in the morning. We got up and left the hotel specifically leaving the "Do Not Disturb" sign on the door knob, not needing the beds made or anybody going through the room with my duty weapon in there. I didn't want to bring my gun over to the island, which would be a pain in the ass having that cannon on my hip the whole time riding bikes with the family. We get back to the hotel room after a fun-filled day, when the first thing we notice is the "Do Not Disturb" sign is missing off the door knob. We go inside the room, immediately noticing the beds are still unkept and an obvious sign that someone had shuffled through our shit! I look in my Trooper bag for my SIG Sauer .40, which is still there—huge relief. Then the wife and I notice that the kids Nintendos and game cartridges are missing. The kids, who are around four or five at the time started crying; now I'm pissed! I head downstairs and contact the front desk clerk, who is clueless and keeps stating our room was not on her list to be cleaned. I keep telling her she's correct because I left the sign on the door but one of the employees with a key still went into our room and stole our property. I tell her that I am a State Trooper and asked for a manager because she is like a broken record, going in circles, with me having to keep repeating the situation, which she couldn't comprehend. She advises me that the manager is at another hotel they have and was on her way to ours, so I go outside and sit on a bench, waiting for her to get there. All of a sudden a St. Ignace City cop and Tribal Police cop roll up and confront me aggressively. I advise them I am a Troop and have no weapon on me, it was in the hotel room, not that it was any of their business, just being polite, I guess. Turns out the twit at the front desk calls 911 on me, saying I'm being disorderly! Are you fucking kidding me? Now I'm triple scoop ice cream pissed! I told that stupid bitch at the front desk I was a State Trooper, showed her me ID, and she still called the cops on me. I tell the young City Kitty and Tribal cop they are all set, they can leave; the St. Ignace cop seemed a little put off, which I could give two shits, and the Tribal cop couldn't get in his car and leave fast enough. He didn't want any part of this shit. I call Dispatch and tell them to send a Trooper to the Holiday Inn to take a criminal report for an off-duty Trooper and his family. At first the Dispatch says it's a City of St. Ignace issue, to which I tell her, tuning her up advising her, "I want Troopers here now."

Two Troops roll up, a male and female. Didn't know the female Troop, but I worked with the male troop down in Detroit. "Hey Bomber, how ya been?" "Could be better." I explain the scenario to him, and he advises, "We'll take care of it, sir!" The Troops find out that the cleaning lady was on that floor and also find out the morons from the hotel and local county jail have criminal trustees that leave the jail on weekends and clean this hotel and who knows does what else on work release. Nice, thieve employees being assisted by jail birds? The Troops go to the jail, and the inmate rats out the hotel employee, who lives about an hour into the UP (Upper Peninsula). She didn't want to go in the room but was coaxed by the other female. When asked why they didn't steal the handgun, knowing it was in a bag that said "State Trooper" on it, she said she wanted nothing to do with it. The hotel cleaning lady stole the Nintendos for her kids. They contacted the thief at around 2 a.m. in the morning, retrieved our stolen property, and received a full confession. The City Kitty (St. Ignace cop) would have never obtained our property, shit he couldn't even leave the city limits. He would have turned it over to some lazy detective and blown us off. If you want something done right, have it done by your own peeps—I learned that as a young Troop. The troops brought everything back to the St Ignace State Police Post, where we retrieved it the next morning from a Sergeant I had previously worked a state fair with. I thought about suing the dipshits at the Holiday Inn but figured it wasn't worth my time having to drive back and forth to the UP. Who has jail trustees clean resort hotels? Morons, that's who! Enough said.

In-car cameras? I never had a problem with video and retired before body worn cameras were purchased by the State Police. I had many instances where the video actually saved my ass. One such incident occurred at the Rockford Post while on patrol in a Blue Goose. I stop this young girl in the city of Lowell for not wearing her safety belt. No biggie, small talk during traffic stop. Her first name happened to be Harley. I said, "That's a cool name. I used Harley motorcycles on patrol for the State Police before we switched to BMWs." Issued her the ticket for seatbelt and then cleared the traffic stop uneventfully, or so I thought. About two weeks later I get called into the PCs office prior to an official IA, him stating the young girl came into the State Police Post with her parents claiming I made sexual comments to her during the traffic stop. WTF? I obviously tell the PC that's a bunch of crap. "She claimed that you said, 'Your parents must have had sex on a Harley; that's why they named you that.' I believe you, Bomber, but we can't find your VHS tape from that day." I go into the tape room and luckily find the tape. We throw it in the VCR, and the traffic stop is just as I said it was. She lied to her parents and to the PC to get out of a seatbelt ticket, slandering me and my work ethic. I wasn't happy and demanded that he turn it over to the Prosecutor's Office for her filing a false police report, but it never happened. I then asked if he could call them back to the post with me there so we could confront her as the liar she was. "Well, her dad is an over the road truck driver, and they say he is too busy to come in." Hmmm, he wasn't too busy the first time he brought his lying daughter to the post. Thanks for the support, Lieutenant, I really appreciate it! Thank God for the video that I found that saved my ass that they didn't care to look for. I also was thankful I was in a Blue Goose instead of on my motorcycle because we don't have cameras on our bikes!

A great friend of mine , another troop named Chris, transferred to Rockford from Lansing. He had a bad rap with some troops calling him cocky and arrogant. I give anyone the benefit of the doubt and don't listen to bullshit or prejudge them. He was third generation MSP. His grandpa, grandpa's brother, and dad were all MSP. We both loved working traffic, using slick top patrol cars to be sneaky, and had a blast being Road Dogs. We were working a snow storm together when he took a crash with a hot mother/daughter that ended up needing a ride to the Gerald R. Ford Airport to catch a flight to Mexico. They invited him to go to Mexico with them. He called me on the phone telling me the story. "Bomber, I have this crash on M-6 with a hot mom and daughter and they want me to go Mexico. What should I do?" Chris was single with no kids. I told him in no simpler terms, "Get your ass on a plane and go. If you don't, you'll regret it the rest of your life!" He ended up going, called in sick for two days after using other days he had off, and said he had the best time of his life. That's one of the once-in-a-lifetime opportunities that rarely come up. Chris was also known for pursuing shitheads on motorcycles that liked to wreak havoc on the motoring public. Weaving in and out of traffic, cutting the lanes at 100-plus mph. Oh hell no, not on his watch. I was usually on my motorcycle when he would get in pursuit with reckless crotch rockets and I would show up after he had caught them, having the bikes impounded. Most of the jokers that drive like morons have no cycle endorsement, no insurance on the bikes, and bend their plates up into the rear bumper so they are not visible. I would roll up on bike and bust their balls with their motorcycles getting towed. "So you think you know how to ride a motorcycle, eh?" We thought about getting little motorcycle stickers to put on his front bumpers like fighter pilots did in World War II!

News Article: "State Troopers put Politicians to Shame!" More layoffs proposed in 2009? Jesus Christ, these fucking politicians are a piece of work! Be it Democrat or Republican, they are all self-serving . What happened to doing the right thing for the citizens of Michigan? It's like a tetter-totter when you were a kid. One kid jumps off, letting the thing slam to the ground for an insane ball busting! It's the same with these moron politicians! Let's make troopers reactive instead of proactive again. Hmm, why are traffic fatalities up? Why are there more drunk drivers on the road? Our Troopers union was always at odds with upper command about staffing during my whole career. Again that newspaper article I saw where the Colonel of the New Jersey State Police stated they were to go under water risking the safety of New Jersey citizens if the Road Dog/trooper numbers went under 2,000! Holy shit, that was nearly twice the number of road troopers Michigan had. Obviously, New Jersey had their priorities straight having a roughly 3,000 staffed department with 2000 being troopers. Michigan at the time had roughly the same with just over 3,000 employees and only having just over 1,000 Troopers, the rest being Sergeants, upper command, and civilians! Talk about too many chiefs and not enough Indians! Crazy thing about it is our yearly budget and New Jersey's budget were close to the same. Last time I checked Michigan's geographical/patrol area was slightly bigger than New Jersey's!

Back on mileage restriction again, thanks a lot, Governor Granholm, Jenny on the block. Third time is a charm during her eight years as Governor! We get a memo from the PC, stay positive, budget cuts, etc., blah, blah, blah! What Governor would threaten to lay Troopers off and put us on mileage restrictions, where we can only drive 30 miles per shift? The bean counters in Lansing actually came up with some bullshit formula to determine how many miles each post could use, to save gas. Traffic posts that put more miles on the vehicles per year would be able to use more miles than complaint posts. That makes a lot of sense, not! I brought up the fact that my police motor got way better mileage that a Blue Goose/patrol car or SUV. They just looked at me with the stupid look they always give and said "NO, any other questions, Trooper Bommarito?" Back to one of my favorite quotes, "**The worst form of**

Police corruption is Incompetence." Stupidity stacks up right behind incompetence.

Shortly after our shooting at the nightclub in Grand Rapids, my partner and I received an award for bravery as listed in the news article above, putting one's life in danger to save the lives of others. They had a nice ceremony in Lansing with upper command, the recipients, and their families. Our Sergeant from the night of the shooting was in his own shooting in the Upper Peninnisula, where he smoked a female active shooter that had gone on a killing spree because she was pissed off at someone or something. Just goes to show there are female monsters also! There is a club in Detroit referred to as the "100 Club." It includes prominent business leaders, athletes, and others in the Metro Detroit area that recognize first responders killed in the line of duty and others showing heroism during the performance of their duties. They also give college scholarships to children of first responders killed in the line of duty. If the kids aren't cutting the mustard, they cut their funds off, which is the right thing to do. In fact, one kid who was screwing up was mentioned, with the board voting to eliminate his free ride to college. They sent a clear message, "Appreciate what your parent did for you sacrificing their lives in public service—don't squander it, kid!" This in an "invitation only" club: if you aren't invited, your ass better not show up. We were inducted into the 57th annual ceremony at the Detroit Athletic Club. We were escorted to the function by our Colonel. We all wore suits and not uniforms due to the political climate in Lansing. Prominent radio personalities gave keynote speeches including Paul W. Smith and George Blahah. My partner and I were sitting next to the Director of the State Police with these two men ripping on the Governor, making her look like an idiot! Wow, I guess we know where he stood. The Colonel genuinely laughed right along with us. Good thing we were wearing suits and not uniforms. Another interesting aspect of the club is they announce the honorees, tell the story of our heroism, and give us a nice engraved watch, being honorary members of the "100 Club." We were treated to hors d'oeuvres, filet mignon, spinach salad, and apple streusel pie for dessert. We then socialized with the big wigs, having cognac and cigars. I'm not a smoker, but in this environment you take one for the team. When our story of the shooting was told, everyone started clapping and cheering for what we had done—strange but cool.

"No Two Dicks on the Same Bike." This was one of our motor unit rules. I'm on patrol on my motor at the Rockford Post when I get a call from a Sergeant at the Drive Track in Lansing telling me that two of my fellow Motor Men are taking a test BMW RTP 1200 to the BMW dealership in Lansing to pick up another one. He's laughing as we're talking, telling me to set up in a median on the freeway to get a picture of those fuckers. Hmm, which way are they going to take? I-96 from Lansing to US 131 or jump off at M-6 then back north? What to do? I set up on M-6 on my Harley waiting with my cell phone camera to get of pic of those guys. Damn it, they took a different route than I thought they would. I head over to the BMW dealership with both of them standing there laughing at me when I pull up. "You really thought you were going to get a picture of us on the same bike, you dumbass?" On a sidenote, this was the first sign we were going to transition to BMWs from Harleys, due to the fact that they were picking up another one for the Drive Track to test and evaluate at the Academy.

Car Deer Crashes: I must have taken at least 100 car deer crashes throughout my career. The number of crashes always picked up in the fall before hunting season started. Dispatch would advise of the location and if the deer needed to be killed/dispatched/euthanized or, in other words, put down, to stop their own suffering. We also carried kill deer permits with us to issue to citizens if they wanted to take the deer home and process it for the meat. Anytime we put a deer down, we had to let Dispatch know how shots were fired. If it took more than one shot, other troops would bust your balls about being a shitty shot. I was on my motor in the middle of the US-131 median when a deer had to be put down, with its rear legs being broken. I hit that thing twice in the torso without it going down. I must have looked like an idiot, chasing a wounded deer down the freeway, shooting at it while trying to avoid it running into traffic, causing another crash, while making sure there was no background targets/cars when I shot at the deer. I shot that thing at least five times before it went down. Damn it, the troops are definitely going to bust my balls over this one. Usually the deer are lying there unable to move when you get on scene, which allows you to put one round in the forehead between the eyes for an easy kill. I've heard of Troops in the UP taking car vs. moose and car vs. bear crashes. We've taken car vs. horse and cows also where they get loose from their farms or ranches and wander onto the roadway getting struck by vehicles. There is the very rare car vs. turkey crash. I never took one and can't imagine driving along and having a 40 lb. turkey blast into my window; talk about shitting yourself when that happens.

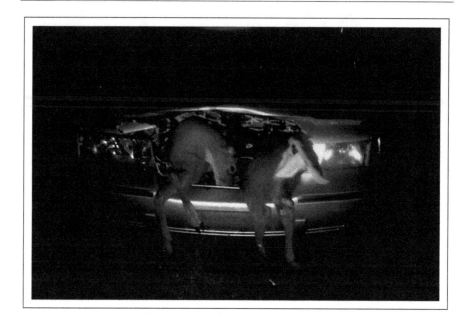

Working as a traffic Trooper for the majority of my career I took a shit load of hit and run crashes. Again, there is no such thing as an accident, they are traffic crashes! This was always one of my pet peeves of shitheads to look for and take aggressive enforcement action on. I was never the victim of a hit and run crash but thought of the victims just driving along and then having some turd run into you and then flee the scene! They are either really drunk, stoned on drugs, suspended, and/or just stupid and unsympathetic! A hit and run crash with no injuries in Michigan is a misdemeanor that carries six points. You lose your driver's license at 12 points. It would be elevated if the crash involved injuries or death. I had probably taken over 1000 hit and run crashes throughout my career. I actually took more in West Michigan than I did in Metro Detroit, which is hard to comprehend. When we were at full staffing we could usually get to the scene before the suspect made it on foot too far, calling a K-9 for a track if their car was not drivable. If their car was drivable, it was even better because we would track down their location from the license plate if obtained and then tow their shit when we found them, basically holding their vehicle for hostage until they came clean. Toward the end of my career, a memo came down from the Legal Department in Lansing saying we couldn't tow their cars anymore as collateral. One more tool they took out of our tool bag, the dickweeds in Lansing. A lot of time they would flag down a car and catch a ride or call a friend to pick them up with their cell phones. We would have extra patrol cars float around the area, looking for suspicious vehicles that might pick up the perps on foot.

As time went on and we were depleted with less and less troopers, it became harder to catch the hit and run drivers. We would have to try and track them down later after cleaning up the crash scene, not having extra bodies to cover the crash and looking for the shithead. This was a problem, especially if the suspect was drunk, giving them time to sober up. It got to the point at the end of my career we had no people working down to minimal staffing, where follow-up might not even occur on the same day, which sucks. If I had enough probable cause, I could try and contact them for an interview, which at times was really hard because they go out of their way to avoid you. I would leave as many appearance tickets for them with a family member as possible and put the onus on them to prove they weren't the hit and run driver. I had a Sergeant at the Rockford Post that had worked on a drug team for years and came to uniform for his next promotion up busting my balls about leaving tickets in a suspect's door. Come to find out the suspect I left the tickets for was the driver and paid his tickets not wanting to go to jail. I never issued tickets where the suspect went to trial and never lost a trial on a hit and run crash. Come on, dude (the Newbie Sergeant), I've worked traffic my whole career. Don't tell me how to do my job, Skippy! He was at the post for less than a year and then moved up the ladder like a nice little kiss ass!

We had motorcycles in Metro Detroit, Lansing, Jackson, and Rockford. We were allowed two or four hours a pay period, every two weeks, to detail/clean our motorcycles. Well, it turns out that one of the Motor

Men on the east side decided to wash his motorcycle naked where his female neighbor could see him. Are you fucking kidding me? What a dumbass! He was suspended and immediately removed from the Motor Unit, thank god! Most of our guys had impeccable integrity and worked hard representing the unit, except for him. Bad apples everywhere, but why this shit. Wash your car or your wife's naked to impress your neighbor, not a State Police Motorcycle.

Morons interfering with traffic stops, does this really happen? Yes, it does. We were doing a multi-agency "Click it or ticket" detail when some asshole pulls up to a spotter/Lieutenant from a local department and starts yelling at him, getting out of his vehicle. Hell no, at least four of us head his way and ended up arresting this drunk asshole for OWI and interfering with a police officer. When you look at the amount of traffic stops I made in the thousands, this would be very rare but does happen. You pull somebody over, some dipshit will drive by and rev their engine or yell something out the window at you trying to distract you. I stopped a couple guys in a pickup on US-131 near Market Ave. in Grand Rapids for not wearing their seatbelts. They were a couple of construction dudes wearing neon shirts, which made it easy to spot the belt violation. They happened to pull over in a gas station parking lot right off the freeway. I exited my Blue Goose making contact with them. I also happened to have a female college intern doing a ride-along with me. I'm talking to them when this schmo comes out of the gas station, interfering with my traffic stop, demanding I move my patrol car. At first I thought this guy is obviously joking! He's not, so I tell him to go back in the gas station and not worry about what I'm doing. I kick the two guys loose with warnings for the seatbelt violations and tell my college intern to stay in the patrol car. I proceeded to go into the gas station and dress down this guy in front of his customers. I noticed the car this clerk had driven to work, running the plate and seeing he had multiple suspensions and appeared to not like the police all that much from his driving record. A few months later I happen to see this dude driving by, not wearing his seatbelt, while on patrol. I drop in behind him, running the plate again, showing him suspended. I stopped him and arrested him for DWLS (driving while license suspended) and towed his car. He was also delivering food for a local restaurant. I had to call his manager to pick the food up. Wham, bam, one in custody, Dispatch, send me a tow truck for a suspended driver. I know what this is all about. Ya you're a dumbass that needs to wear his seatbelt and not drive without a license, especially delivering food!

I was on patrol in Kent County on afternoons on my Harley when Dispatch advised Ionia troops in the next post over to the east were in pursuit of armed robbery suspects heading west toward Kent County. Well, shit, we have a no-pursuit policy on the motors, so what to do? I call one of my Trooper buddies in a Blue Goose and tell him to pick me up at the gas station on 10 mile. I pull my bike up to the door and tell the gas station clerk to keep an eye on my motor; since we don't have keys to them, someone could swipe it. I jump in the Goose with the straight leg Troop and off to the races we go to get into that pursuit. I tell a Troop acting-Sergeant at the post (that I had seniority on) over the radio, "Hey, I dropped my bike at the gas station on 10 mile to jump in a car and get in that pursuit." Silence over the radio, he doesn't know what to say, but I know he was thinking, "Oh shit, what do you mean you dropped your bike?" "Have faith, I'm me, fellow Trooper, I know what I'm doing." There were many times during my 15 years on the bikes that I boogied ass back to the post to get in a patrol car to stop or assist with a pursuit. Most of the time for deadly force situations, carjackings, murder, armed robbery, kidnapping, etc. Well, we weren't needed; the Ionia troops caught the RA suspects after they crashed out. No harm, no foul.

GRPD contact some dude in a church parking lot, turns out to be a doper meth head, drags one of the officers across the parking lot, and peels off into a nearby subdivision. They won't let them pursue the shithead!? I am close on my police motor, so I boogey back to the post and jump in a Charger. I cruise to the subdivision, knowing he's hunkered down. I drive right by the asshole, we look each other in the eye, chase is on. I try to pit him out before he leaves the sub, spinning around and then chased him back where he crashes into a stop sign. I jump out of the Goose and go hand on with him, when the fight's on. One arm here, punch at me there, we go down on the ground, and then my savior arrives. A little old lady came into the street hitting shithead with her broom, bam, wham, he quits fighting and gets placed into custody and then off to jail. Put that little old lady in for an award!

Various acronyms and quotes that you learn in the military and law enforcement—here are but a few. FUBAR: Fucked up beyond all recognition, FIBIFY: Fuck it before it fucks you, FNG: Fucking new guy, ESR: Eat, sleep and repeat. My fave: "The worst form of police corruption is **incompetence,**" "If they give you sugar, treat them nice; if they're an asshole, give them spice," "If you looking for sympathy, look between 'shit' and 'syphillis' in the dictionary," "Same shit, different shovel," TOT: Turned over to, "Trooper lane, Trooper speed!" "Mess with the bull, get the horns!" "Don't start no shit, won't be no shit!" NFA: No fun allowed.

Hot as balls summer day in the mid-90s. I'm at the BMW dealership in Wyoming looking at the RTP 1200 police bikes when a customer flags me down and says there appears to be a vehicle fire at an industrial complex behind the building. I call it in to Dispatch to send Wyoming Fire. I roll up on my State Police Harley seeing a compact car backed into a row of hedges. There are a couple of employees standing around, looking, so I tell them to go into the business and grab a couple of fire extinguishers, no space for one on my police motor. At this point the car is fully engulfed in flames. Wyoming Fire arrives on scene. They get the fire extinguished and wave us over with a glazed look on their face. "Hey, Trooper, there is a body behind the wheel." "What the fuck?" The Wyoming officer and I go over to the car. Sure as shit, there is a dead body in the driver's seat. Turns out an older woman in her 80s had got lost, backed her car into the hedges trying to turn around, and possibly had a heart attack. The heat from the exhaust caught the hedge on fire and subsequently her car. Weird thing was the car was not running when I got there? I jump on my Harley and tell my Dispatch I'll be clear. TOT Wyoming Police and Fire, I'm out.

Neon yellow traffic safety vests? For the first 15 years I was in the State Police we never wore traffic safety vests. Some department somewhere, maybe over in the UK even, started the trend that spread like wild fire. Anytime we were on a traffic detail and working an outdoor function we had to wear those stupid vests. Of course ours had to say "State Police" on them. They tested three different types in the field before picking one for the entire department. I was on scene at one critical incident/shooting when the District Captain showed up, saw me wearing the vest, and asked me, "Bomber, what are you doing wearing that stupid vest?" "Uhhh, sir, I was told to wear it while performing traffic duties." "That doesn't apply here, take that stupid thing off." "Sir, yes sir." We would come to use the vests at most details, NASCAR races, classic car cruises, festivals, etc.

Piss tests (urinalysis)? Our Troopers Association in its infinite wisdom in one of the contract talks decided to allow the State of Michigan and department to perform random piss tests on its members. I thought this was crossing a fine line of violating our rights. If you have some turd that clearly has a drinking or drug problem, hell ya, give them a test! But to randomly do it was bullshit. Of course I had to take three of these stupid "random" tests in my last five years in the State Police. All came back negative of course, but the first time I was actually working the road when they called me on the radio advising to report to some urgent care clinic. I had to go in uniform to some clinic with civilians and sit there again in uniform. How fucking embarrassing. I busted my ass to become a Michigan State Trooper. Never again, the next two tests I was randomly picked for I told my post commander I will not go again in uniform, fuck that! I made sure to go in civilian clothing. Thanks for nothing to our Troopers Association/union throwing its members under the bus. When we were in Recruit School we had a Sergeant who was arrested for drunk driving while in uniform in a Goose come talk to us about his problem. Fuck him, his stupid ass should have been fired! Whenever a department member would get popped for drunk driving we would refer to his name again and again.

Budgets: "Police Work Cost Money." No shit! At the start of my career with the Michigan State Police, budgets were not an issue. We had a Republican Governor who saw the big picture and built us to some of the highest numbers of road Troopers our department and state ever had. Our department was one of the only ones that generated monies for the state. If I write a $150 speeding ticket, which I wrote a ton of over my career, that generates money in fines and court costs for the state and lower jurisdictions depending on which court you're in. Our yearly budget ran from October 1 till September 30. At the start of September every year under Engler we would basically have unlimited overtime. Work as much as you want, we have a ton of money to get rid of. If we don't use our assigned funds, we might lose them next year! Our interdiction teams, especially in Detroit and the 5th District, which covered the I-94 pipeline between Chicago and Detroit, always had large seizures of drugs and high-dollar amounts of drug money sometimes ranging from $100K to $500K. The biggest sucking vacuum of state funds was the Department of Social Services, which doled out welfare with Bridge Card and other social programs. I am not against giving a hand up, but I am totally against free handouts. My parents divorced when I was a young kid, around five years old. My mother was on food stamps until she could get on her feet. My dad paid very little child support and was a cheap ass most of the time. Unlimited social welfare programs are not sustainable at the taxpayers' expense. When Governor Engler left office and Jenny on the block took his place she cut our budget and put us at the bottom of the barrel as far as priorities go. The state had plenty of money left over with a budget surplus, but the State Police budget was not a priority for her. Mileage restrictions three times, banked leave time, trooper layoffs, etc.

"Bikes on the Bricks" held in Flint, Michigan. We sent most of our motor unit; over the 15 years on the bikes I probably only went three times. I had never been a big fan of driving around slow cones and over two-by-four boards having a 1000 lb. Harley Davidson motorcycle fall on my ass! It was a cool experience having motor officers from all over the state show up and even some outstate dudes. Some Louisiana State Troopers came up, not sure what the Michigan contact was, but it was still cool having them there. It was a three-day event that we called a "Motor Refresher," so departments would pay for expenses and let you ride on duty time. Hmm, kind of a scam, but will take it. For all the details and shit weather, we rode in on regular patrol, and during motorcades it was nice and the higher-ups in Lansing throw us a bone. What to do at night in Flint? Not much, let's go drinking. Flint PD actually had a party bus set up to take us bar-hopping, so we didn't have to drive; probably a good thing because most of us got our liquor on and stayed out way too late, having to do slow cones the next morning. Most of the slow cone exercises were the same that we've done for years from the "Northwestern Course." The key hole, intersection, bump and go, etc. The main parking lot for the exercises was paved good, and the other lot sucked balls with lots of cracks and uneven pavement. I guess trying to do the exercises under shitty conditions makes you a better rider? The best riders would compete at the end for first place, and I was **never** one of those best riders. I knew my limitations and rode within them.

Traffic stops and tickets were primarily what I dealt with on a daily basis working out of Metro/Traffic Posts. Thats what Lansing wanted us to do, keep the motoring public safe, so I did my damndest to oblige! They wanted us to write at least one ticket per patrol hour, but then they changed it to one contact per patrol hour. We had troops at the Rockford Post that were lazy as fuck, would sit in the median and wait to be dispatched to traffic crashes. I took the stance that I work for the citizens, and they deserve an honest day's work for an honest day's pay! I learned my work ethic from my Recruit School Trooper, later Sergeant at Jonesville, which ironically was all complaint/investigative work, very little traffic. We had a small two-mile stretch of US-127 near the Jackson County line of freeway. Other than that, it was all M-Roads, US-12, M-99, county two-lane hard-ball roads, and a lot of dirt roads. If the speed limit wasn't marked, it was 55 mph unless in a residential area/subdivision. I actually did try and work a lot of traffic at Jonesville when not taking complaints, which was challenging.

Dispatch? Hmm, where do I start? I guess I could have written about Dispatch when I first became a State Trooper at the Jonesville Post, or when I worked in the Metro; nah, I'll wait till I am at my last post, Rockford, to talk about all three work sites. When you see a car that has a bumper sticker that reads, "Dispatch—We tell Cops where to go" with a donut on it should say it all. The Jonesville Post had a central-ized civilian Dispatch with a civilian administrator that had just started right before I arrived there. Prior to this, the state would have a civilian dispatcher at the post or desk sergeant dispatch troops to calls. The Hillsdale County Sheriff's Department would do the same and have deputies or dispatchers send their Deps. to calls. Hillsdale city and other small cities would be dispatched by either the state or county. It was done like this for years with half the time one department didn't know what the other one was doing and vice versa! This was probably the worst way to dispatch resources for a small county. The newly opened Central Dispatch allowed all Police, Fire, and EMS to be dispatched by the same dispatchers. They would put out a call in different parts of the county with some deputies or troops not answering up because they were lazy or didn't want to be bothered taking certain calls. "State and County Cars for a call in Camden Township." Crickets could be heard chirping on the radio. Camden Township was one of the shitty good ol' boy areas with a lot of CSCs and bullshit calls. The senior troops and Deps. didn't want to be bothered. Dispatch finally wised up and asked cars on patrol for their location. "State car 19-07, what's your location?" "County Car 41-08, your location." Ha, got you, you sons a bitches. It forced them to give their location before the call, and then Dispatch would send the closest car. I was forced to midnights with a senior troop when I was at Jonesville. We would go to Central Dispatch for an hour, hour and a half periodically. Come to find out the senior troop was banging one of the dispatchers, and I had to be called as a witness when they busted his ass. I would hang with the other dispatchers and as a cub, kept my mouth shut until called in on the carpet. "Trooper Bommarito, your are being interviewed as a witness and not a primary subject." Fuck, I only had a year in and didn't want spotlights on me. The Metro and Rockford dispatchers were the same, most were competent, some not. Call out your stops, don't call out your stops?

News Article: "Cop Makes the Call on Texting Teen." Should read "Trooper," whatever; most reporters don't know the difference or care! The first day that Michigan's new "Texting while driving" law came into effect I just happened to be working on my Electra Glide in blue. I look over to the right of me on a nice July afternoon and see a young kid wearing a cookie monster hat looking down at his cell phone, texting. I gave him to the count of five and then said, okay, that's long enough; here's my first stop for the new "Texting while driving" law. I turn on the police lights on the Harley, then blurp my siren to get his attention. I contact this young man who was 16 and a new driver, and he admitted texting. He could not produce a valid driver's license, so I have him step from the vehicle and sit on the curb while I run some file checks on him. He did come back valid with the name he gave me, so I wrote him the $150 ticket for texting and issued a dismissable ticket for not having his license on his person. "Me give Cookie Monster" two cookies (tickets) for his troubles. Next thing I know I get a call from Dispatch saying to call the post. Oh shit, what now? It appears I was the first law enforcement officer in West Michigan to write the new texting ticket to a motorist and one of the local TV stations wants to interview me and do a news story on it later! Really? Okay, I guess. The young man's parents weren't too happy about having to pay for the $150 ticket, hoping he learned his lesson.

No motorcycles in February in Michigan, lots of snow. The Motor Men would just patrol in cars from December 1 through April 1. My motor partner and I happened to be working on afternoons in patrol cars with our post K-9 as the other car in the post area. That makes three troopers in all of Kent County. Our K-9 handler goes home sick, shit happens. My motor partner and I double up to a two-man car per the contract and for officer safety. The desk Sergeant, who happens to be out of my Recruit School, calls us on the radio, inquiring what we are doing. Being a former district rep with him in the same Association, I remind him that per the MSTPA contract if we have less than three Troopers working in the post area after dark, we are allowed to double up on patrol. He knows this well yet still decided to be an asshole, questioning what we were doing. We come into the post at the end of the shift and see someone wrote on the dry erase board, "Please leave the lights on,

Troopers are afraid of the dark!" I had been in shooting a year prior and thought to myself, "I'm afraid of the dark" "Fuck you, Sarge, classmate!" I didn't get promoted to desk Sergeant as fast as possible to get off the road; who's afraid? He also had the gall to compare us to deputies and city officers with my response being the Sheriff's Department is putting out 20 cars across the county and the City of Grand Rapids has around 40 officers covering the city during most shifts. We have **two** Troopers working in the entire County of Kent, and you're going to bust our balls about doubling up and being afraid of the dark? Fuck off! I wrote a memorandum to the PC concerning the incident that ended up biting us in the ass in the spring when we got back on our motors. He turned it on us, saying if we didn't have minimum staffing to his liking, we couldn't ride our bikes. We knew where we stood with him, he didn't do the right thing talking to his Sergeant but played games later on. What a sign of a shitty leader! My Motor Lieutenant from the east side would have went toe to toe with the PC and threatened to pull the bikes from Rockford, but I figured I'm a big boy, I can fight this battle on my own. My motor Lt. was a little peeved I didn't keep him in the loop and the trickery from the post Lt. Oh well, you live and learn. I learned that my PC had integrity issues and was an administrator, not a leader!

Livonia Police Officer Larry Nehasil, 48 years, old killed in the line of duty trying to apprehend two brothers wanted in connection with several home invasions. They were conducting surveillance on the two brothers inside a fresh home invasion, when one of the brothers ran out the back door of the house. Officer Nehasil took off after him with a gunfight ensuing during the foot pursuit. Both the suspect and Officer Nehasil exchanged gunfire, with both dying from their wounds. My old Partner, Topher was really close to Larry, working a detail with him. We attended the funeral and paid our respect to the hero that gave his life to keep these two shithead brothers from victimizing anyone else. Rest in peace, Officer Nehasil.

Trooper Jeffrey Werda, 43 years old, killed in the line of duty in a single-car crash while responding to a pursuit Saginaw County deputies were involved in. Jeff was my friend and a Great Troop. We worked many details in Detroit together and kind of had the same personality. He bitched about command and the stupid shit they do but still did his job to the best of his ability. His father-in-law was a retired Troop, and his two brothers-in-law were both Troopers. His wife was the daughter and sister to them. His death was definitely a hard-hitting blow to the MSP family. He was working single-officer patrol at approximately 1:00 a.m. when he went lights and sirens to back up the deputies. Word is he came around a blind corner with a posted deer crossing and swerved to avoid the deer, leaving the roadway, rolling his patrol car over in a ditch, and getting partially ejected from not wearing his seatbelt. I always think if he had a partner with him, which was his right and call, maybe the partner would tell him, "Hey, Jeff, slow down around this curve," or "Hey, Jeff, put your seatbelt on." I escorted his body as part of the motor unit, and this was a tough one. Jeff, we miss your witty personality and think about you often. Rest in peace, brother, Trooper Werda!

Officer Eric Zapata, 35 years old, shot and killed in the line of duty responding to a call of shots fired. He and another officer had responded to the call when a man standing on his porch pulled out a handgun and opened fire on the officer. The man then fled between houses and ran into Officer Zapata, and they exchanged gunfire, with Officer Zapata being shot in the chest and head, being fatally wounded at the scene. The coward that killed Officer Zapata then committed suicide. I assisted the Kalamazoo Department of Public Safety with the funeral detail on the MSP Motors. Strange feeling doing the detail where I went to college at Western Michigan University. I ended up meeting Officer Zapata's son years later at a gun range in Grand Rapids, of all places. Nice kid, I gave him one of my Troop business cards and told him if he ever needed anything to give me a call. Rest in peace, Officer Zapata!

Semitruck full of cattle rolls over on midnight in the Rockford Post area. A two-man car with a female Troop and male Troop respond to the scene. Some of the cows have to be put down due to being injured too badly in the crash. The female Troop doesn't have the heart to shoot the cows, so instead of having her partner do it she hands a Michigan State Police–issued shotgun to the truck driver to dispatch the cattle. Holy shit! Was her partner surprised! Hmm, what if the civilian she gave her shotgun to wigged out and smoked the two Troops? Remind me never to work with her on midnights!

Every year we have performance appraisals issued around our anniversary date when we came in the State Police listing our performance as a Trooper, where we are excelling and where we might need improvement, etc. It took me sixteen years to receive an "**Outstanding**" on my appraisal mainly due to the arrival of the "E" Electronic tickets/citations. We could now print those on our in-car computers or on a little tablet we used on the motorcycles. I was always downgraded for my penmanship being hard to read, but now with the E tickets, peeps could read my tickets thanks to technology. The commendation from 6th District HQ read as follows: "Congratulations on receiving an outstanding performance appraisal. Receiving 'high performing' in all rated competencies is something to be proud of and demonstrates your character through your actions."

On my MSP motor headed to funeral of retired Sergeant's/dispatcher's father that had passed away. There were three other Troopers in patrol cars that were with me rolling on I-96. We pass the Alpine exit in the city of Walker when one of the Troops in a car says there was a fresh stabbing at the Motel 6, which is just off the freeway exit. We hit the next turn around and haul ass to the motel, arriving the same time Walker PD units arrive. I look to the top of the walkway/overhang and see blood dripping down to the lower level. We immediately run upstairs and see a large white male lying on the walkway. He had been slit open from the center of his chest down and around though his belly. His eyes were glazed over, and he had no pulse, which told me he was dead. A Walker officer (whose own funeral I would be at shortly after this) was putting on medical gloves to do CPR, and I told him, "His chest is ripped open, you can't do CPR on him, he's gone." We covered him with a blanket from a motel room and proceeded to look for the monster that did this to this poor guy. The Monster was described as a white male that some knew as being homeless. We got a name on this turd. We canvassed the area, unable to locate him. He supposedly got on a bus just after the gutting/murder occurred. The victim was a big burly, married, family man from Indianapolis, Indiana. He was staying at the Motel 6 while in town as a cable contractor working in Michigan. Further investigation revealed that the two men had words over him being loud and obnoxious on the lower level, harassing other people. The suspect went upstairs, pulled out a large fishing-style filet knife, and gut him like a pig. I have seen a lot of death and callousness throughout my career, with this incident being one at the top. One of our state police K-9s was doing a search, looking for this monster in a local homeless camp near the freeway when he tripped and accidentally shot his own police dog with his shotgun. We heard the shot fired and thought, "Shit, he got him" until he came running out of the woods carrying his police dog in his arms. I gave him and his K-9 police dog an emergency escort to a veterinary clinic nearby; what a fucked-up day in the life of a Trooper! We never made it to the funeral service for the Sergeant's father. The Monster was picked up out of state, extradited back to Michigan, receiving 40–80 years in state prison. He will never see the light of day again.

CHAPTER 10: THE GREAT RE-ORG!

2011 ROLLS AROUND, and we were finally set free from the Canadian Granholm running the State, thank God! Things are starting to look positive, the US and state economy are turning around from the 2008 recession. Rick Snyder, the self-proclaimed nerd, becomes Governor and decides that because four out of the 10 most violent cities in the U.S. are in Michigan, he is going to send State Troopers into those cities to try and reduce crime. The higher-ups in Lansing call this the "SCP–Safe Cities Partnership" initiative and decided to pull the trigger on this idea. Good idea, but wrong implementation. Okay, Michigan has four out of the top 10 most violent cities in America—Detroit, Pontiac, Flint, and Saginaw. If you were born and raised in Detroit or somewhere else in Michigan, not a big surprise! The Gov. and our first female Director of the State Police decide to send Troopers into these cities, which is a great idea, but does it with staffing that is ridiculously low. Then on top of it, you're robbing the rest of the state, especially in rural areas, to send Troops to those four cities. They claimed to run Trooper Recruit Schools to covers the numbers, not mentioning that many Troopers were retiring at the same time! When the Benton Harbor riots kicked off in the the 90s, more than a hundred Troopers were mobilized and sent to quell the shitheads wreaking havoc in the much smaller city of Benton Harbor than the other four most violent cities. Then you have to make sure the Troopers are in two-man cars for officer safety because they are dealing with mainly shitheads that don't want to be dealt with. The numbers sent to patrol these "safe cities" was a joke. You put a couple two-man cars in Detroit in a Blue Goose with the red bubble on top, and all of a sudden, crime is going to drastically reduce? Case in point, I'll use a military analogy since I was in the Cavalry, when you declare war on an opponent you send in overwhelming forces to strike with shock and awe. You stop everything that moves, you take every turd to jail that asks to go to jail, etc. That was not done, they tried putting a Band-Aid on four dams (Detroit, Pontiac, Flint, and Saginaw) that were getting ready to explode. The Governor was trying to say he was reducing crime in those four cities without doing what really needed to be done, smoke and mirrors. It would be like sending your kids into a candy store and telling them they can only get sugar-free candy. WTF, Governor?

New Governor means a new Director of the State Police, time for a new reorganization of the State Police. Here we go again, what stupid ideas are they going to come up with now? Every time there is a regime change they try and reinvent the wheel when it doesn't need to be reinvented? "Look what I've accomplished." The economy turned around after the 2008 recession. More tax revenue coming into the coffers. Our new Director decided to close half the State Police posts across the state turning them into detachments to save money and only stay open during banking business hours Monday through Friday 8 a.m.–5 p.m. leaving a desk Sergeant at the post to answer phones and command to do whatever they do. They had after-hour emergency phones at the front of the post for night and weekends! Are you fucking kidding me? Case in point domestic assault in front of the post at midnight while a female victim is getting her assed kicked if she can even make it to the phone to call a Trooper back to the post, who could be one mile or 30 miles away! They closed the Grand Haven Post, making it a detachment of the Rockford Post, which was stupid enough. Grand Haven should have been a detachment of the Hart Post, which was closer. Now we also had a mass transfer policy that came along with closures allowing Senior Troops from around the state to transfer to other posts and bump junior Troops to other posts! Who were the morons in Lansing that came up with this plan? The ones that get paid the big bucks! Back to one of my favorite quotes that I quote throughout the book, "The worst form of Police Corruption is **Incompetence!**"

More car-deer crashes. I took a lot of car-deer crashes at the Jonesville Post, not so many at Metro. Car dogs, mainly pitbulls, the official dog of Hood Rats in Detroit, more than car-deer crashes. Rockford was a combination of Jonesville and Metro, a great place to work with Grand Rapids (having Hood Rats) being the second largest city in Michigan and out Kent County being rural, with lots of Wood Ticks out in the country. The car-deer crashes in Rockford were sometimes obliteration like something you'd see in a horror movie. We took a car-deer crash on US-131 at the south end of the county, where a deer darted into the side of a small SUV. The deer basically exploded inside, covering a young couple with guts, feces, and deer piss. I was the 2nd Troop on scene after one of my afternoon partners beat me to the crash. Holy shit, I couldn't believe my eyes. The deer exploded on impact in the interior. We gave the couple emergency blankets and a ton of hand gel to try to clean up. There was no immediate clean up of this mess. The young lady was crying, and I didn't blame her. If I were her boyfriend, I would be crying also. I was on my motor, and Dispatch advised there was another deer that was struck but still alive running in and out of traffic on US-131 near 10 mile. I found the deer, pulled over on the median side on my motor, and tried to approach the deer to put down before she took off on me. If we do have to dispatch (kill) the deer, we have to let Dispatch know how many shots we fired and with what weapon. I took one shot at her with my SIG and missed. She ran across the freeway and jumped a fence. No more shots by me, especially with traffic driving by on the freeway. Can you imagine trying to dispatch a deer and hitting a citizen in a vehicle driving by? Not this Trooper!

Being a union representative is like being a defense attorney. I have to represent my members, Troopers, and Sergeants to the best of my ability. Only problem is when you have staffing issues with post command and the assistant post commander and MSPTA vice president teaching Recruit Schools together and are long-lost buddies, that poses a problem. Little did I know this until I was getting cock-blocked by that vice president who was giving the Lt. information to circumvent me and issues he didn't feel were all that important. I actually Trooped with him at the Jonesville Post and thought we had a good rapport. Silly me to be so naive. We had three counties in West Michigan that the Rockford Post patrolled: Kent, Ottawa, and Muskegon. Minimum staffing per the contract was at least four troopers for the three counties, which is still ridiculously low! You would think that the lieutenant would want as many troopers working for officer safety as he could provide, not! "Well you know, Bomber, since we technically don't patrol or take calls in Ottawa County, it doesn't count for staffing." Okay, Noob, let's go with that, and I'll file a grievance on your ass faster than your head can spin! He knew he was wrong and would lose a grievance looking like a dipshit to higher command in Lansing maybe stifling his rise up the promotion ladder, so he intelligently backed off.

Ferris State University, home of the Bull Dogs, is about an hour north of Rockford. The university has been known for having a strong criminal justice program for years. They run a police academy recognized by MLEOTC/MCOLES, graduating certified police officers. Turns out they had patrol cars that resembled our MSP Blue Gooses, same color, which back in the day would not be allowed. A group of the students decided to after class take some of the MSP look-alike patrol cars off campus and initiate fake traffic stops on local citizens. They got caught and hopefully got kicked out of school and charged with impersonating a police officer. You're not cops yet, dumbasses! MCOLES, which sets the standards for Michigan law enforcement, decides that no off-campus traffic stops for training can be made anymore. We did that with Blue Gooses during my recruit school and during Motor School on the freeway system surrounding the capital in Lansing. Staff were in unmarked cars with us initiating traffic stops on them on high curbs and high-traffic areas for an accurate learning experience. All future MSP and other Academies had to conduct this training on the Drive Track or other private property area thanks to the dickheads at Ferris and Morons at MCOLES.

I am a huge University of Michigan fan growing up on the east side, "Go Blue!" I stop a guy for speeding in Grand Rapids for doing 20 mph over the limit. No biggie, he's a cool dude, so I write him a 5 mph over ticket, which carries no points on the freeway. He had a badass license plate U of M vanity with the "Megatron." I also told him his plate was sweet and I was a big U of M fan. About a year later, a desk sergeant calls me on the radio when I'm on patrol and tells me a citizen dropped off a license plate to the post for me to have. I go into the post at the end of my shift and that "Megatron" plate is sitting there waiting for me. Wow, what a surprise, took the plate home, and it's still hanging in my garage to this day. I wrote the guy a five-over ticket, and he took the time when that plate expired to drop off to a State Trooper that liked his plate; great positive contact on a traffic stop even with enforcement action taken!

Walker Police Officer Trevor Slot killed in the line of duty, 41 years old. The Fee-bees (FBI) were following/tracking two bank robbery suspects as they robbed the Ravenna Bank in Muskegon County. They let them rob the bank and never engaged them coming out, hmmm, were we afraid, Fee-bees? Trevor was killed assisting State Police Troopers with a pursuit of armed bank robbery suspects in a rolling gun battle when he attempted to deploy "Stop Sticks." The suspects ran him down at over 100 mph outside of his patrol vehicle. They obliterated Trevor, crashing in a ditch as a result of losing control when they murdered him. They then exited their SUV and engaged in a close-proximity gunfight with three Hero Trooper friends of mine. By the grace of God, the shitheads lost the gunfight, both being fatally wounded during the gunfight. Trevor was a court officer at the 59th District Court in Walker. He left the court when he heard that Troopers were in a pursuit with these shitheads shooting at the troopers pursuing. He decided to get ahead of the pursuit and deploy those stop sticks. I never deployed stop sticks during high-speed dangerous pursuits, especially one with the suspects shooting at the police, trying to stop them from pursuing. That's as desperate as it gets for them trying to get away. I learned that from working in Detroit and seeing too many cops intentionally run down by turds trying to get away. I used them once in Detroit, where we drove up alongside a slow drunk and threw them from the passenger window in front of the drunk's car; didn't work, so never used them again because they are way too dangerous. Trevor or any other officer would have been justified to use deadly force by shooting at those dudes with a rifle when they drove by. I had seen Trevor at court on various occasions and was at the Motel 6 when that contractor was gutted. Trevor was a great guy that didn't deserve to die like that, being run down like a dog. I had the honor of escorting Trevor along with other motor officers at his funeral. On another sidenote, Trevor's wife had stage 4 cancer and died shortly after her husband was murdered, leaving two young daughters with no parents. Rest in peace, Officer Slot!

News Article: "MSP Rockford Troopers Receive Bravery Award." The 3 troops that engaged those monsters in a rolling gunfight and close-quarter gunfight that mowed down Officer Trevor Slot and 2 other Troops involved in the pursuit were recognized in Lansing for their bravery on September 13, 2011. Great job, Troops, We're damn proud of you Boys!

Working afternoons toward the end of the shift during winter off the motors when I was dispatched to a car-vs.-pedestrian crash on I-96 W/B near Cascade Rd. I arrive on scene and see a body lying face down in the right lane of travel. I shut down the lane and call for a couple more cars for traffic. I checked on who appeared to be a white male in his mid-30s. One of his legs was missing, and he was clearly deceased. I covered his body with an emergency blanket and called for an accident investigator and the Medical Examiner's Office. I look on the ground and see a baseball card that I assumed belonged to his young son, boy with same last name, which it was. Damn it, what the hell happened here? Gentleman that hit him felt horrible as anyone would. He said he was going on vacation and asked if he should cancel. Hell, no, I told him. Go on your vacation and get away for a while. Turns out the victim went out celebrating with his work buddies bar hopping some local pubs on Michigan Ave. in Grand Rapids. He was a salesman and closed some big million-dollar deal. His buddies throw him in a cab to take him home. I track down the cab driver later on, and he says, "Yup, he was blasted!" I tried to take him home but he wouldn't listen and actually jumped out of my cab running away on foot on Cascade Rd. He ran onto the freeway, where he was struck by the car. It was after dark, and he had mostly dark clothing on him. I had to interview his wife, which sucked, and she stated he did have a drinking problem. Even more sucky, she said she was on the phone with him when he was struck. He kept telling her I see lights coming at me! Sliding doors, maybe the buddies should have called his wife to pick him up?

We transitioned to BMW RTP 1200 police motorcycles from the Harley Davidson Electra Glides in 2012. The BMWs were much lighter and faster than the Harleys. I resisted at first because the Harleys finally had the ABS (antilock braking system) that most other motorcycle manufactures had for years. Harley beefed up the engine with a little more speed and put a badass-sounding exhaust on the Electra Glides. I started the motor unit in 2002 riding a piece of shit 2000 Harley that had basic strobe lights and a stator problem that shut the bike down randomly, needing to be towed. The Harleys were also heavy, weighing over 1000 lbs. with the rider on board. I resisted the Beemers at first, then once I transitioned, I did not want to go back to a Harley. The BMWs were definitely Bad Aspirin!

We carried M-4 rifles and Remington 870 .12-gauge shotguns in our patrol cars, so why not put a rifle or shotgun on the BMW? Michigan State University had M-4 rifles on their Campus Police bikes. BMW actually made a mount to go on the bikes. The post commander had put out an email asking if anyone needed equipment, so I asked for a rifle mount for my BMW. The BMW dealership in Wyoming installed it, I put my rifle on, and was on patrol with it for three days or so when some dink in Lansing found out and threw a fit. The inspector in charge of equipment authorization was pissed because he wasn't in the loop. Then the Drive Track guys in Lansing find out about it and pick my motor up to run over to Lansing for testing and a demo for the Executive Council (director and Lt. colonels). They thought the rifle looked too intimidating on the motor and had the Drive Track remove it. Are you fucking kidding me? I was so pissed, almost quitting the unit because of their ineptness at decision-making. At the time we had no gun mounts in our patrol cars. I would take a .12 gauge and rifle on patrol and leave in the long gun bags when some schmo could break the window and steal one of my long guns. The M-4 motor mount had a locking mechanism on it that could be set to desired times for release when an unmarked button was pressed on the handle bars. It could be set to 5, 10, 15, second for that lock to release, etc. That was way more secure than our patrol cars. So if I ride on a motor and need a long gun, I'm fucked. Campus cops must really be intimidating to the students at MSU (Michigan State University); thanks, Lansing Executive Council!

Keys to the Blue Goose: The trailer on YouTube by Buoy 22 Films is actually pretty cool. Our department and the MSPTA jointly invested somewhere in the amount of $300 grand to make a documentary/

reality show about the Michigan State Police. One of my Recruit School instructors, who ended up becoming Colonel, was the narrator on the teaser trailer. The film crew filmed the motor unit at the Drive Track doing our refresher exercises, sometimes dumping the bikes as we do. The project got scrapped and never came to fruition. As far as we knew the department and our union lost our investment, damn more tax-payer monies and MSPTA dues out the window. We should have at least sued them for the money back.

Shifts worked? Eight, 10, or 12 hours. I worked every imaginable schedule in the State Police that some scheduling Sergeant would come with and the PC would approve that gave them the most visibility. It was always about visibility to the public, make it look like there are more Troopers on the road than there really are! This came from the top in Lansing. The higher-ups fought extended workdays against the Troopers union for years. Most old-school PC's wanted the standard eight-hour shift. Days worked 6 a.m.–2 p.m., afternoons worked 2 p.m.–10 p.m., and believe it or not, midnights worked 10 p.m.–6 a.m. I worked noons most of my career, even on the motors. We weren't supposed to ride after dark, which was a problem in the fall (fall back, with the time change). Most PC's let that slide as long as you were out writing tickets though. I didn't mind working 10s, but 12s were horrible and dangerous on a motor. I always said riding a motorcycle on patrol is like time and a half in patrol car or SUV. Eight hours on bike is comparable to 12 in a car. The heat, lifting the bike up and down on every stop, and mentally being on a motorcycle kicks your ass. I did this for 15 years, not complaining, just saying! Some of the Troops liked working the extended workdays because it gave you more days off during the year, not me. I was one of those guys that liked going into work on nice sunny days so I could ride my motor and write a shit load of tickets to people that deserved them.

Pay for Performance: This was a program extended to the upper command of the State Police, mainly post and team commanders (lieutenants) for keeping their budgets in line with Lansing. When I first joined the State Police they had monies to get rid of at the end of the fiscal year, which was September 30. Come September 1, they were frantic to have any overtime not used to be used so it wouldn't reduce their budget for the next fiscal year. Hmmm? I remember working my ass off throughout the month of every September earning a lot of money to work traffic details, fugitive sweeps, or other details they would come with to burn the money. Fuck it, they're offering it, I'll take it! If a post or drug team commander meets their budget requirements, they get a monetary bonus at the end of the year. We're talking thousands of dollars for sitting on their ass making money off the backs of the Road Dogs. Then we get a Governor that decides she's cutting all budgets across the board including the State Police. Okay, maybe that was a good thing in certain areas including PFP. This was one positive, out of all the horrible things she did including putting us on mileage restrictions and laying off Troopers. She leaves after her eight-year term, thank God, then the next Governor gets in, the self-proclaimed "nerd," and he puts the pay for performance back in effect! Whoop, here we go again, "We don't have money for that or this because that would affect my end-of-year bonus!" One of my favorite Sergeants, who we called "Pallet Head," put it best, it was like "Baskin Robbins 30 flavors" flavor of the week with command.

Motorcycle patrol does have its times with strange occurrences. Most people have no idea who you are, even being a State Trooper in full uni-form on a fully marked MSP blue motorcycle be it a Harley or BMW! I pull next to this looker (hot chick) on her driver's side at a red light. I'm looking directly at her when she picks her nose. "Don't do it!" She looks at the booger then eats the damn thing! She guns it when the light turns green. Holy shit, she still has no idea who I am. I pace clock her at approximately 15 mph over the posted speed limit for close to a half a mile. I initiate a traffic stop on her vehicle and contact her like I would any other traffic violator. I never said one word about the booger she just ate, write her a 5 mph over speeding ticket, and go about my business, again never mentioning the tasty booger she had just swallowed. Gross!

Under 100: There was a national initiative where Law Enforcement Command decided to enact policies to reduce duty-related deaths. Sounds good on paper and at meeting with do-nothing administrators, but in reality doesn't do shit! The use of seatbelts, in-car-cameras that turn on at 85 mph, use of cell phones, etc. The incentive was to reduce duty-related deaths to under 100 nationally, which skyrocketed when Covid hit. I religiously wore my seatbelt, some cops don't. My friend Trooper Jeff Werda wasn't wearing his during a pursuit/crash that cost him his life—his choice. When we worked in Detroit, I would bust his balls, saying to wear it, it would say it was hard to get off when they had to bail out of the Goose on shitheads real quick in the 'hood. Hmm, three ways to look at things: your way, my way, and the right way! They changed our patrol car cameras to turn on at 85 mph or faster, which was every time I was going after a speeder. No cameras on the motors, so I could do 120 mph with no issue, stupid shit. It was a huge distraction, so I just left the camera running all the time, with command complaining I was using up too much storage space on the computers; damned if you do and damned if you don't! I hope this isn't true, but with the direction law enforcement is heading, a huge uptick in assault and murder of police, etc., I don't think they will ever reach their goal of under 100!

Troopers are assisting Walker PD at a Motel 6 off I-96 looking for home invasion suspects/crew that had been hitting houses all over the area. The lone male surprisingly answers the door to the motel and lets the Coppers in. If shitheads are overly nice or cooperative, that's a huge red flag something bad is about to happen. A Walker officer puts Mr. Nice

Guy into his patrol car handcuffed up front with a senior citizen ride-along in the front seat of the patrol car and leaves him alone to go search the motel room—huge mistake. The dude prys the sliding glass aside, jumps behind the driver's seat of the patrol car, which is running, and kicks the old-timer out the passenger side door. He throws the patrol car in reverse and stomps the gas, headed toward a Trooper, who opens up on him with his .12-gauge shotgun. Back to drive toward another Trooper, who lights him up through the windshield, somehow missing dickhead. The Troop was a firearms instructor and a hell of a shot—the bad guy was very lucky. They call it out on the radio, "Shots fired, a Walker patrol car was stolen, he tried to run us down!" I'm at Subway in Grand Rapids on meal break. Fuck, I jump in my Goose, being it winter time. I take off at the same time calling for GRPD and Kent County advising what happened. I get on N/B US-131 with police car after police car headed toward Walker, the Cavalry is a coming, boys! Meanwhile back at the ranch, literally he drove the stolen patrol car up a side road and tore the in-car computer out, throwing it in the roadway, then ditching the patrol car at a horse barn off Baumhoff Rd. He was smart enough to know the computer had GPS, allowing Dispatch to track his ass. With 15-year Trooper instinct, I found the stolen patrol car parked behind a barn with a GRPD officer. Thanks to fresh snow, it was clear where the turd ran. Thank God he couldn't get the Walker officers .12-gauge shotgun out of the locked gun rack to use on us. A K-9 unit tracked his ass running across a farmer's field about a half a mile away from the ditched patrol car within minutes. Remember the John Wayne quote, "Life is hard, but it's really hard when you're stupid!"

Betty Ford, the former First Lady, passed away in 2011. I was assigned with various other motor units to assist with the funeral escort on my Harley. President Ford had already passed a few years prior, and he was interred at the Gerald R. Ford museum in downtown Grand Rapids. We picked her body up from the Gerald R. Ford Airport with family after flying in from California, where she passed, and escorted them to the museum, where they had a nice ceremony to lay her to rest next to her husband. It was mid July and hot as hell but a detail that I was honored to participate in. The funeral service was very nice and fitting for the former First Lady."

Trooper Paul Butterfield, 44 years old, shot to death on traffic stop in Manistee, Michigan. I was working on my motor when Dispatch put out an officer had been shot but very little else. They never said Trooper, which should have been said! He initiated a traffic stop on a shitbox pickup for loud exhaust, walked up to the driver, and was shot in the head by a 19-year-old Monster. He fled the scene of the murder and swapped the pickup for a Pontiac Grand Prix and tried to flee the area with his 19-year-old pregnant wife, where he was confronted and shot by Troops from the Gaylord Post later that night. We had a incompetent Sergeant working at the post that afternoon that sent cubs/young troops up there to assist. Myself and three other more experienced Senior Troops being involved in shootings ourselves were so pissed off he didn't send us. Send the new guys that will be scared, why don't you, Sarge! Turns out he had a loaded gun in the truck and was suspended and didn't want to go to jail, so he executes our Trooper. I didn't know Paul personally, but he is still a Troop and a US Army Veteran like myself, so it hit home. I went to the trial on my own time when I could and got a chance to look that piece of shit in the eye as he was gimping on the elevator on crutches. He had a bullet removed from one of the Gaylord Troops that had shot his ass. I gave him the mean eye, and he looked right back at me like a little pussy. He went to Jackson prison after being convicted of murdering Paul and hung himself shortly after arriving. He must not have wanted to deal with what lay ahead? Rest in peace, Trooper Paul Butterfield!

I was tasked with working a three-day detail with three other Motor Men/Troopers escorting bicyclists fundraising for the Make a Wish Foundation. We started in Traverse City escorting them to Brooklyn, near MIS (Michigan International Speedway). This detail was one of the most rewarding and heartwarming I have ever participated in. This was my 15th and last year on the police motors. They put us up in hotels, had us at all the rallies at night, and fed us at every meal. What a great detail for the kids and feather in the helmet of the motor unit!

I was on patrol on my MSP motor when I attempted to pull over a woman directly in front of me. I can't even remember what the hell I was stopping her for. I turn my police lights on, no response from her. I blurp my siren, which is really loud at the bike, not being exposed under the hood like in a patrol car. Still no response, she keeps on driving. Out of frustration, I yell out, "Pull over, dumbass." She hears that, finally pulling over to the right shoulder. I get in her grill for not stopping initially, write her a ticket for whatever it was she violated, and kick her loose. Not surprisingly she calls the post to complain about our contact, and I get called into the APC's office being asked what happened. No IA (Internal Affairs) pulled, just a man-to-man conversation, which we had in the early days. I told the Lt., I did say it loudly, not knowing she would hear me yell that but not my siren. Luckily I didn't have my PA system on my helmet mic turned on; then it would have been super loud me calling her a dumbass! Never lie when being interviewed by command, way worse than what you might have done! The Lt., calm and cool, says, "Okay, Bomber, don't do it again!" "Sir, yes sir."

Better to be judged by 12 than buried by 6? That was what we were told as young cubs/Troopers when we first started our career. Basically we were told to do what you have to do to go home at the end of your shift. The closer I got toward retirement, it became "Do what you have to do, not get time off, criminally charged, or lose your pension." I saw many Cops, Deputies, and Troopers become reactive instead of proactive with the negative climate and feckless command and politicians that didn't have their back.

Throughout my entire career, starting at the Academy in Lansing, we were given "Performance Appraisals" once a year usually around our anniversary date from coming in the MSP. My annual date was March 10, 1996, so every year I had a review around that time to see how I was performing as a trooper. Our shift Sergeant would look at our performance over a year period and rate us in different areas including investigative skills, patrol generated activity, dealing with peers and the public, etc. When I was a new Trooper, Sergeants would keep notes on their Troopers throughout the year and use that as the basis for the yearly review. I always got downgraded on my penmanship/legiblity of tickets issued, my handwriting wasn't the greatest, but I knew it. I would get downgraded on that throughout my career until we switched to computer-generated UD-8s (traffic tickets/citations). My response to my piss-poor writing was I have a bachelor's degree and can't go back to elementary school to learn how to handwrite better cursive again. My parents did divorce when I was five years old around the time I would have started writing, just saying. As I progressed in my career, some lazy Sergeants would not keep notes on their troops; they would tell them to keep notes themselves, which is stupid, or ask them for significant things that they have done over the last year? Really, Sarge? Your job, not mine.

The State of Michigan has car pool lots near most of the major interstates where people can leave their vehicles and catch a ride to work, etc. There are people that use those lots for nefarious reasons, criminals that break into cars for visible valuables and cut the catalytic convertors out from underneath to sell for scrap metal. Other people meet there for sexual romps. I always ran through car pool lots performing property inspections, looking for crime afoot or suspicious situations. I rolled into the lot on West River and US-131 observing a white male in a pickup with his head back on the rest but not sleeping, hmm? Something strange there. I exit my patrol car when another white male pops up from the driver's lap area with the driver scurrying to get his pants on. The male passenger was giving the driver a blow job at three o'clock in the afternoon. I asked both for ID, and the male passenger refused to produce ID. He was immediately removed from the truck and placed in handcuffs and then secured in my patrol car. The driver produces his Michigan license and advised he used to be a sergeant with the Kent County Sheriff's Department, shit! The Rockford Post is in Kent County! I don't recognize this dude, so he must have left before I transferred over from Detroit. I never placed the ex-sergeant into custody with him willingly giving a full statement, stating he met the passenger online and met at the car pool lot for oral sex. The passenger was a flaming asshole from New Jersey, so I lodged him for R&O and gross indecency between males. I called an on-call prosecutor to run it by him getting the okay to lodge Jersey and go complaint and warrant on the ex-Sergeant. Turns out the ex-Sergeant is also a convicted felon and registered sex offender. The head prosecutor in Kent County, not the on-call I talked to, decided to drop all charges on Jersey and continue with charges on the ex-Sergeant? Are you fucking kidding me? Boy, was I pissed. Stick it to the guy that's an ex-Dep./Sgt. and give the contemptuous shithead from out of state a free pass!

Perks of the job of being a cop, if wanted: free coffee, free meals or half off the bill, free dry cleaning. What about free dates? There were many an opportunity working as a Trooper having women ask me out before I was married and after. A lot of flirting and sexual innuendo thrown at ya! Booze, broads and Blue Cross! We were told by Senior Troops when we were young cubs that's the shit that will get you in trouble. You guys make decent money, have great benefits (Blue Cross/Blue Shield), so watch your ass concerning women. They would love to have your bennies and pension! I stopped by a Shell gas station to get a soda on my police motor when the clerk, who happened to be a looker, said, "You can have that pop for free if you bend over so I can see your ass!" It appears the high leather boots and breaches turn certain women on. Not the first time flirtation happened while on the motors. Maybe a part of the reason why I stayed on the unit for fifteen years. Other troops would meet women at Tim Hortons on coffee break. One buddy of mine met some chick after her boyfriend was killed in a rollover crash on the freeway. He went to give death notification, then within two weeks was sleeping with her. Not my cup of tea, good for him! We all knew which restaurants were "on the plan." Uniformed cops 50% off your meal bill or the entire meal for free. A lot of times we would stop somewhere for lunch when a thoughtful citizen would grab the waitress and pick up the bill. Sometimes they would want to remain anonymous. I look back and remembered some dink instructor at the Academy schooling us recruits on how wrong it is to take a free cup of coffee. Really? Big difference between the cup of coffee and some citizen offering a bribe to get out of a ticket, which never happened. I had plenty of women flirt trying to get out of tickets, which usually got them a full shot biscuit (ticket) writing them for what I had stopped them for instead of giving them a break such as 5 mph over instead of 20 mph over!

On my MSP motorcycle on patrol near my house in Rockford when Dispatch advised a father on his bicycle with his young son in tow was struck by a car on Belding Rd. near Blakely in Cannon Twp. and the female driver appeared to be intoxicated per witnesses at the scene. I was about a mile out and passed my wife and kids running hot lights and sirens to the crash. Erie for my family passing the crash scene where Poppa Bear Trooper was. I arrived before the ambulance, making sure the father and young son, around four, were okay. Luckily they only had minor injuries, thank God! The drunk female and a drunk male passenger in her vehicle could have easily killed them! He was milling around the scene constantly interrupting me when I was asking her questions. He told her not to answer any of my questions, so I finally had enough of his running his pie hole and put him in handcuffs sitting on the shoulder. I told a volunteer firefighter to watch his stupid ass until my backup arrived. I couldn't hog tie his ass and throw him over my saddle bags on my BMW, would be pretty funny though. After performing sobriety tests on the slushy female, she failed miserably and went to the Kent County Jail for OWI causing injury. Her mouthy companion went to jail for R&O and disorderly intoxicated. I gave the little boy a "Trooper Teddy Bear" to calm him down from all the excitement and getting thrown threw the air like a circus clown. His dad was extremely thankful. They were riding on the shoulder of the roadway with traffic when she hit them from behind shooting them both through the air. He was pulling his son in a carrier that we actually had for our kids. We called it a bike chariot. I told his dad it might be a good idea to ride on the trails instead of roadway shoulders where traffic is doing 55 mph. They were not the safest place to ride bikes, especially with young children. I stopped the same dad for speeding about a year later, and he told me he should have listened because he was on his bike on the side of the road and got hit again. I stopped him for 72 mph in a 55 mph a mile away, just saying. If the drunk lady had hit them at 72 mph, he and his son would both probably be dead!

One of my Recruit School/Academy classmates showed early signs that trouble was ahead. He was married with a couple young kids during the Academy, which could be a huge distraction. I remember him arguing with his wife a couple times in the parking lot on Sunday nights when we came back after weekend break. One time I looked over, and she was crying. Luckily I was single during the Academy, having no distractions, especially opposite sex ones! Staff never saw what we saw or maybe didn't address it, not sure, doesn't really matter. He ended up getting assigned to the Kalkaska Post just south of Traverse City. Word had gotten out to our classmates that he got in some female trouble and hot water, hanging out in bars, causing problems off duty. I had heard that he had lost his job as a Troop, then disappeared off the radar. I was at the Rockford Post years later when word came out that he snapped, killing his wife and all of his children except one, then committed suicide over in Ionia County, which was the next county east of Kent. Damn, goes back to my saying and belief that we live among monsters!

Fatal car crashes occur all the time in metropolitan areas with large population centers and traffic. I had probably taken/investigated at least

50 at this point in my career. Metro Detroit 10 years, Grand Rapids 11 years. More cars, more cars crashes, simple concept. We are always at minimum staffing during holidays, go figure. I'm working noons on Thanksgiving when I'm dispatched to a semitruck rollover crash on M-6 E/B to the N/B US-131 freeway. Upon my arrival, the semi appeared to be driving too fast for the conditions, slammed into the guard rail, and rolled over in the ditch. The driver was a K (fatal) at the scene. Son of bitch, what a way to start Thanksgiving. My buddy Chris shows up to help with the scene, which took the entire shift, tying up the only two MSP cars in Kent County. Dispatch keeps calling us asking when we're going to clear, busting our balls, with the same response going back. We are both Senior Troops and not putting up with their bullshit. Call in other Troops or midnights Troops early. Huge surprise, it's Thanksgiving and nobody's going to answer their phones or come in early. It's just the way it is! Command fucked up by not staffing appropriately to begin with. The driver was not from Michigan or the United States, which made death notification almost impossible. It took us half the shift to find out where this guy was from and how to get in touch with immediate family. We had an accident/crash investigator respond to the scene who was new to the job. He took the truck driver's property and brought it back to the post. Big mistake, Skippy, we always send property with the medical examiner and the body so family can recover at the morgue and not have to be traveling all over the place for their personal belongings. Now I had to go back to put that into property, which didn't need to be done. I finally made it home late, missing Thanksgiving with my family, but hey, at least I had plenty in the future to celebrate, not the same for the truck driver. You have to put things into perspective sometimes. I had to double back on Black Friday the next morning at 6 a.m. on day shift, working on about four hours of sleep. As soon as I check in with Dispatch, 61-61 copy a pickup/pedestrian injury crash on Alpine near four mile. I hadn't even had a chance to grab a hot cup of Joe. I arrive on scene, again only two Troopers working in all of Kent County, one of us coming from Grand Haven in Ottawa County (thanks, Great re-org) to find out it's

a K (fatal) car crash. A homeless lady darted out in front of a mother and her daughter doing some early Black Friday shopping. So much for discount shopping. I felt horrible for the driver, her daughter, and the dead homeless lady. "Dispatch from 61-61, send me the ME [Medical Examiner] to pick one up, please." This time I made sure her property went with them like it's supposed to. Long day working on another fatal, went home and had a nice dinner, thankful to be with my family, holding hands around the table and saying a prayer for the two people that had died on my watch.

State Troopers handle/police many traffic crashes throughout their career, even more if they work the road and are at a traffic post, which applied to me. Other than my just under two years at the Jonesville Post, the rest of my career was spent at traffic posts until I retired and walked out the door of the Rockford Post the last time. I took a serious injury crash on the Beltline near Plainfield Road one afternoon, where a young man and another vehicle collided head-on with him being transported to Butterworth Hospital in Grand Rapids. I was still at the crash scene when I received a call through Dispatch from staff at the hospital saying the young man in the crash was not going to survive. I cleared the scene and was able to contact his mother, who lived in Rockford but didn't have any transportation because he had been using her vehicle when the crash occurred. I rushed to pick her up in Rockford and was running lights and sirens to get her to the hospital downtown before her son passed. A Sergeant working at the time heard my radio traffic and told me to quit running hot with lights and sirens activated. Dispatch told him the circumstances, but he didn't seem to give a shit! Whatever, what a dink! I kept driving lights and sirens and turned off the siren whenever I had to call Dispatch. This isn't my first rodeo there, Sarge! Sometimes you have cool Sergeants that get it and other times Sergeants that are incompetent Noobs, which happened to be the case here. Is there some official order that says I can't drive fast with civilians in the patrol car? Sure there is, but fuck it. I'll take the hit on this one, her son is dying, damn it! We made it in time, and she was able to see her son before he passed. Nothing ever came of my blowing off the Sergeant and come to find out she was a prominent professor at one of the local universities. She wrote a nice heartwarming letter to the PC thanking me for my compassion at a very sad time in need. I would do the same thing over again, family comes first, even for the public we "Protect and Serve"!

Riding a motorcycle for the Michigan State Police for 15 years allowed me to participate in a multitude of details including funeral details. We escorted fallen officers from various agencies including our own fallen, retirees, and military killed in action in Iraq and Afghanistan. The greatest honor I had during all those funeral escorts was where my friend Chris's (a former Motor Man) teenage son, Chris Jr., was killed by a shithead drunk driver up in the UP (Upper Peninsula). Chris's ex-wife had taken Chris Jr. and his sister up north to attend a Green Bay Packer game, his favorite team, for his birthday! The drunk hit them head-on at night, causing a horrific crash. Chris Jr., who was critically injured, still had the strength and compassion to check on him mom and sister before he passed. Myself and my Motor School buddy Tram Dog rode our BMW (newly issued) police motors to the Upper Peninsula with the rest of the Motor Men from the eastside trailering their bikes. It was October and the further north we rode, the shittier it got weather-wise. We had packed our saddle bags with whatever would fit. I met Tram in Gaylord since I was at Rockford and he was in Detroit. We had on winter gloves, balaclavas, and of course long john underwear! When we arrived at the Mackinaw Bridge it got even colder and windier across that bay! We paid our toll fee to cross the bridge. On Michigan State police motors in uniform going to a funeral and still had to pay the bridge toll; whatever, take your dollar and stick it! Here we go, start accelerating up the Mighty Mack, talking on a tac channel, where no one else can hear us. Tram kept saying, "This is bad, Bomber," as we're swaying side to side looking down at the crashing waves against the bridge pillars. Holy shit, maybe we are going to die? Maybe we'll get blown over the bridge rail like the infamous

Yugo? Oh shit, here comes the wet metal grate now. If you've never rode over wet grating on a motorcycle, it leads to an instant code brown, where you potentially shit yourself! "We're not gonna make it, Bomber," says Tram. I respond on the tac channel, "Bullshit, Tram, down shift and hit the gas; we're gonna make it over this bitch!" I knew from flying planes and helicopters in high winds in the Army, more rpm's and throttle give stability. We made it over the bridge and pulled into the St. Ignace Post parking lot to check our underwear for a code brown. A female Troop pulls into the lot in her Goose, gets out, and says "I heard two crazy fuckers on motorcycles were crossing the Mighty Mack in high winds and come to find it's two Troops, you crazy bastards!" When we told her we were on our way to Chris's son's funeral she immediately understood. We have turned down dignitaries including presidents for less severe weather, not for Chris's son, a hero that had the fortitude to check on his mom and sister after that crash, probably knowing he was dying!

On patrol in a Blue Goose at night with a college intern/US Army vet-Afghanistan Purple Heart recipient later to become a troop and referred to as Nuggets. Grand Rapids PD stops a carload of turds at the speedway on Leonard and US-131. A female bails on foot from the suspect car. We are close by, so I hit the next side street over with Nuggets killing my driving lights/vampire mode. I swept up, and down about three blocks and come across some "Karen" running down the street. I jump out of the patrol car telling Nuggets to stay put. She sees me coming and kicks the overdrive on hauling ass. At this point in my career I am no spring chicken but still have a little nitrous in my tank even with that 30 lb. gun belt on! I chased her approximately two blocks yelling, huffing, and puffing behind her, "Stop, State Police," just like our hood light. She cuts into a backyard trying to ditch me when I close the gap on her. I lunge out at her when she tries to climb a chain link fence with me grabbing her shirt. She falls backward onto me lying underneath her on the grass. I forgot I had a nice $100 pair of Ray Bans in my left shirt pocket. Crunch, smash, crackle, they are toast. I get handcuffs on her stupid ass, then hoofed it back to the Goose, where we drove her back to the GR Unit and turned her over to them because she had some warrants for her arrest held by them. (That's why she bailed on foot.) I turned in a complaint and warrant to the Kent County Prosecutor's Office for her for R&O, which was authorized. About six months later I received a check at the State Police post made out to me for $25, then three more checks each for $25 totaling $100. I had put in the report that my glasses were broken during the arrest, and they made her pay me for the Ray Bans! Holy shit, there still is justice out there; it even surprised me, I wrote them off as a loss.

Shots fired in Grand Rapids residential area near Plainfield and I-96. I'm close on my Police motor, so I head to the scene. The house was just cleared by GRPD with four dead in the home. All the officers that exit the house look like they're in shock when I pull up on my motor. They asked myself and one of our commercial vehicle officers to stay at the scene and close off the street. A monster who was determined to be on a drug rampage, went into the home, executed his wife, in laws and young daughter running out the back door. He then fled the scene of the first shooting and went on a killing spree all over the Grand Rapids area on a mission to kill his exes (girlfriends/wives and family). He was able to find other exes, killing again, then had a road rage incident in Wyoming with a stranger, shooting him in the process. The guy he shot had previous surgery with a metal plate in his head that stopped the bullet from the monster, lucky bastard! I thought about going back to the post to get in a patrol car and grab a couple long guns, but I figured this joker is going to flee the area and beat-feet somewhere else like maybe Chicago or Detroit, both cities the same distance from Grand Rapids. Turns out he was all doped up and on a killing spree, not giving a shit about nothing but his idea of retribution! He got in a shooting with GR officers downtown by their PD, then headed back to the house I was at on perimeter. I was talking to a reporter from Channel 13 news off the air and actually told him he might try and come back to the original shooting scene to shoot more family members, then word comes out of the radio during the pursuit with this schmuck he's back toward the original crime scene! I jumped on my motor and left the scene headed toward the pursuit coming our way. I thought to myself, "Here we go again, another shooting with another monster, and all I have is my SIG! Fuck it, it's him or me, I'm not going to let him kill any other innocent victims. My wife was watching on the news and actually saw me drive off on my police motor, scaring her to death. After already being involved in a shooting, I had the mindset I'm going to get in a gunfight with the monster and kill him or be killed, there's no, "State Police, drop the gun" with the prick! He crashed in a ditch on I-96, ran up to a house, and kicked the door in of a home right of the freeway and took some folks hostage. I met some Troops at the end of the block, jumped off my police motor, and grabbed a rifle in case he decided to carjack someone again and take off toward the end of the block, where we had set up a roadblock. This was the first time in my career I had been involved in an actual roadblock, waiting for a shithead to try and ram us. He stayed in the house for a few hours until he came down off his drug high, stepped out on the front porch, and shot himself in the head. What a coward!

CHIPS, the TV show, was one of my faves when I was a young kid, who would think I would have that gig for fifteen years with the MSP! Ponch and Jon rolling on California freeways. Eric Estrada came to Grand Rapids Harley for a public relations show. I brought one of our MSP Harleys to the dealership for him to use and took a photo with Eric and my boy Dom.

On patrol on my motor when I stop this dude on West River near Pine Island for lane use, suspected drunk driving. He turns onto Pine Island near the Circle K gas station and pulls to the right, bouncing off the curb. I conduct an OWI (operating while intoxicated) investigation and determine he's drunk. I call for a Troop car for transport to the county jail. My buddy Bruce rolls up. I tell Slushy to stand by the curb he bounced off when pulling over. As I walk over to Bruce, he has an "Oh, shit" look on his face. I look back and my arrestee cuffed behind the back falls over forward like a California Redwood that had just been cut down. Timber, face first on the concrete! Bruce and I look at each other saying, "Holy shit" in unison, trying not to laugh our asses off. We run over and pick him up with blood gushing out his nose, a bloody lip, and "road rash"/ gravel on his face. We call for an ambulance to be on the safe side and bandage his face until the paramedics arrive on scene. He looked like a mummy with gobs of gauze wrapped around his entire head and face to stop the bleeding. They transport him to Butterworth Hospital for a medical clearance, which worked out better so we could get a blood draw on the OWI. Mr. Slushy told a couple of nurses and the doc, "These cops beat my ass!" Bruce was such a smooth talker with a soft voice, responding, "No, we didn't, sir. You're so drunk you fell on your face." Luckily Bruce's in-car camera was activated when he pulled up just in time to catch the fall. We got the medical clearance and took him to Kent County Jail for lodging. Case closed, never heard from him again! My friend and fellow Trooper Bruce Cojeen passed away after having a heart attack while I was finishing this book. He retired five years before I did, and I saw him on many occasions after he retired. He was a happy-go-lucky guy who worked many types of different part-time jobs after retiring like most cops do. He use to always say, "Bomber, you need to retire and get the hell out" before I did retire and then, "Bomber, I'm so glad your retired" after I did! A Great Man that will be missed by his family and so many others! We saw each other last when he came out to a Thursday Night Pay Day Choir Practice just before the holidays. I was honored to be asked by his family and MSP staff to be a pall bearer at his funeral. Godspeed Brother, Trooper Bruce Cojeen!

Retired MSP F/Lt. Joseph Zangaro, 61 years old, killed in the line of duty on July 11, 2016, as a security supervisor at the Berrien County Courthouse when an inmate killed him and Court Officer Ron Kienzle, 63 years old. The inmate was a bad dude pending trial for a violent rape and kidnapping. He was trying to escape when he overtook a female deputy and took her service weapon. Hmm? Why would they have a female Dep. watch this Monster when he was charged with committing horrific violence on another woman? He exchanged gunfire (female Deputy's weapon) with other officers before finally being killed. Rest in peace, Joe and Ron! It was an honor to participate in the funeral service for you, gentlemen, on my MSP motor.

On my police motor when myself and a straight leg troop get dispatched to a fatal Jeep Wrangler crash on M-6. Per witness, dude was driving recklessly, lost control, and was ejected from not wearing a safety belt, killed instantly. The crash scene was easy to investigate, single vehicle, no belt, dope in Jeep. We go to a nice house in Byron Center to do a death notification. Weird, we pull up, all the shades are drawn, and the basement windows are covered with card board? Hmm, it appears something is afoot here. We see a female looking out the shades in the middle of the day. Hello, State Police, please come to the door. She won't come to the door, when I finally yell though the window, "If you know a 'John Doe,' he was killed in a car crash out on M-6." She opens the door and goes into a meltdown. "Jesus Christ, he's my husband." Turned out they had an illegal marijuana grow operation in their basement. She thought we were there to bust them for the dope, which we did, calling in a Drug Team detective to process the house.

Most citizens and criminals don't know motorcycle cops are cops until it's too late. I was on patrol in downtown Grand Rapids on my fully marked MSP motor when I look up ahead and see this dude bust out the front door of a local pizzeria with what appeared to be a couple of waiters/employees on his ass, chasing him on foot. Hmm, I decided to investigate further by downshifting and hitting the throttle turning my police lights on, catching up to him fairly fast. It appeared that he D&D (dine and dashed), failing to pay for his bill at the pizzeria. I hit my air horn to get his attention, which scared the shit out of him. He realizes I'm a cop and tries to kick it in gear, zigging and zagging, trying to flee and elude me on foot. Really, dude? My right leg happened to slip off the foot peg and kick him in the ass, down he goes. I jacked my brakes hard, put the bike down sideways, and jumped off the motorcycle and onto his stupid ass, with bracelets (handcuffs) soon to follow. He was down and out faster than a calf in a cattle rustle! I called Dispatch after having him sit Indian style, asking for a transport car to take home slice to jail. The two waiters came running over, thanking me for catching the thief with big smiles on their face. Case closed, Perp turned over to GRPD for eating pizza without paying!

Similar incident in downtown Grand Rapids again, as above I was on patrol on my MSP motor. There was a festival going on at Rosa Parks Circle. One of my straight leg Trooper buddies was on patrol in his Blue Goose when GRPD Dispatch advised there was a white male with a knife threatening to stab people if they didn't give him money. I head up Monroe St. and see the shithead being chased on foot by a couple GR cops and my Trooper buddy Mark. He tries to taser his ass while in foot pursuit, "Pop," but misses at full stride. "Oh, hell no." I do a quick U-turn. The perp is opening up the gap losing the Coppers on foot until I fly by them on my motor, again the dude having no idea who I am or that I'm right on his ass. He ran to a closed building, trying to get into a locked building, clearly out of breath. I get off my police motor, calmly put the kickstand down, not dumping this time, and body-slam his ass on the ground. The other guys showed up also out of breath, thanking me for catching their perp. He had tossed the knife during the foot pursuit, but a GR officer saw him toss it and grabbed it as evidence. There were some civilians that were at the tail end with their cell phones on. "Whatever, you get to see a turd that threatened to stab your cohorts at the festival get taken down like the weasel he was! Tot GRPD at the scene for felonious assault and resist and obstruct the police, case closed!

I spent 23 years in the Michigan State Police and got along with the vast majority of Troops, command, and civilians in our agency. After the "Great Re-Org," I had the unfortunate pleasure of having to work with and deal with a horrible Troop that came to our post. He was lazy as hell and somehow suckered his way in the post court officer position. Actually he probably got the position because he was buddies with the APC. I was working mids with a hard-charging Troop that transferred to the Rock from Flint. He had arrested some chick that had a warrant for her arrest where she bonded out with approximately $1,000 cash, which is pretty high for a misdemeanor warrant. The money/cash was not put into the "Bond Box" by the Troop and never documented and taken to the court to satisfy the warrant by the court officer. She was rearrested about a month later on the same warrant. Hmm, that's strange and should never happen! The Desk Sergeant never caught the money missing from the receipt book entry; hmm, that's also strange! My partner was contacted by the court inquiring where the money was because they had received notice to cancel the warrant when the original arrest was made and bond was posted. We tried to contact the court officer at home. "Where's the money on this arrest, dude?" "I'm busy. I'll get back with ya." He blew us off for days. We advised a Sergeant of the situation, and the money turned up all of a sudden. A supervisor had to pinch him on where the money was. He said he had forgotten the cash, again approximately $1,000, in his clip board. Really? The Sergeant gave the information to the APC, again the court officer's buddy, who blew off the incident stating he was one of the most well-off Troops at the post. "Are you fucking kidding me, Lt.?" I told my partner to drop a UD-93, IA complaint against this pogue. He didn't want to because he was new to the post, and he didn't want to cause any waves. I raised a stink and should have contacted Lansing IA myself since post command was going to do nothing about the incident. A woman was falsely arrested because of this cat! Command left this mope in the court officer spot, which at a minimum he should have been removed from and put back on the road, taking calls. The rest of my short time in the department leading up to retirement I had to deal with the puke. I would be missing subpoenas for court, which cost me overtime and affected my pension. He would kick warrant requests back, which I had rarely have happened in the past. I couldn't prove the dink was doing it on purpose, but it was pretty obvious. I had words with him on multiple occasions, once pretty heated argument at the post when a Sergeant intervened when I told the court officer to go fuck himself and get me my subpoenas on time. Same shitty Troop was pinched for drunk driving after I retired. I pegged this asshole as a bad apple from the first time I met him. His ass should have been fired or criminally charged instead of just bouncing him to a different post.

Cops with beards? Don't like it, never have. I think it looks totally unprofessional. We had a Black troop when I was down at Metro who tried for years and years to force the department to let him grow a beard while wearing a uniform. He actually had a medical reason, the bumps, which caused him to break out on his face when he shaved. He took his case to arbitration and lost. The department had him working as an undercover trooper not requiring the wearing of a uniform. I agree with the department's stance on this one, no beards or goatees in uniform! That was years ago though; in today's environment he probably would have won that arbitration hearing and would be sporting that beard, just saying. Ever hear the term "bearded clam"? Just saying!

I stopped by the Rockford Post during patrol for who knows what when I run into one of the ES (SWAT) guys who we called "Ball Sack." He was all suited up wearing a sniper/guilly woodland camouflage suit. "Whats going on, man? Who do you plan on killing today?" Ha, he said he was assigned to sit in the brush near one of the "car pool" lots running surveillance on people specifically looking for catalytic convertor thiefs. I started laughing so hard I thought I was going to piss my pants and have to go home to change my motor uniform! Now that's some funny shit, the elite of our department, what a great use of resources, not!

What to do when on patrol dealing with a gang or large group of motorcycles? Most young cops would be scared to deal with Motor Heads, not me. Being a motorcycle Trooper I knew how to deal with these idiots early on. I would look for the asshole driving the worst, popping wheelies, doing burnouts, etc., and stop them. When their peeps would stop with them, which you would have happen, I would point to my offender and tell them he is getting a ticket, but if you don't get your ass out of here, you're going to jail and I'm towing your motorcycle. That worked **all** the time; they would drive down the street and pull over, waiting for the buddy while he got a ticket. Easy way to deal with packs of motorcycles!

On patrol on my MSP motor when Dispatch advised there was a vehicle fire on US-131 N/B ramp to Post Road. Deputies and a MSP Sergeant beat me to the fire. It didn't turn out to be a vehicle fire but a suicide by fire! Some dude in a rental car from New Jersey exited the freeway pulling over on the left shoulder before the top of the ramp at the traffic light. He gets out of the car and methodically makes a bed out of magazines and newspapers. WTF? He douses the papers with gas, lies down, then himself before lighting himself ablaze. I arrive on scene and immediately smell that distinctive smell of burnt/charred flesh that I have smelled before. They had extinguished the dude on fire before I got there and the Fire Department. The MSP Sergeant gave the call to the Deps.; he must not want to have been bothered, I guess. We never found out what he reason for killing himself was. Does it really matter? Just another fucked-up situation we have to deal with on the job. Shortly after this incident I was again on patrol on a nice summer night with a beautiful sunset when Dispatch advised there was a dead body behind the car pool lot on Post Road near the US-131 N/B ramp, close to where our Jersey Dude smoked himself. A couple of young Troops beat me to the call. I pull in the car pool lot on my motor, got a horrible whiff of the smell of death, and pulled right out. I never went back to look at the body or talk to the troops, didn't have to. I called them on the radio to make sure they were all set and blurping my siren when they said yes. A young couple had gone for a walk and stumbled onto the body. That body had to have been out there for a while with the smell around there and you can definitely tell the difference between a dead animal and human. I was surprised nobody had called sooner. Turned out a middle-aged woman parked her car, walked north of the lot into the weeds, and smoked herself with a handgun. There didn't appear to be any foul play like a staged murder suicide. Two suicides that close to each other, creepy!

I was in a Blue Goose on patrol dispatched to investigate a crash on Belding Road approximately a mile from my house. Upon my arrival there was an extremely sloppy drunk female that had crashed her vehicle into a ditch. I had her take a seat in the rear of my Explorer so I could ask her some questions before performing sobriety tests. She got pissy and jumped out the vehicle forcing me to chase after her ass and place her into custody without any sobriety tests or PBT. Made my job easy just get a search warrant for blood except for the fact that I wrenched my right knee and barely could walk. I advised Dispatch for assistance with no other Troopers available, big surprise. My knees killing me at this point pain 8 on a scale of 1 to 10 and I have to deal with the sloppy, drunk bitch that's refusing to do anything I ask of her. I got a search warrant for her blood and had a doc at the ER look at my knee. Turns out I tore the meniscus wrestling with her ass up against a wrecker she tried to run around. I was off for the next month having to get immediate surgery from being in so much pain, part of doing the job, I guess. A Sergeant advised this moron wanted to file a complaint against me saying I mistreated her until he told her she jacked my knee resisting arrest, causing me to have knee surgery; she then changed her mind and apologized. This took me right into my last two years on the job.

I would set up in parking lots on M-Roads (Michigan) to shoot laser at speeders off the freeway to get a break from the ditch (freeway). By the time the speeders saw me and hit the brakes, it was too late. Bing, bing, bing, one after another, lot to lot. One summer day I was set up in a church parking lot in a 55 mph zone only going after 70 mph and faster, which was usually one after another. I'm shooting my laser at cars coming at me when some lady and a couple teenagers approach me sitting on my police motor. I thought they were going to thank me for my service or offer me some water, seeing me working hard, sweating my nads off.

The woman asked me to leave their church lot because they had a youth group of troubled teenagers and them seeing me was upsetting some of the kids. Wow, it was like I was sitting in a methadone clinic parking lot, not a church! Easy fix, I went about a 1/4 mile up the road and set up there to tag speeders where they would have to pull into the church parking lot when I turned my lights on. Bing, bing bing, every car now was pulling over there where the troubled teenagers and moronic woman had to now see me doing my job and my scary police lights on the scary State Police motorcycle. Most people support the police and would be thankful that a Trooper, deputy, or police officer was nearby. I guess Idiots go to church too!

My last day on patrol in October 2015 on an MSP motor I decided to wear my "Old School" uniform. Leather jacket, breeches, high shine Chippewa boots, tie, and open-face helmet. What's Lansing going to do kick me off the Motor Unit? I'm rolling towards the Post for the last time on the motors when a large buck deer stops on the right shoulder looking at me. Holey Shit, it was like he was sending me off, take care Motor Bomber, I won't dart in front of you causing you to crash, God Speed!

CHAPTER 11: THE LAST TWO

THE LAST TWO! We call it the last two because our pension we have been working toward our whole career is based on the last two years that we are in the department. All the overtime, including court, details, holidays, etc., affect what our FAC (final average compensation), or pension, will be. Our base pension is 60 percent plus any of the above mentioned and averaged out over the last two years. Different departments have different pensions and requirements. If we had the "Best two," my pension could have been set after the attacks on 9/11. "Operation Stone Garden" patrolling the US-Canadian border was unlimited overtime plus all the court overtime in Metro Detroit, I would have been all set and not had to bust my ass working mids and going to court my last two years on the job.

Literally a week into the start of my last two years I was working speed enforcement on US-131 near 54th St., in the city of Wyoming, when I observed a black Chrysler 300 in the left lane at a very high speed. I activated my radar in my Goose and obtained a reading of 90 mph in a posted 70 mph zone. I proceeded to follow the car, which exited at 54th St. I turned on my police lights and chirped my siren to get the car to pull over on a traffic stop. The Chrysler accelerated at a high rate of speed attempting to flee and elude. I called out the pursuit with Dispatch, also advising the shift sergeant and other troopers for backup. The driver of the Chrysler ultimately ran a red light at 52nd St. and M37 T-boning a passenger car traveling NB. I was about a half mile back observing a large cloud of smoke and came across a violent crash scene with debris everywhere. "What do I got? What do I need?" I immediately called for Fire and EMS, knowing there would be serious injuries turned out to be a multi-fatal crash. The 21-year-old female college student was driving north when the suspect ran the red light at over 100 mph hitting her in the door splitting he vehicle open and killing her on impact. The 15-year-old in the passenger seat of the fleeing car was ejected, not wearing his seatbelt, and also killed on impact. The 16-year-old suspect/driver of the Chrysler was semiconscious in the burning car, mumbling for help. He was pinned in the driver's seat. I yelled for a Kentwood firefighter that had just pulled up on scene, asking him to help me get the driver out of the burning car. It was later determined that the boys were cousins. They had been drinking and driving around, smoking dope, when I attempted to pull them over. The driver was also driving without a license, being suspended. His 15-year-old cousin that died had a felony warrant for his arrest held by Kent County Sheriff's Department for escaping from a Youth Detention Camp. I had never in my career come across a 15-year-old with a felony warrant for their arrest! We'll never know, but my intuition says the 15-year-old told his cousin to hit it when I lit them up, not wanting to go back to the Youth Camp being a Saturday and they were in party mode. The case went to trial with the prosecutor charging the 16-year-old as an adult since he was only two weeks away from 17 when the crash/deaths occurred. You're considered an adult at 17 in Michigan when it comes to criminal cases. He was charged with two counts of second-degree murder for killing the innocent 21-year-old college girl and his cousin. He was offered a plea deal at the preliminary hearing to dismiss one count of murder and only do 10 years in the State Penitentiary. He turned it down! We went to trial, where he was convicted, being found guilty on the two counts of second-degree murder, being sentenced to 27 years in prison. It appears he should have taken the plea for 10! During the trial, the defense attorney asked if I would do anything differently, to which I replied, "No." I did everything I was trained to do per department policy and had no crystal ball or insight letting me know the outcome of that pursuit. The outcome was a horrible tragedy that was caused by one person, the teenager that went to prison for 27 years. I think about that innocent girl often; may she forever rest in peace.

The Michigan State Police Chaplain Corp is a great organization that serves the religious needs of department members and families. I did the background investigation of our post chaplain when I was at Metro. Chaplain Michael O'Mire, aka Chappy, had an impressive background also serving as a Chaplain in the US Army before coming on the to State Police. He also had his own church congregation in Troy up in Oakland County. Chaplains do everything from providing grief counseling with death or sickness, helping troopers involved in critical incidents, acting as marriage officials, and a multitude of other functions. He was at my wedding and said "Grace" before dinner, come on now. Chaplain O'Mire participated in a great deal of ride-alongs with many troopers in the Detroit Metro area. He was always there if the Troops needed an ear and didn't care if we used profanity, which was huge to me. He encouraged us to lay it all out. Anytime we had a shooting, which was often in Detroit, he would show up and support the troops. Anytime a troop was charged criminally he would also be there knowing they needed support just a little more that some others! I enjoyed my time in the 2nd District having Chaplain O'Mire there for support. When I transferred over to the Rockford Post in the 6th District I was in a shooting on New Year's talked about previously, we won, bad guy lost. It was a pretty traumatic incident my partner and I dealt with and the Rockford Post chaplain was nowhere to be found. Hmm, doesn't this guy care about the troops? I guess I was spoiled by Chappy. I called him and talked for a while, appreciating his support. I also had another critical incident toward the end of my career, again a new post chaplain to Rockford nowhere to be found. No biggie, I knew I could always count on Chappy!

Campaign Hats, to wear or not to wear, that was the question. My last two also happened to be the 100th anniversary of the forming of the Michigan Department of State Police. Troops have been trying to get campaign hats brought back for years with the brass in the department always shooting it down. "Do we want to look like drill sergeants in the Military?" Well we were supposedly a semi-militaristic organization, State Police, huda, huda, huda. The colonel finally made a command decision and decided to bring back the "Smokey Bear" campaign hats for the anniversary who knows for how long after that, it was a big secret. Also strange was we were told to keep our garrison hats just in case! They also had throw back Dodge Chargers in black with a gold arrow on the sides put out in the field for the 100th anniversary. Each post was to receive two going to troopers that had the most arrest activity, which didn't make any sense. What does arresting people at a complaint post have to do with the car you drive? Now a traffic post like Rockford or the Metro Posts had everything to do with it. The Chargers have the V-8s with the hemi for speed, i.e., pursuing crotch rockets and speeders. I talked the post commander at Rockford into giving one of the Chargers to my buddy Chris, who was third-generation MSP: his grandpa, grandpa's nrother, and his pops. Our department paid approximately $300,000 to outfit everyone in the Uniform Division with those campaign hats. Some look great in a campaign hat (pic me and Ron), but others look like a soup sandwich. I preferred the garrison hat myself but was okay with the campaign for the anniversary. We actually received the hats late in the middle of the year missing half of the celebration. About a year later the colonel put it up to a vote to keep or get rid of the campaign hats. The vote came in to keep the hats, which wasn't to her liking, so she held another vote that mysteriously changed to switch back to the garrison hats. Stupid is as stupid does (*Forest Gump* quote). California, Massachusetts, New Jersey State Police have both, so why can't we keep both? Nope, no more campaigns, we just wasted $300K of the Michigan taxpayers' money, which they had no clue about. We could wear the garrison in the fall/winter and the campaign in the spring/summer. They did produce a 100th anniversary SIG Sauer .40 caliber semiauto pistol that they let enlisted, retirees, and civilians the opportunity to purchase, which would be approximately

5,000 people. Sig only produced 90 pistols, which was crazy to me. I bought one, of course. How many 100th anniversaries do you have? I should have bought more; a captain in our department bought 10 of the 90 produced. They also made a sweet knife made out of elk horn from the UP with the 100th anniversary logo on it; got one of those too!

I had a couple of run-ins with a local GRPD Officer and Kent County Deputy that were notable. Lest, keep in mind over a 23-year career as a Traffic Dog, I've stopped judges, doctors, attorneys, politicians, corrections officers, and a multitude of cops from many different agencies. City Kitties, County Mounties, Super Troopers, Feebees (FBI), Secret Service, ATF, marshals, damn, I think I've stopped 'em all! These two were a couple of peaches I needed to mention. I met the GRPD oficer when his daughter was involved in a crash with a Meijer grocery semitruck on US-131. He was on scene (off duty) before I got there. When I arrived he was a HUGE dick! I rolled up not knowing any of the parties in the crash or him; never seen this dude before. Turned out he was in some computer crime unit, explains why I never ran into him on the road! First words out of his mouth, "You're not interviewing my daughter." Really? That makes my job easy. I'll just find her at fault and issue her a ticket, smartass! He finally decided to let me talk to her after I spoke with the truck driver. The truck driver stated they both changed lanes at the same time, and he didn't see her. I found them both at fault and didn't issue either one a citation, easy fix, that's my discretion. About a year later this same GRPD Officer got popped by the county for drunk driving.

My contact with a the Deputy was on a traffic stop on US-131 for improper lane use. Lansing wanted us to strictly enforce the lane use law because people were bitching it wasn't being enforced enough. Easy for me because that was one of my pet peeves also. "Stay right except to pass" signs about every two miles on Michigan's freeway/highway system, yet morons still hang in the left lane, screwing traffic up. Simple concept, if you're not passing, stay the hell to the right, right? I was behind this dude for approximately three miles, which was way more that required, with him continually looking in his rear-view mirror at me. I'm in a Ford Explorer blue Goose slick top (no bubble), MSP blue, so he knew who I was. I finally pull him over after checking to see if he was wearing his seatbelt, which he was, and issued him a ticket for improper lane use. I'm at court when some guy approached me in the hallway/lobby asking if I could cut his client a break on a ticket I wrote him. I was thrown off because all I had were informal hearing, which don't have attorneys; formals hearings with the prosecutor have this. "Hello, Trooper, I'm the counselor, Dewey, Cheatem, and Howe. You wrote my client, a Kent County Deputy, a ticket for lane use. Can we have that dismissed?" I ask his client why he didn't identify himself as a deputy when I stopped him, I would have kicked him loose; now it was too late. He said his department had a policy where they couldn't identify themselves during traffic stops. Bullshit flag thrown. WTF, dude, now I'm pissed. Take your attorney that's not even supposed to be here and set up a formal hearing. This Deputy and his attorney are obviously full of shit, here we go. They move the hearing over to the neighboring Ottawa County due to a conflict with the judges knowing both of us. Turns out he's a transport Deputy, doesn't work the road, which is why I never ran into this cat either! We go to a formal hearing over in Ottawa with a female judge who seems to be pissed to have to hear this traffic case. I get on the stand to give my testimony, behind the guy for three miles, your Honor, no move over, pretty simple. The Deputy gets on the stand and claims it wasn't three miles and there was traffic to the right, so he could't get over when I was behind him, which was bullshit. I tell this young Ottawa prosecutor representing me to ask him why he didn't identify himself as a Deputy when I stopped him. His response, under oath on the stand, "I didn't feel I did anything wrong, that's why I didn't identify myself." Wow, what a lying piece of shit, he just perjured himself. I told this to the noob sitting next to me, the young prosecutor, who looks at me dumbfounded. Object and tell the judge he just perjured himself, you idiot! The judge ended up dismissing the ticket. Boy, was I pissed. I got up walked out. If nothing else, I got five hours overtime to be applied toward my pension; thanks, judge!

My squad Sergeant and I are at the post at the end of an afternoon shift I worked when we're watching Fox News on TV with some protest going on in Dallas, Texas. Holy shit, we saw the live execution of five Dallas police officers that were there trying to protect protestors. We looked at each other with that look on our face. Did you see that shit? Horrible to see Police Officers killed on live television.

A young Trooper I had worked with on midnights was working days by himself when he stopped a pickup truck on the Beltline with a stolen plate on it. He gets this 19-year-old kid out of the truck and tries to place him into custody. The fight's on as this turd twists and turns with the suspect falling on top of the Trooper. The whole incident is caught on video. You can hear the punk on top of the Troop saying, "I'm going to kill you," as he's punching him in the face. He gets off him, runs to the pickup, and takes off with the young troop now pursuing. Hmmm? Attempted murder. I would have smoked this asshole while he was on top of me saying he was going to kill me! Kent County Deputies eventually catch this turd. A District MSP Sgt. shows up to the scene not involved in the pursuit and give a local TV interview about the pursuit. He talks about how our Trooper never put any citizens in danger, his speeds weren't excessive, blah, blah, blah.He should have said this teenager tried to murder one of my troopers, and he should be thankful he's not dead right now! Really Sarge?, what a puss! They charged the turd with multiple felonies, and he was given a ridiculous plea by an assistant female Kent County prosecutor that actually had the ovaries to bust the Trooper's balls at the preliminary hearing, "You've obviously never had a felony case before?" She's obviously never had a man lying on top of her punching her in the face, saying he was going to kill her! This asshole stopped by the State Police post with his grandpa to pick up some property after the hearing. Luckily we had a Desk Sergeant with the balls to tell him and his grandpa to get bent and get out of his post. "Get an order from the court to pick up your property, asshole!"

Homeless in Grand Rapids: Some years back after I was a Troop for a while some liberal federal judge determined Michigan's "Panhandling" law was unconstitutional. Hmmm, more than one way to skin a cat! When I transferred to Rockford/Grand Rapids I was approached by a gentleman who stated he ran "Mel Trotter," which was a nonprofit that helped the needy and homeless. He told me most of the people out panhandling downtown made more money in a day than I did. He stated most of them were drunk and/or high on drugs, which disqualified them from going to his place; they had to be sober. After that conversation with him I made it a priority to keep the slushies and dopers off the ramps and sidewalks, keeping them from harassing the good citizens of Michigan. On first contact I would give them a warning, which worked most of the time. They would see my rolling up on my police motor. "Shit, here comes that asshole Motorcycle Trooper." If they didn't want to leave, the next step was a ticket for pedestrian on the freeway. See, they could panhandle on the city streets, but it was still illegal for them to be on the freeway ramps for safety; they might get run over, traumatizing the poor citizen that ran their STUPID ass over. If they refused to leave after getting the ped ticket, I would arrest them for disregarding a police officer and disorderly conduct/intoxicated and call for a transport Blue Goose to take them to jail.

Working midnights my last two years kicked my ass; never could get or stay on the same sleep cycle. My partner and I are downtown in Grand Rapids assisting GRPD with a bar fight at one of the umpteen bars they have kicking it every weekend when were dispatched to a white female walking on US-131 near Pearl St. in the left lane of traffic. We boogy ass up there and luckily come across her on the left shoulder. She is highly intoxicated not knowing where she is at 2:30 in the morning. She's a pretty, young college girl in her early 20s. We grabbed her license to find out where she lived to take her home. We debated on taking her to jail, which we had done in the past with drunk pedestrians walking on the freeway. She advised she was out partying with her roommates when they left her with no ride home. We basically saved her life from either getting run over or swiped by some turds looking for a good time! She blew a .16 on a PBT, which isn't that bad, but we all know alcohol affects different people in different ways. Happy drunks and shitty obnoxious drunks, etc. It was a miracle she didn't get waffled on the freeway; been there, seen that before. We decided to take her home, waking her roommates up and giving them an earful for leaving her at the bar by herself. We thought about calling her parents but decided not to because she was over the age of 21. We gave her an appearance citation for drunken disorderly, being highly intoxicated, putting herself in danger, and motorists in danger, having to swerve around her. I've done way too many death notifications throughout my career; thank God we didn't have to do one for her!

On patrol in a Blue Goose when I was requested by another troop to standby on a suspended driver he stopped on US-131 N/B near West River Dr. I roll up and talk to the troop, who said he was on a mission for the sarge at the post and had to clear. The dude he stopped had a carload of groceries and asked that he not tow his car. Sure, no probs. I never went up to the car, no reason to. A car pulls up in front of the vehicle, and a guy gets out. He appears to be the person the suspended driver called to pick him, the car, and groceries up. I call him back on the public address system to verify he had a valid driver's license. Do people show up to scene with the police drunk and not valid? YES! He came back valid and had a slight attitude that I would question him about having a license. Just doing my job, no more, no less. I cleared the scene of the traffic stop and headed to the post. As I'm pulling into the post parking lot, Dispatch advises there is a serious injury crash on US-131 N/B at West River Dr. Hmmm, there was another troop close to the scene that responded. I cleared the post to go assist him. On the way down Dispatch advises the crash is a K (fatal). Turns out the car had a manual/stick shift transmission, and the guy that showed up to pick up the car didn't know how to drive a stick! The car owner/suspended driver spent about 10 minutes trying to teach his friend how to drive a stick. Are you kidding me? He goes to pull out, again never driven a stick before, pulls right in front of a large truck, killing himself. Wow, what a horrible tragedy. What were they thinking? Wow, dead over some groceries.

A laser is a Motor Man's best friend. We had radar on the Harleys, which was okay, but I preferred a laser, which was way more accurate at picking out speeders! When I had a Harley, for the first eight years on the motors I kept my laser in the right saddle bag like most motor cops, which was a pain in the ass! There was a puck looking knob on top of the saddle bags that had to be twisted and latched or the bag would open up at high speeds, flapping in the wind. We would put foam padding in the saddle bag to hopefully keep the laser from getting damaged. I would find good hiding spots/fishing holes to park my motor and shoot laser coming at me most of the time. Every once in a while one would be in and out of traffic go by me, and I would shoot them in the ass, to see the look on their faces as they went by me. They had that "Fuck, I'm fucked" look on their face. The lasers technically would go out to infinity, but we usually accepted readings of 1,000 feet or less for court purposes and testimony. A radar would sometimes pick up the wrong vehicle or give false high speed readings near large vehicles or semitrucks, which was called "Batching." At the start of my ninth season on the motors I was a senior Motor Man, so I was given a brand-new BMW 1200 RTP to ride on patrol. The transition course in Lansing was super easy, way easier to do the cone exercises than on the Harley. I really liked my Harley but loved that BMW. At first, some citizens were busting our balls for going to the BMW, but I used to say, "There's nothing wrong with a Chevy Cavalier, but wouldn't you rather have a Cadillac?" That usually shut most whiners up. When we transitioned to the BMWs there was a laser holder/scabbard that mounted on the frame for easy access and protection from damage.

We had a district meeting with the colonel at the American Legion in Rockford, where she decided to go around the state and talk about the Ferguson Shooting. She came with three hotties in dresses that weren't hard to look at all dolled up. That was the only thing that made the meeting worthwhile. What in the hell does Ferguson, Missouri, have to do with Michigan state troopers? Some turd stole some cigars from a party store, assaulted a uniformed police officer trying to kill said officer attempting to take away his firearm, the police officer used deadly force, where deadly force needed to be used and was justified, case closed! "If you hate people, you're in the wrong business." What the fuck, colonel? We looked at each other and rolled our eyes. We hate a lot of people as should you, Ma'am! We hate the monster that shot Trooper Paul Butterfield in the head when he walked up on a routine traffic stop. We hate the Michigan militia shithead that killed Trooper Kevin Marshal because he didn't believe he had to live by the rules like the rest of us! We hate rapists, murderers, and a whole lot of other monsters in society. Yes, Ma'am, there are a lot of people we hate that you should hate too! We could't get out of there fast enough listening to bullshit that had nothing to do with us!

The Colonel, who was said to only have an associate's degree, started pushing education enhancement, which is fine but the MSTPA had been asking for years for the department to pay or partially pay for college courses. She decided to have Troopers rated in their yearly performance appraisal on taking classes that again they would not pay for or now finally partially pay for, big deal. I had received my bachelor's degree in aviation from Western with a minor in business before I joined the State Police. In fact most of the road troopers I knew and worked with all had at least a bachelor'a degree. I told my rating sergeant I was not going to participate in her education program! What could he say, I was in my last two years in the MSP and surely didn't need any more education, especially with the bullshit they were pushing. I had a Psychology Professor at my community college, who was a great instructor. He put it bluntly, just because you had a college degree didn't mean you were any smarter than the next guy! Again that coming from a PhD holder! He said a "BS degree stood for bullshit, MBS stood for more bullshit, and PhD stood for piled higher and deeper!" Our Colonel must not have taken his class.

I blew out my left knee/torn meniscus working a two-man midnight car after the Great Re-Org. We were on patrol on I-96 when we lit up a car exiting on Alpine Ave. in Walker. The car pulled over to the right shoulder with the front seat passenger bailing out of the car on foot. My partner secured the driver and peeps in the back seat. I leaped out of the Blue Goose chasing the passenger on his heels, I thought. He jumped over a fence like a gazelle that I didn't see. I hit that fucker at full stride flipping over it blasting my knee and getting a face full of dirt and gravel. Fuck, that hurt! I lost him but knew he was hunkered down close. We called for a K-9 trooper whose dog eventually found his stupid ass hiding in some bushes. He ran because he had some misdemeanor warrants for his arrest. I ended up having some scratches in my right eye having to see any eye specialist to clean my eye out and also needed surgery on my left knee. Another reason why I hated working midnights, the older you get, the less shit you can see, i.e., the wire fence that tore me up. Note to self, "Don't chase turds on foot in the dark when you can't see what's about to ruin your day, week, and month."

Working midnights with a new partner, also a motor trooper like myself. My regular partner called in sick, go figure. We actually had a great shift arresting two drunks from the time we doubled up at 6 p.m. We were sitting stationary by the Van Andel Arena in downtown Grand Rapids when a crotch rocket drives by a GPRD unit that was pulling into the police station garage. The schmo on the motorcycle revved his engine as he went by the GRPD unit, looked over at us, and hit gas, taking off at a high rate of speed. We followed the dude, who attempted to drive on the Blue Bridge, which is a pedestrian bridge with no motorized traffic allowed on it. I'm driving, so I pull up in front of him before he see us so he can't cross the bridge. He stalled the bike when my partner jumped from the passenger seat and told him to get off the bike. He did not comply, trying to start the motorcycle back up, when I jumped out of the driver's seat and ran to his left side. All three of us fell over to the right with my partner having the bike fall on him primarily. We get dumbass into custody. He had a slight odor of intoxicants on his breath but didn't appear to be drunk. No cycle endorsement, no insurance, and expired plates on the motorcycle. We issued him three misdemeanor appearance tickets and released him. We also towed his bike, which he kept whining about like a little girl. Be thankful we're not taking you to jail, stupid! I took pictures of the motorcycle to be on the safe side because it fell over on the right side due to his actions. The wrecker shows up, tows the bike, case closed, or so we think. About a month later a Sergeant lets us know the schmuck hired an attorney, stating that we assaulted his client and damaged his motorcycle. This lying prick was trying to jam us and get out of his tickets, easy to see, which you could see happening more and more with these idiots. Some asshole lieutenant from Lansing actually wanted us charged criminally. The Kent County prosecutor threw out the tickets and told the MSP Lieutenant, "Nah, no charges on the troopers." He should have tacked on a felony charge for R&O on the dude for trying to take off on my partner and dropping the bike on him. They gave him what he wanted, dismissing those tickets for being a lying prick! Whatever, he still had his sled towed that night and had to pay the tow bill and weekend storage fees, also having to insure the motorcycle before the tow yard would release it; ha, take that! Here comes the administrative interview. I was given a one-year letter in my personnel file for calling the dipshit "stupid" on camera; really, that's all you can come up with, you noobs? I've called criminals and others "stupid" too many times throughout my career. Remember one of my favorite "John Wayne" quotes, "Life is hard, but it's really hard when you're STUPID!" I retired six months after this incident, thank God, things were getting very STUPID with the State

Police and law enforcement in general. Funny thing, I receive a letter from MSP Human Resources in Lansing about six months after I retired letting me know the one-year disciplinary letter was being removed from the personnel file. "No shit, morons, I'm retired and don't have a personnel file!" Back to my favorite quote again, "The worst form of police corruption is **incompetence!**"

A year before I retired, our illustrious Director decided to drastically reduce our authority imposing a dereliction of duty on Troopers and sergeants allowing criminals to flee unless it was a known felony they were fleeing for. Duh, that makes a lot of sense since fleeing and eluding in and of itself is a felony! What a joke and how embarrassing. I had five pursuits in the first year of my last two in the State Police after my pursuit fatal where the defendant went to state prison for 27 years. Three out of the five were bad dudes and one crazy bitch that were all convicted felons on parole that went back to prison, where they all belong. The female perp carjacked a vehicle during a traffic stop in Grand Rapids had and tried to run one of our young Troopers down. That crazy bitch once tased and arrested after crashing in the city and fighting Troopers ended up having a felony warrant for child abuse, intentionally burning her kids with cigarettes as discipline. I don't usually go to sentencing hearings, but I did for her. I walked into a packed courtroom at circuit court. "Good afternoon, Trooper, good afternoon, your Honor." The judge called her a menace to society and sent her back to prison for 10 to 15 years just on our charges alone, not including the child abuse case. Bye, bye, have fun in prison, you crazy bitch! After the Colonel curtailed our pursuit policy, I had another pursuit while working construction zone overtime on US-131, trying to keep the workers safe. I had this dude coming at me and the construction workers at 85 mph in a posted 45 mph zone. I immediately take off after him when he blazes by some workers going off road onto a dirt road near the freeway. He went "Dukes of Hazard" on me going down some back roads, then crashing into a farmer's fence, taking it out, with me hitting the same.

I went airborne at the end of the pursuit actually breaking the frame on a Dodge Charger I was in. He bailed on foot and was caught a short time later being drunk with a 12 pack in the car. Again, another prison parole absconder that would be going back to the state penitentiary. I contacted the farmer whose fence we trashed. First words out of his mouth, "Did you catch that son of a bitch, trooper?" "Yes, sir, we did." "Don't worry about the fence. I'll string it back up." I had five "NPI's" (no pursuit initiated), where we turned on the police lights, the suspects failed to stop and/or hit the gas and took off. Per the new State Police policy we had to turn off our emergency lights and sirens and just let them go. We had PIT and boxing in training that was a waste. We had a great policy before she decided to castrate us that allowed supervisory monitoring and well as trooper discretion. We only use the tPIT technique under 45 mph at safe locations and never on motorcycles. This appeared to be overlooked because of a trooper working in Detroit that decided to tase a criminal fleeing on a 4 Runner that lost control and ran into the back of a parked pickup truck. That was a use of force issue more than a pursuit issue there, Colonel! If anyone had skin in the game, it was me where an innocent college girl was killed by two cousins in the pursuit that I had. I wouldn't wish that horrible experience on anyone, yet we still have to enforce the laws and maintain civility in society.

Now MSP Command was saying to get a plate and follow up on it later. Really? My first "NPI" was a guy I attempted to stop on West River near US-131. He was wandering all over the road and appeared to be intoxicated. He kept going, got on the freeway, and I had to let him go turning my police lights and siren off and advising Dispatch of the same. If I had pursued the guy, now I would face discipline and/ or termination. I now had an imposed dereliction of duty as the new policy I had to adhere to; damn, I couldn't get out the door fast enough. What a disservice to the citizens of Michigan. I tracked the registered owner down hours later, who was a white male in his forties that lived with his mother in Grand Rapids. He denied fleeing my traffic stop, of course, thanks again, colonel! After running a criminal history on the schmuck, Dispatch advised he was on parole for murder years prior. He was stalking a young woman setting her house on fire burning her alive. He spent time in prison for murder and arson. This asshole could be a serial killer and had a dead body in the back of his SUV, guess we'll never know! All I could do was write him a reckless driving ticket because we finally got a partial admission that he had been driving and he didn't know I was behind him trying to stop him. This was the time when I was embarrassed to wear the uniform with one year out from retirement. I couldn't get out the door fast enough. The light on our hood of our Blue Goose that read "Stop State Police" didn't mean anything anymore. It should read "Flee State Police." We became one of the few State Police agencies throughout the country with such a restrictive pursuit policy, even more restrictive that liberal California! A second incident out of the five "NPI's" I had involved getting dispatched to a car blocking the roadway at the top of a freeway exit ramp at the traffic light. Dispatch advised the driver appeared to be intoxicated and slumped over the wheel. My partner and I pull up behind the suspect car and turn our police lights on. His head pops up, he throws the car into drive, and takes off through a red light. A taxi driver who called it in says, "Aren't you guys gonna take off after that car?" "No, sir, we now have a 'No Pursuit' policy unless they are a known felon!" "Did he tell you he was a convicted felon?" The taxi driver was dumbfounded. We apologized and told him he could write his state rep to complain about our imposed dereliction of duty! One of my favorite quotes that's written in my Retirement Shadow Box, Proverbs 28:1: "The Wicked flee when no one Pursuith, but the Righteous are bold as a Lion."

I stopped writing tickets and working about two months out from retiring, which would have been around Christmastime. One of the last tickets I wrote was to a 16-year-old kid on a graduated license. I clocked him on the Beltline Rd. at 95 mph in a posted 55 mph zone. He was trying to get home before 10 p.m., which was state law for his age and driving level. I called his parents, who came to the scene of the traffic stop to pick them up. His dad was so pissed he jumped in the car and took off. Mom came back to talk to me, and I told her early Christmas present for your son, I did write him a ticket for 95 in a 55 so schedule a court date, I'm retiring soon, and I won't be there at court, hint, hint! If the trooper doesn't show up for court for whatever reason, the court dismisses the ticket.

My last day on patrol with the Michigan Department of State Police was a midnight shift with my partner Adam, the "Keebler Elf." We didn't do shit, why would we, met the rest of the shift at a Coney Island for breakfast went back to the post, then made my last radio call to our Dispatch Center in Gaylord. Veni, Vedi, Veci (Latin for I came, I saw, I conquered), I came to the State Police 23 years ago, saw a great career and, conquered the job by leaving the department in one piece, not like many of my friends that were killed in the line of duty. Rest in peace, brothers and sisters!

I took a few weeks off burning time, then took my equipment back to Lansing HQ and the Academy. Potus, a Sergeant buddy of mine, took me. I did the "DROP" by dropping my shit off in Lansing. I actually got to sit on my old Rockford Hog, Motor 6161 that I used on patrol that was in the MSP Museum now, pretty cool! I bought both my issued side arms, which the department allows you to do, and picked up all my retirement accoutrements for my retirement party to be held two months later in nicer weather. Michigan is pretty damn cold with snow still in early March. My retirement party was held at the Gerald R. Ford FOP lodge in Grand Rapids. We had bag pipers, a nice video collage of my career, and a nice photo collage of my fellow Michigan Troopers killed in the line of duty while I was on the job! A great time was had by all. I love the Michigan State Police and have no regrets about my career; hopefully things are cyclical, and the state will get a decent Governor that appoints a Colonel/Director with the <u>balls</u> or <u>ovaries</u> to do the right thing by the Troopers and the Citizens of Michigan!

EPILOGUE:

LAW ENFORCEMENT and policing is a pretty simple concept. There are good guys and bad guys, the same way it's been throughout history. When bad guys commit crimes, the good guys need to address it! One of my good friends, Topher, had a great analogy. The citizens/people in society are like sheep. You need sheep dogs to protect the flock of sheep from the predators like wolves, coyotes, foxes, etc. When you lock the sheep dogs away in the kennels because they might be too aggressive, the predators have a field day on the sheep! He actually has a tattoo of a sheep dog on his arm showing how strongly he feels about that analogy. That same Trooper has been in three shootings in his career, one of them smoking a dude with a machete threatening to kill his girlfriend!

Most politicians and law enforcement command stood by and supported the cops on the beat when I first became a young Trooper in the mid-90s. Over my career and after retirement you could see how they were gradually changing. Now the Road Dogs/street cops were the bad guys and the criminals were the victims of the system. What a huge crock of shit! We used to have politicians and police command that stood up to these assholes and their liberal agendas. Now it appears they are feckless and afraid to do the right thing. The extremely small/extremely loud voice of radical shitheads doesn't need to be shut down, they need to be drown out with the voices of common sense people that want law and order in a civil society. Just before I retired, the MSP was excluding a large number of great applicants that had visible tattoos, which included many military combat Veterans. Now they allow male Troopers to have "man buns" and finger nail polish! WTF? Who knows what they are allowing female Troops to do? Stop State Police doing the wrong thing, and do the right thing!

Throughout my 23-year-career as a Trooper I've been called many names. The bad including, "asshole, cracker, nigger (by Black suspects I've arrested, go figure), faggot, dumbass, pussy, pig," and others. Some good names include recruit, Vinny, Bomber, Burrito, Sir, Motor Man, hero, and the best **"Trooper!"** The title Trooper is the one I am most proud of and always will be! I still remember sitting in that chair with my classmates back not too long at at the Michigan State Police Academy graduation in July 1996 and the Director/Colonel calling my name, Trooper Christopher Bommarito. Wow, what a great name to be called! The Trooper is and will always be the backbone of the Michigan State Police.

I had a great career with the Michigan State Police and love the history of the department and what we once stood for. I have no regrets about my service to the citizens of Michigan. I was able to ride police motors for 15 years loving the TV show *CHIPS* as a kid! I am optimistic that someday we will again have politicians in Lansing and upper command in the State Police that take care of the Troops in the best interest of taking care of our citizens. Let them do the police work I was allowed to do when I swore and took an oath to serve the citizens years ago, not the way it is now. When it comes down to it just like I told all my cubs, when you get frustrated, remember you don't work for the Governor, the Colonel, or Post Commander. They come and go, you work for the citizens of Michigan. When you stop someone for driving like an asshole and cars drive by and beep their horn thanking you for stopping that dude or chick, that's who your work for! You work for the young child that was molested and/or raped by an adult! It was an honor for me to be the last Road Dog/Motor Man to retire from the Michigan State Police Rockford Post that had been serving the local community and citizens of Michigan for over 85 years. Lansing closed the Rockford

Post shortly after I retired and opened up a Mega Post/District HQ/ Crime Lab in Grand Rapids.

This book is dedicated to my two fellow MSP Motor Men friends that were killed in the line of duty doing what they loved, patrolling on a MSP motor, Trooper Chad **"Wolfman"** Wolf and Trooper Tim **"Gator"** O'Neill. It is also dedicated to my older brother, Richard Dominic Bommarito, who died from a long fight with muscular dystrophy at the age of 15. **"Donny"** was my Guardian Angel, watching over me during trying times as a Trooper with the Michigan State Police.

REFERENCES:

Quote from *Game of Thrones*, Tyrion Lannister character, page 1

Journey song " Don't STOP Believing," page 2.

News article, *Detroit Free Press*, November 15, 1994, "Michigan State Police Looking to Fill 250 vacancies," page 15.

News article, *Hillsdale Daily News*, August 2, 1996. "Jonesville Post Welcomes New State Trooper," page 35.

News article, *Jonesville Independent News*, August 21, 1996, "State Police Investigate Driving Incident," page 39.

News article, *Detroit Free Press*, July 22, 1999, "I-94 Crash Kills 4 after Tiger Game," page 61.

News article, *News Herald*, October 10, 2000, "Woman Takes Command of Trooper Post," page 68.

News article, *Detroit News*, September 1, 2001, "Attack on America," page 68.

News article, *Detroit News*, June 27, 2002, "Retirements cost MSP," page 95.

News article, MLive, February 22, 2005, "State Trooper Charged with Drug Possession," page 105.

News article, *Detroit Free Press*, April 2, 2004. "Michigan State Police Investigators Claim the State Attorney General Impeded the Probe of the City of Detroit Mayor," page 108.

News article, *News Herald*, July 1, 2005. "Quick Action by Off-Duty Officer Helps Save Toddler," page 117.

News article, *Detroit Free Press*, April 3, 2005, "Troopers Jobs May be Cut," page 119.

News article, *Detroit Free Press*, May 11, 2005, "Trooper Held in Homeless Man's Death," page 120.

News article, *News Herald*, June 15, 2008, "Trooper Read Lips," page 122.

News article, *Detroit News*, June 8, 2007, "Troopers Told Park It," page 144.

News article, *Grand Rapids Press*, August 25, 2008, "Motor Cycle Troopers Return to Rockford," page 146.

News article, *Detroit News*, April 10, 2008, "State Troopers Put Politicians to Shame," page 154.

News article, *Grand Rapids Press*, January 1, 2009, "Exchange of Words Sparked Grand Rapids Nightclub Shooting, Police Later Killed Alleged Suspect," page 149.

News article, *Grand Rapids Press*, March 20, 2009, "Troopers Honored for Heroic for New Year's Morning Shooting," page 151.

News article, *Grand Rapids Press*, July 10, 2010, "Cop Makes the Call on Texting Teen," page 162.

News article, *Grand Rapids Press*, May 14, 2009 "MSP Rockford Troopers Receive Bravery Award," September 13, 20111 page 163.

The New Testament Bible, Proverbs 28:1, page 197.

Cover Photo courtesy of Trooper Casey Trucks/Motor Man Rockford Post.

Printed in the USA
CPSIA information can be obtained
at www.ICGtesting.com
CBHW052016141123
1883CB00004B/30